HAUNTED HALLS

HAUNTED

Ghostlore of American College Campuses

Elizabeth Tucker

UNIVERSITY PRESS OF MISSISSIPPI ☾ JACKSON

HALLS

www.upress.state.ms.us

This volume is supported in part by a subvention from the
English Department at Binghamton University.

The University Press of Mississippi is a member of the Association of
American University Presses.

First printing 2007
∞
Library of Congress Cataloging-in-Publication Data

Tucker, Elizabeth, 1948–
  Haunted halls : ghostlore of American college campuses / Elizabeth Tucker.
    p. cm.
  Includes bibliographical references and index.
  ISBN-13: 978-1-57806-994-1 (cloth : alk. paper)
  ISBN-10: 1-57806-994-7 (cloth : alk. paper)
  ISBN-13: 978-1-57806-995-8 (pbk. : alk. paper)
  ISBN-10: 1-57806-995-5 (pbk. : alk. paper) 1. Haunted universities and
colleges—United States. 2. Ghosts—United States. I. Title.
  BF1478.T83 2007
  133.1'22—dc22

                              2007009961

British Library Cataloging-in-Publication Data available

CONTENTS

ACKNOWLEDGMENTS

I want to thank my husband, Geoffrey Gould, for his generous support and wise counsel throughout the preparation of this book. His wonderful photographs bring out the excitement and mysteriousness of college ghostlore. It was a joy to work with him.

My son, Peter Gould, and his friend, Ashley Bleck, have helped me to see how students find meaning in ghost stories. I especially want to thank Ashley for photographing the stairwell in Cheney Hall at the State University of New York at Cortland, haunted by the ghost of Elizabeth. My father, Frank H. Tucker, offered insights from a historian's perspective, and my sisters, Margaret Mitchell and Sarah Owens, shared their thoughts about Indian ghosts and other supernatural phenomena. My cousins, Martha Harris, Susie Whalen, and Anna Roth Hays, told spine-chilling ghost stories on hot summer afternoons.

I am very grateful for the assistance I have received from friends and colleagues while collecting legends for this study. Linda Dégh, my mentor at Indiana University, generously offered advice and helped me to find legend texts, as did Lydia Fish, my first folklore professor at Buffalo State College. Important help also came from other kind friends who shared legend texts and insights: Janet Langlois at Wayne State University, Nancy C. McEntire at Indiana State University, Joseph P. Goodwin at Ball State University, Elissa Henken at the University of Georgia, Bill Ellis at Penn State Hazleton, Carol Burke at the University of California at Irvine, Frank de Caro at Louisiana State University, Susan Deer Cloud at the University of Massachusetts, Donald Allport Bird at Long Island University, Henry Glassie at Indiana University, and James P. Leary at the University of Wisconsin.

I want to thank my friends and colleagues at Binghamton University who have supported this research project: David Bartine, Ruth Stanek, Susan Strehle, William V. Spanos, Nancy Henry, Philip Rogers, Robert Micklus, and Nina Versaggi.

Others who provided valuable assistance include Ruth Aten at Indiana University, Christina Hope at Marist College, Alan Dundes at the University of California at Berkeley, Rosemary Hathaway at the University of Northern Colorado, Kim Jones at West Virginia Wesleyan, and Charles Lamb at Rochester Institute of Technology.

I want to thank my research assistants, Kristen Fusaro and David Schaaf, for their excellent work collecting legend texts and suggesting revisions. Darlene Gold kindly read my introduction and offered some wonderful insights; Claudia Martin offered helpful information about nineteenth-century female characters.

Many thanks to all of the undergraduate students at Binghamton University who have generously shared stories with me, especially Courtney Kelly, Lauren Moscowitch, Jessica Torres, Jason Ginsberg, Iris Hsieh, Sandra Van Vooren, Mackenzie Harris, Dianne Harris, Kristin Lau, Alicia Maston, Jessica Montera, Jacqueline Minichiello, Joanna Pelizzoni, Justin Phillips, Paul Lee, Samantha Schulman, Ken Shiraiwa, and Matthew Steward.

I am grateful to the publishers and societies that have given me permission to reprint my previously published essays. "Ghosts in Mirrors: Reflections of the Self" was published in the *Journal of American Folklore* 118:468 (2005): 186–203 and is reprinted with the permission of the American Folklore Society (http://www.afsnet.org). "Marbles on the Ceiling: Emerging Campus Legends" was published in *Contemporary Legend* 7 (2004) and is reprinted with the permission of the International Society for Contemporary Legend Research. "Spectral Indians, Desecrated Burial Grounds" was published in *Voices: The Journal of New York Folklore* 31 (2005): 10–13; "Legend Quests" was published in *Voices: The Journal of New York Folklore* 32 (2006): 34–38. Both are reprinted with the permission of the New York Folklore Society.

I want to thank August House Publishers for giving me permission to reprint an excerpt from W. K. McNeil's *Ghost Stories from the American South* (2005): 77.

I also want to thank all of the archivists who have given me permission to include texts from their files: Pamela Dean at the Northeast Folklore Archive at the University of Maine in Orono, Rebecca Fitzgerald at Mount Saint Mary's College in Emmitsburg, Maryland, Patricia Hodges at Western Kentucky University in Bowling Green, Margaret Rauch at Wayne State University, Kelly Revak at the University of California at Berkeley, Randy Williams at the Fife Folklore Archive at Utah State University, and Peggy Yocom at

George Mason University. Information about the texts from each archive is included in the text and in the list of references cited.

It is also a pleasure to thank Mark Sceurman and Mark Moran, webmasters of the fascinating *Weird New Jersey* website, who gave me permission to include one of their best college ghost stories in my manuscript.

I am grateful to Craig Gill, my editor at the University Press of Mississippi, for his wise counsel and encouragement. I also want to express gratitude to the reviewer of my manuscript, who made some very helpful suggestions.

Lastly, I want to thank Alan Duesterhaus at Tennessee Wesleyan University in Athens and Christopher Tuthill at the University of Maine in Orono, who contributed pictures of beloved campus figures which, according to campus lore, now roam their institutions as ghosts.

HAUNTED HALLS

Chapter One

CAMPUS GHOSTLORE

An Eerie Presence

Two weeks after Halloween in the millennial year 2000, I found a desperate e-mail message that had been posted on a national housing listserv. A director of Residential Life at a small liberal arts college in New York City had sent the following plea:

> *My students swear that one of our residence halls is haunted. The building is very old and does have a lot of history (fires, suicides, etc). At first, I thought that students were playing jokes on each other but now it is at the point where some of them aren't sleeping and hate being in the building. They speak of being touched in the middle of the night, lights turning on and off and an eerie presence . . . Has anyone ever dealt with a "haunted" residence hall? If so, how was it handled?*[1]

When I received this e-mail, I had just finished an eight-year term as Faculty Master of a residential community at Binghamton University in New York. One hall, Sullivan, had a reputation for being haunted. Students living in this building had told me about seeing faces in mirrors, hearing furniture move around by itself, and feeling the presence of something disturbing that could not be explained in rational terms. I had thought about writing an article for a folklore journal on our campus's haunted hall.[2] But this unexpected e-mail, forwarded by a friend who knew of my interest in the supernatural, convinced me that an article about one hall's haunting would not be enough. If Residential Life professionals were asking one another for help with hauntings on national listservs, the phenomenon merited broader study.

When I looked closely at the Residential Life director's e-mail, I saw that it emphasized one residence hall's age and history, including fires and suicides. This emphasis fit the kinds of questions that freshmen and sophomores in my folklore classes asked when they heard a place might be haunted. "How old is the building?" was usually their first question, followed by "What happened there before?" To test the validity of supernatural experiences, my students relied on the evidence their senses gave them, telling memorates (personal experience stories) about what they had seen, heard, felt, and smelled. They also paid close attention to legends about past tragedies. Sometimes, however, it was difficult for them to speak about hauntings without fearing that friends would criticize them. Just as the Residential Life director who wrote the anguished e-mail put "haunting" in quotes, many of my students hesitated to admit that they took supernatural phenomena seriously. Some of them found religious faith to be the solution to unwelcome hauntings, and eventually, the Residential Life director at the small college in New York City came to a similar conclusion. After she asked a priest to bless the haunted hall, students assured her that the eerie presence had vanished.

In this book I present a broad spectrum of college ghost stories, asking what makes these texts meaningful to students. When students have shared their thoughts about ghost stories with me I have listened carefully, trying to perceive the stories on the students' own terms. After many conversations and archive visits, I have found that ghost stories entertain and educate students, offering a unique blend of excitement, mystery, and danger. When students gather to tell ghost stories, they get to know one another better. Although ghost stories have more than one kind of meaning in a college setting, they primarily initiate entering students into a new community and a new stage of life. This process works best for students of the traditional age range, between seventeen and twenty-two. The anthropology professor Rebekah Nathan, author of *My Freshman Year* (2005), discovered how complex and difficult college life can be for contemporary young people while going "undercover" as an entering freshman at the university where she taught. My own study examines the challenges of college life through narratives told by students, especially those who have recently started college in a place that is new to them. Away from home, struggling to handle academic and social pressures, freshmen of the traditional age range listen closely to legends of past tragedies. Many college ghost stories offer explanations about what happened to murder, suicide, and accident victims and to persecuted minority group members, including African American slaves and American Indians. Hearing such narratives, freshmen gain a deeper understanding of historical and psychological horrors in relation to current social problems. They also learn that worst-case scenarios, such as lovelorn women hanging themselves and all-night studiers overdosing on drugs, need not apply to themselves. The subtleties of such stories reveal much about the dangers and delights of college life.

College ghost stories comprise one lively form of the legend. Folklore scholars have persuasively asserted that legends fulfill an initiatory function for adolescents. Students who enter college after graduating from high school are young adults, but they also fit the pattern of late adolescence, in which many adjustments to adult life take place. According to Linda Dégh, "To be involved in the legend experience belongs to the initiation into adulthood; like other transitory steps at critical turning points in the life cycle, it is a rite of passage, appearing as a particularly fearsome strain both physiologically and psychologically" (2001: 252). Dégh has shown that the legend integrates narration with action, making it possible for young people to test what stories tell them through personal experience (1969: 2001). Alan Dundes's psychoanalytic approach has brought out important symbols that appear in college legends, especially those about fraternity initiations (1971: 2002).[3] Simon J. Bronner's *Piled Higher and Deeper: The Folklore of Student Life* (1995) takes a socio-psychological approach, examining various kinds of ghost stories. And Bill Ellis's study of adolescents' folklore of the supernatural explicates the close relationship between legends, play, and rituals of rebellion (2004).

My own study examines social, psychological, and cultural elements. The intricacies of college storytelling, embedded within the matrix of campus life and cultural history, suggest a need for analysis with a social, psychological, and cultural orientation. For each legend text, I apply the appropriate kind of theory. Legends about reflections of ghosts in mirrors, for example, call for psychological analysis, while legends about spectral Indians necessitate cultural analysis. Close scrutiny of college legend-telling shows how ghost stories initiate students into college life and young adulthood. Through sensory evidence of ghostly intrusions, students probe the nature of reality while adjusting to academic stress and residence hall social life. During this process, intriguing questions arise. Do ghosts exist, or are they just projections of an overactive imagination? Is it possible to have an extra roommate who is not alive? If an Indian ghost appears outside a residence hall, what does that mean? Can messages from ghosts console, guide, threaten, and warn? While confronting such questions and searching for answers, students discover important aspects of their emerging adult selves.

The prototype for young people's search for truth is the Grimms's story number four, "The Youth Who Set Out to Learn What Fear Is" (Aarne-Thompson tale type 326). In this folktale, a young man goes on a quest to understand fear: first in a church, then near gallows where a dead man is hanging, and finally in a haunted castle where roaring and howling noises, as well as sounds of bodies clattering down a chimney, test his endurance. Although the young man sees and hears many terrible things, the only stimulus that makes him shudder is a bucket full of cold water and squirming fish. Through the evidence provided by his own senses, he finally learns how it feels to be afraid.

College students pursue much the same quest: to experience fear and to understand danger. Their setting is a residence hall or another building that is supposed to be haunted. With long corridors, mirrors, locked rooms, towers, tunnels, and spooky basements, many college halls resemble the buildings found in nineteenth-century literary ghost stories and Gothic novels. It is not surprising, then, that students make these buildings the settings for legends highlighting fearful confrontations. By telling ghost stories, students transform their college buildings into mysterious and magical places. Within these structures, amazing things can happen.

According to a recent study, going to college increases students' belief in ghosts. Two professors—Bryan Farha at Oklahoma City University and Gary Steward Jr. at the University of Central Oklahoma—conducted a poll of 439 students that showed seniors and graduate students were more likely to believe in paranormal phenomena than freshmen were. High on the list of subjects that inspired belief were haunted houses, psychics, telepathy, and channeling (Britt 2006). This study supports my observation that students actively seek confrontations with the supernatural while completing other parts of their education.

In gathering narratives for this book, I have obtained as broad a selection of students' experiences as possible, conducting interviews and obtaining material from archives in Maine, Maryland, New York, Virginia, Indiana, Kentucky, Michigan, Colorado, Utah, and California. The earliest texts come from the 1960s, when American folklorists first maintained archives. Although I cannot cover all college ghost stories, I have tried to represent a number of regions, types of institutions, religions, and ethnicities.[4] Most of the students whose stories appear here are of the traditional age for undergraduate studies, seventeen to twenty-two, but a few are somewhat older. I hope that this study will encourage more specialized studies of students' ghost stories as fieldwork continues.

Shades of Meaning

Before introducing more specific material, I want to identify key terms and scholarly approaches, as well as literary traditions that have nourished the development of the ghost story as a genre. Any search for meaning depends on careful definition of terms and contexts. When I began my research, I worked my way through a thicket of varying terms, concepts, and methods of classification. This section outlines that range of possibilities, suggesting which approaches seem most productive for study of college ghostlore. It also offers an overview of the kinds of ghosts that inhabit haunted halls on college campuses today.

According to the *Random House College Dictionary*, the word "ghost" has eleven meanings, the first of which is "the soul of a dead person, a disembodied spirit imagined as wandering among or haunting living persons." The antecedents of "ghost" include the Middle English *goost*, the Old English *gast*, and the German *Geist*, all of which mean "spirit." This Anglo-Germanic orientation limits the definition of "ghost" to some extent. In Asia, for example, ghosts have a close connection to ancestor veneration.[5] However, "the soul of a dead person" and "a disembodied spirit" make good general definitions.

"Ghost" is not the only term Americans use to identify supernatural phenomena. "Specter" and "spook" usually suggest a strange or terrifying ghost; "haunt" or "hant," especially common in the South, refer to the ghost's habit of visiting a place; "apparition" applies to visible ghostly figures; and "shade" denotes a pale figure that is only a shadow of its former self. Folklorists use the term "revenant," based on the French verb *revenir*, "to come back"; in this case, from the realm of the dead. I use the terms "ghost" and "revenant" in this study, with "spectral" as a descriptive adjective.

For Americans, the word "spectral" has particular meaning because of what happened during the Salem witch trails in the early 1690s. Reliance on "spectral evidence" to convict villagers of witchcraft demonstrated the Puritans' belief in the power of invisible shapes or spirits of evil-doers. Some of the people who testified at the trials described horrifying apparitions; others spoke of spectral assaults that resulted in injuries. In her article "Mutations of the Supernatural," Ann Kibbey makes the point that Puritans had a strong interest in investigating "intrusion of supernatural power," which could affect and transform "otherwise ordinary lives" (1982: 136–37). Some of these intrusions offered proof of God's benevolence, but many of them frightened and disturbed the Puritans. George Lincoln Burr reminds us that Salem witchcraft narratives were "no fairy tales"; instead, they represented "the intensest of realities" (1914: xv). Transmission of stories from one person to another raised the fear of supernatural forces to a high level. In *America in Legend*, Richard M. Dorson explains how ghost stories circulating at the time of the Salem witch trials helped to persuade Salem residents that those accused of witchcraft deserved to die (1973: 23–26). Scholars today continue to give what happened in Salem close attention, considering the meaning of the witch trials' heritage. Alison Tracy suggests that "the Puritan crisis (re)produces for its modern readers a pleasurably chilling version of a seventeenth-century encounter with the contingency of selfhood even as it evokes for its audience the intimidation of a less pleasurable encounter with the fragility of our own identities" (2004: 35). This statement eloquently expresses the close connection between selfhood and spectrality. Although much has changed in the more than three hundred years since the Salem witch trials, many contemporary Americans seek evidence of supernatural influence as avidly as the Puritans did.

Fascination with ghosts and uncanny events has resulted in several thriving literary genres. The Gothic novel of the eighteenth and nineteenth centuries captivated readers with lurid descriptions of sinister monks, bleeding nuns, innocent young women, and dashing young men moving through the labyrinthine pathways of haunted castles and cathedrals. The first Gothic novel, Horace Walpole's *The Castle of Otranto* (1764), introduced the first spooky castle of this kind; later novels, such as Matthew Lewis's *The Monk* (1796), further developed the Gothic scenario.

British and American ghost stories flourished in the nineteenth century, when spiritualism was spreading rapidly; confrontations with spirits of the dead seemed to occur during séances with mediums and more informal experiments. Magazines such as *Household Words* (founded in 1850) and *All the Year Round* (founded ten years later) regularly published short fictional narratives about haunted mansions, spooky graveyards, and other spectral sites (Dalby 2002). Ghost stories of the Victorian era gave such authors as Henry James and Edith Wharton the inspiration they needed to write their own psychologically oriented stories of hauntings. Henry James's novella *The Turn of the Screw*, with its finely tuned ambiguities and evocative images, offers an especially good example of the literary ghost story of the early nineteenth century (James 1999).

The sociologist Avery F. Gordon defines ghosts in relation to haunting, "a paradigmatic way in which life is more complicated than those of us who study it have usually granted" (1997: 7). Admitting that sociologists do not usually study ghosts, Gordon explains that ghosts constitute presences that make us painfully aware of important absences. "Being haunted," Gordon says, "draws us affectively, sometimes against our will and always a bit magically, into the structure of feeling of a reality we come to experience, not as cold knowledge, but as a transformative recognition" (1997: 8). Her focus on magic and transformation neatly demonstrates the vitality of folklore of the supernatural.

Following the example set by Gordon's postmodern study of haunting, Jeffrey Andrew Weinstock states that ghosts are "unstable interstitial figures that problematize dichotomous thinking" (2004: 4). Weinstock emphasizes the ghost's role as an interrupter, a deliverer of a wake-up call that needs to be heard: "The ghost is that which interrupts the presentness of the present, and its haunting indicates that, beneath the surface of received history, there lurks another narrative, an untold story that calls into question the veracity of the authorized version of events" (2004: 5). College students excel at finding and sharing such untold stories. These stories become part of their education, an alternative view of the past that offers insight into the present.

One important aspect of American students' education is learning about their country's complex racial history. According to Kathleen Brogan's *Cultural Haunting* (1998), some ghost stories emphasize ghosts' ethnic identity. For ethnic groups that have suffered at the hands of the dominant culture, such stories provide a vital link to unresolved issues of the past. Brogan suggests, "Stories of cultural haunting record the struggle to establish some form of historical continuity that allows for a necessary distance from the past—breathing room, as it were. They can be read as cautionary tales about the proper function of memory" (1998: 9). Renée Bergland's *The National Uncanny: Indian Ghosts and American Subjects* (2000) explores how American literature has turned Indians into ghosts, spectralizing their involvement in American history. In chapter 7, I examine how ghost stories about Indians serve as subversive histories that foreground the process of cultural haunting.

Folklorists' studies of ghostlore have tended to concentrate on storytellers in certain regions of the United States. W. K. McNeil, author of *Ghost Stories from the American South*, notes that there are surprisingly few ghost story collections from the South, although that part of the country is rich in folklore of the supernatural (1985: 23). One of McNeil's and my favorite studies of southern ghostlore is William Lynwood Montell's *Ghosts along the Cumberland* (1975), which presents beliefs and omens related to death as well as narratives about ghosts. Another good collection is Ray Browne's *A Night with the Hants and Other Alabama Folk Experiences* (1976). In the Northeast, some of the best studies of ghostlore include Louis C. Jones's "The Ghosts of New York: An Analytical Study" (1944), which compares New York ghosts to European ghosts, and Emelyn Gardner's *Folklore from the Schoharie Hills* (1977). All of these regional studies pay particular attention to older informants, because of their in-depth knowledge of local traditions. An exception to this trend began with the works of Linda Dégh, who, while gathering midwestern legends about the supernatural in the late 1960s, analyzed patterns of adolescents' storytelling.[6]

Simon J. Bronner's *Piled Higher and Deeper: The Folklore of Student Life* (1995) offers an insightful analysis of ghost stories in a college setting. Among these forms, Bronner explains, are resident ghosts, lovers' ghosts, fraternity ghosts, suicidal ghosts, and others (1995: 148–57). Bronner makes the point that college ghosts help entering students to feel at home: "As if to both personalize the place and underscore its strangeness, new students are introduced to a resident ghost" (148). He notes the difference between fraternity/sorority ghost stories, which emphasize the importance of cooperation, and stories of solitary, miserable ghosts, who have not formed close attachments to their fellow students. Non-Greek ghosts are more likely to commit suicide than students inside the Greek organizational structure (153).

Most college ghosts are students, but some are professors, college presidents, and other staff members. Usually professors make relatively quiet ghosts. Although they have become shades of their former selves, they walk through classrooms and move chairs back and forth in their offices as they follow familiar routines. As a busy academic, I sympathize with these professorial ghosts whose work seems to be eternal, although life itself is finite. I have collected a few narratives about students' visits to places that professors are supposed to haunt, but these are certainly not the most exciting ghosts on college campuses.

Many campus ghost stories feature children who died from natural or unnatural causes. After their deaths they haunt the places where they died, entertaining and disturbing the students who live in their former home. Child ghosts run around, throw balls, and leave tiny handprints on windowpanes. At Florida Southern College in Lakeland, Florida, for example, the ghost of Allan Spivey, who died in 1932 after being bitten by a rabid dog, throws a ball in the corridors of Joseph-Reynolds Hall (Barefoot 2004: 41). Students at Gettysburg College in Maryland have told stories about "Blue Boy," who stands outside dormitory windows, moaning "I'm cold!" (Nesbitt 1991: 76–79). Child ghosts remind students of their pre-college days, when they could run and play freely. Freshmen who have just started living in college residence halls may find that child ghosts make their new domicile seem more like home. Mischievous young ghosts that run around a residence hall enliven everyday life, just as younger brothers and sisters do at home. Emphasis on very young ghosts also reminds listeners of tragic cases in which children have suffered accidents and become crime victims. Innocent children who died young sometimes become protectors of the living. Chapter 6 includes a legend about a young rape victim who warns male students to beware of sexual assault.

Most child spirits seem innocent and good, as do many of the spirits of adults on college campuses. Some of these good spirits save students from peril, guarding stairways and other dangerous places. There is a strong connection between these caring ghosts and saints and angels of the Christian religion. Catholics have a long tradition of belief in guardian angels, which offer daily protection and solace. Since the New Age movement began in the 1960s, guardian angels have belonged to mainstream popular culture. Such books as Joan Wester Anderson's *In the Arms of Angels: True Stories of Heavenly Guardians* (2004) encourage expectations of angelic support. Saints offer help in certain situations; Saint Christopher watches over travelers, Saint Anthony finds lost objects, and Saint Jude supports lost causes. Saint Thomas Aquinas and Saint Catherine of Alexandria, two patron saints of scholars, have special meaning for college students. Invisible but powerful and comforting, helpful ghosts have much in common with saints and angels. Some Christians believe in ghosts as well as saints and angels, while others feel ambivalent about spirits that do not belong to church dogma.

In contrast to benevolent spirits, some college ghosts threaten and horrify those who perceive them. Distinctions between good and evil predominate in stories about possession, such as the "haunted hall" e-mail with which I began this chapter. Learning to recognize sources of evil is an important aspect of the quest to understand fear. Some legends link threatening, apparently evil presences with recognition of the perceiver's own potentially dangerous behavior. In chapter 4, I explain how disturbing apparitions, sounds, and tactile sensations help students recognize a "shadow-self" that they must learn to keep under control.

Among the many legends about worrisome ghosts, stories about persecuted members of minority groups deserve particular attention. Stories about ghosts of African American slaves have circulated widely on southern college campuses. Ghosts of American Indians are not as well known, but an increasing number of stories about Indian ghosts has appeared in campus oral tradition and on the Internet. Ghost stories about torture of slaves remind listeners of unjust suffering. Stories about Indian ghosts tend to focus less sharply on persecution, but they present a disturbing view of what happened to North America's original inhabitants. Because stories about Indian ghosts are less well known than stories about ghosts of slaves, I take a close look at Indian ghosts in chapter 7.

In contrast to the seriousness of Indian ghosts, ghosts of animals comprise an entertaining segment of college ghostlore. Some animal ghosts, such as Old Coaly at Penn State, teach students how their campus was built. In November 2004, Sam, a freshman at Penn State in University Park, said, "If you go into the game room or study lounge in the basement of Watts Hall, you might hear the noisy braying of a mule coming from behind the door of a basement storage room across from the laundry room. That would be Old Coaly. Coaly was one of the original pack mules that worked to build Penn State in the 1850s, or so I'm told."[7] This is a good example of a story that educates and amuses at the same time. The incongruity of a mule braying near the basement laundry room is so funny that the listener has to laugh. Another spectral mule named Pedro, at the University of California at Berkeley, is supposed to whisper the answers to exam questions in students' ears.[8]

Other ghosts represent small animals that died in campus halls. Ted, a student at Southern Methodist University in Dallas, Texas, sent an e-mail message in the spring of 2003 that explained what happened when construction workers building Dallas Hall accidentally killed a squirrel: ". . . they decided to bury the squirrel under the building so it could watch over all the students in the hall. Ever since, late at night, students swear they can hear the running footsteps of a 4-legged animal in the hallway, which is believed to be the squirrel" (Motif E423.2.12). Other small animal ghosts include hamsters, rabbits, and ducks. Most of these spirits are friendly, with the possible exception of a judgmental duck spirit who disapproves of beer drinking. That story appears in chapter 4.

Ghosts add a sense of excitement to college life. Campus spirit, a positive attitude shared by members of a campus community, sometimes takes the form of a campus ghost. For example, Emory University in Atlanta, Georgia, has a time-honored ghost named Dooley who looks like a skeleton (Motif E422.1.11.4, "Revenant as Skeleton"). First identified in 1899, Dooley supposedly died of alcoholism and then joined Emory's faculty, using his bones to teach human anatomy. Brittany, an eighteen-year-old freshman at Emory, sent a description of her university's ghost to Binghamton University student Mackenzie Harris in the spring of 2005. Her message, sent on AOL Instant

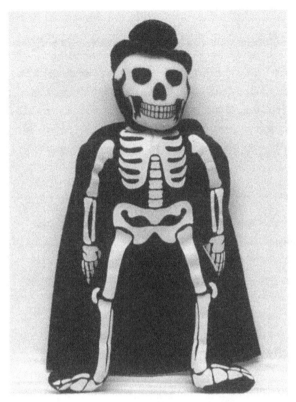

This representation of Dooley, Emory's beloved ghost, was purchased in the campus bookstore in the fall of 2005. Photograph by Geoffrey Gould.

Messenger, takes the loose, semi-poetic form that is characteristic of IM messages:

> his name is Dooley
> and he is a skeleton . . . and he walks around campus
> and he's not allowed to talk
> and it's really weird
> everyone calls him Lord Dooley . . . he's like an eternal spirit here
> he's like on our Facebook
> i'm sure you can find it online . . .
> it's like a big Emory tradition.

This description shows Dooley's importance to Emory's students. While he is Emory's "eternal spirit," he is also a community member who appears in Emory's *Facebook*, an online guide for meeting fellow students and others on campus. While shopping in their campus bookstore, students can buy small representations of Dooley, as shown in the photograph. Dooley has the power to release students from class; during his week in the spring, if he appears in a classroom and shoots his squirt gun, the professor must let students go.[9] Who would not love such a ghost? Like the "Lord of Misrule" of medieval times, he joyfully subverts familiar routines and changes the usual power structure.

Some college ghosts defy folklorists' usual kinds of classification. Most scholars identify ghosts as spirits that haunt; vampires, the blood-sucking undead, are different creatures. So how can we classify the following story?

Gas Guzzler

> The Gas Guzzler in Vestal is rumored to be haunted. Supposedly a murder of a little boy happened there some time ago. The story was that he was murdered by his parents in front of the gas station. So now when you drive by the gas guzzler, you can see the shadow of a little boy and your tank runs out of gas.

Aaron, a nineteen-year-old Binghamton University student, told this story in the fall of 2004. Strangely, the murdered boy's ghost seems to drain students' gas much as a vampire would suck people's blood. This unusual ghost/vampire hybrid kills nobody. It just removes gas, an important and increasingly expensive commodity that gives students the power to get around town by themselves. Two freshmen with cars of their own told me that this story scared them more than any other ghost story they had heard on campus. The "Gas Guzzler" legend has a cognate in children's folklore; Simon J. Bronner notes that in the legend of "Knock-Knock Street," a woman runs over a little boy and drives away with the boy's hand stuck to her car (1988: 145). While this legend warns children to take care, the "Gas Guzzler" story focuses more on confronting fear and conserving gas.

A different classification problem applies to a ghost that rearranges all the furniture in the room of a college residence hall but leaves no other clue of its identity (Motif E599.6, "Ghosts move furniture"). Poltergeists, identified in studies of the supernatural for many years, move things around and cause damage; furniture rearrangement disturbs people but does not harm them or their property. Disorder is not as severe as destruction, but it serves as a trope for things that we cannot easily understand. Furniture-moving ghosts are audible but invisible. How can we categorize the sense of a supernatural "presence" that has no clear form? My answer to these classificatory questions is that we should rely on sensory evidence and not worry too much about traditional classifications. In this study I work with college students' own categories, which rely heavily on sense perceptions. These perceptions form the heart of their stories, offering listeners evidence to accept or reject.

Many college ghost stories are told as true, and for a number of tellers, they are true. W. K. McNeil says, "Whether or not ghosts exist, they are psychologically real" (1985: 23). Linda Dégh decries the current "irrationality explosion" but asks "Are we certain that the noises in old houses, the sights, screams, footsteps, the stopping and starting of old clocks, rocking chairs, and music boxes are not caused by restless spirits? No, we are not" (2001: 6–8). I will go one step farther here and say that some of my colleagues and I have had experiences that are difficult to identify by rational means. Barbara Walker's term "out of the ordinary" works well for narratives about what some people who live and work in college communities have experienced. Walker asserts that "we live in an imprecise and ambiguous world, which in its inexactitude allows for the awesome, the inexplicable, the wondrous" (1995: 1). In this complex world, ghost stories tell us about exciting, sometimes frightening possibilities that widen our dimensions of meaning.

Early Campus Ghostlore

Not many American colleges and universities have kept chronicles of their early folklore of the supernatural. Some campus newspapers have published articles about ghosts around Halloween, when folk tradition draws attention to the spirits of the dead (Santino 1994). Although most institutions of higher learning have compiled their own histories, few have included resident ghosts in their historical records. Some shining exceptions to that pattern have included Mount Saint Mary's University in Emmitsburg, Maryland, Sweet Briar College in Sweet Briar, Virginia, and the University of Northern Iowa in Cedar Falls, Iowa.

Mount Saint Mary's College, founded in 1808 by Father John DuBois, is the oldest Roman Catholic independent college in the United States. According to Lisa Villard, who wrote a paper at Mount Saint Mary's on "The Legends of the Mount," a priest foretold the erection of a church at the present location of Mount Saint Mary's in the early eighteenth century. When Father John took one of his many trips through the South, he followed a light on the mountainside, thinking it might be coming from a settler's cottage.

Monument in the Williams family graveyard at Sweet Briar College, where the ghost of Daisy Williams has played tricks on students. Photograph by Geoffrey Gould.

No matter how far he walked, he could not catch up with the light. Finally, Father John stopped, made a cross from two sticks, and attached it to a tree. Later, he came back to that location to found Mount Saint Mary's—and then he learned about the prediction of the eighteenth-century priest. This wonderful story of the college's founding resembles the saint's legend, in which amazing and miraculous events form the center of a narrative.

Another legend of Mount Saint Mary's concerns a slave, Leander, who was punished for stealing by having his hand cut off. Lisa Villard's version of this story explains that the former slave quarters were located on the spot where Phillips Hall now stands; students who listen very carefully can hear the slaves' cries and screams. If students do not lock their windows, they may get a shocking surprise: Leander's hand crawls up the side of the dorms at night, looking for a window through which it can crawl. Here we can apply the traditional motif E422.1.11.3, "Ghost in the form of a hand."

Dennis Hauck's *Haunted Places: The National Directory* mentions that Mount Saint Mary's keeps files of ghost stories; some students have said that administrators keep the files in a locked room where students must not go (1996: 207). When I visited Mount Saint Mary's in the summer of 2003,

I discovered that there was no locked room, just a kind archivist, Rebecca Fitzgerald, who helped me to find Lisa Villard's paper and several others. Since the folklorist Marie Campbell once taught at Mount Saint Mary's, the college has a good collection of folklore of the supernatural, including legends about black masses in the campus grotto in the 1970s. Taking a walk past some of the residence halls, I met two resident assistants (RAs) who told me stories about things that had happened at their college: a nun's and priest's joint suicide after an illicit relationship, a room with blood pouring from its walls, the ghost of Father Bruté in room 252 of Bruté Hall, and a shadowy image of a man in a mirror. The two RAs also mentioned a ghostly horseman that rides over an underground tunnel and a spectral Civil War soldier, buried upside down, who still shouts "Turn me over!" At Mount Saint Mary's, students take pride in their resident ghosts. It is worth noting that Gettysburg, advertised in tourist literature as one of America's "most haunted" towns, is just a few miles away.

Another famous campus ghost is Daisy Williams, the daughter of Indiana Williams, who founded Sweet Briar College near Lynchburg, Virginia. Tragically, Daisy died of pneumonia at the age of sixteen in 1884. Her grieving mother, who died in 1900, left instructions in her will for Sweet Briar, her home—once a thriving plantation—to be transformed into an educational institution for young women in Daisy's memory. During the years since then, Sweet Briar administrators, professors, and students have warmly remembered Daisy and her mother. The Monument Hill graveyard reminds members of the campus community how much Daisy and her mother mean to them. When I visited that graveyard in the summer of 2003, I met a Sweet Briar alumna and an elderly man whose grandfather had attended Daisy's funeral. Remembering what his grandfather had told him, the man described mourners' sadness as they watched Daisy's horse pulling her coffin up the hill to the cemetery. The horse had to struggle because the hill was so steep, and the mourners noticed that someone had tied Daisy's gloves around the horse's neck. Later, Daisy's grieving parents donated a window to their church in memory of their daughter. These details, carefully remembered and retold, show how strongly Daisy's death affected those who knew her.

It is only natural, then, that stories about Daisy continue to be told at Sweet Briar, which was founded in memory of her life and untimely death. Some of the most meaningful stories appear in Martha Stohlman's *The Story of Sweet Briar College* (1956). Stohlman recounts the story of a catastrophic fire in 1927, which almost destroyed Sweet Briar House, the center of the original plantation. After college firefighters, two local fire departments, and students put the fire out, an instructor went over to view the remains of the house:

> As she stood by the sundial in the boxwood circle, she saw a woman and a little girl slowly approach the house, hand in hand, from the garden on the left of the house. They stood for a moment and surveyed the ruin, then . . . they climbed the steps, passed through the burned doorway, and entered the front hall. The amazed spectator followed quickly to the place where they had disappeared, but no one was there (1956: 170).

This moving personal experience story, published in the *Sweet Briar News*, comforted students and faculty members after the fire. The story reminded everyone that Daisy and her mother were still there, watching over the campus community.

Sweet Briar's website, "Ghosts of Sweet Briar College," offers a wealth of stories about Daisy and her mother: some from personal experience, others from older legends.[10] One of the most amusing stories on that site is "Daisy Drove My Car," which tells of two female students' lighthearted visit to the graveyard on Monument Hill late at night with their male friends. The narrator, Kerri Rawlings '97, remembers that she carefully set her car's emergency brake. When her friend Joey asked whether students honored Daisy Williams, Kerri facetiously answered, "Yeah, we have to face the monument five times a day and bow." Kerri's answer apparently made Daisy angry, because the car started to roll downhill. Scared to death, the four young people jumped into the car and left the graveyard as fast as they could. "To this day," Kerri says, "I get goose bumps when I think back to that warm July evening when I had my encounter with Daisy" (Rawlings 2000). When some of my own students read this story on the Internet, they laughed with delight, saying it was one of the best ghost stories they had ever heard. Stories like this one give students the message that beloved ghosts can participate in their daily lives, both playing amusing tricks and scaring people out of their wits.

Stories about campus ghosts often circulate around Halloween, when students are in the mood to hear about supernatural subjects. Halloween parties became common on college campuses by the last decade of the nineteenth century. At the University of Northern Iowa, students celebrated Halloween in the 1890s by carving pumpkins, pulling taffy, and playing games. By 1911, they were serving kegs of cider to party-goers, whose fortunes were told by a visiting witch. An "All College Spook Party" took place in the mid-1920s. At this point, ghost stories took their place on the Halloween agenda, along with games, stunts, poetry readings, and costumes. Residence halls and clubs developed their own Halloween traditions, some of which included haunted rooms. When horror movies became popular in the 1940s and 1950s, students used favorite films to help create a spooky atmosphere.[11]

Another important aspect of the University of Northern Iowa's ghostlore has been entertainment of local children. In 1915, university students helped an elementary school perform a Witch and Ghost Drill. By the mid-1960s, students were putting on various kinds of parties for children, including trick-or-treating in the residence halls. Fraternities organized spooky events, and students living in residence halls tried to find original ways to entertain their young guests. These philanthropic events balanced out the occasional Halloween pranks and property damage, some of which resulted from massive food fights in the residence halls.

The University of Northern Iowa has two well-known ghosts: Zelda and Augie. Stories about Zelda, known as the "spirit of the theatre," have circulated since 1963. She used to live in the basement of the Old Auditorium but moved to the Strayer-Wood Theatre when it opened in 1978. Students say that Zelda is a helpful ghost, because she once made an electrical cable fall on the only seat in the theater that was empty. She shouts insults, cries like a baby, plays the piano, and opens and closes doors.

UNI's other ghost, Augie, is supposed to have been a soldier at the time of World War II who died in Lawther Hall when it functioned as an infirmary. Students associate him with Lawther's attic but have heard him all around the building. Typically, Augie has taken posters off walls, moved them to the middle of women's bedrooms, turned on radios, and made the radios play while unplugged. He has also made a TV screen turn blue and flashed the message "Good Night" on the screen while walking toward a female student's bed. "Augie's Attic" was the name of a haunted house event held in Lawther Hall every year between 1980 and 1997. These haunted houses raised a good amount of money for other residence hall activities, with as many as a thousand people coming to see the spooky scenes that students had created.

College and Camp

To clarify how campus storytelling initiates its listeners, I want to compare American colleges to "sleepaway camps": residential camps where children stay for as short a time as a week or as long as two months in the summer.

Aaron Karo, who wrote his very funny *Ruminations on College Life* shortly after his graduation from the University of Pennsylvania in the spring of 2001, compares college to camp: "The first week of college feels kind of like camp. You've got enough clothes to last you a few weeks, you're sleeping in a little bed, and you write letters to your parents and friends. After two months I was like, 'OK, this has been fun, but the summer is over now, time to go home.' The RA was in the hallway stopping dazed kids from leaving. They were all packed up saying, 'Wait, you mean this isn't camp? But it feels just like camp! What? Four more years?'" (2002: 6). In this humorous description, the resident assistant or RA seems less like a Residential Life staff member than a camp counselor. The students, who are just "kids," feel so homesick that they can hardly concentrate on their life at college. Karo's description makes students laugh because it approximates the truth. The first weeks of college *are* very difficult, and some students wish they could retreat to the comfort of home.

For most American students, going to college means greater independence, excitement, and stress. Whether they go to college in their hometowns or far away, students must learn how to function on their own, without their parents' constant guidance. It has become customary for parents to take their college-bound children on long shopping excursions to prepare for separation and change. These shopping trips serve as rituals of preparation, in which parents and their children acquire bedding, bathroom supplies, and other objects to create a comfortable nest away from home. For many parents, these rituals do not seem unfamiliar, as their college-bound children have already made the more limited transition from home to summer camp.

During the months of July and August, American pre-freshmen and their parents troop down the aisles of stores specializing in college supplies to buy the necessities of college life. In the summer of 2005, the website of Bed, Bath and Beyond included a guide for entering students, "Survival 101: Your Info Source."[12] Sections of this guide offer advice on choosing the right college, writing admissions essays, storing clothes, doing laundry, and coexisting peacefully with a roommate. A sample piece of advice is "Keep your fingers crossed. The roommate from hell may turn out to be your best friend." With "survival" as their keyword, prospective freshmen and their parents know that something serious and harrowing will soon take place. If they buy all the proper equipment, they may feel ready to confront this challenge.

In their first months of college, students undergo an initiatory experience that will prove their abilities, both in the classroom and in social situations. This experience seems especially significant because American society has an uneven set of rituals to acknowledge children's transformation into adults. Teenagers can drive at the age of sixteen and vote at the age of eighteen, when they also become eligible for military service. Students aged eighteen or older do not need to share information about their progress in college with their parents. Strict laws about underage drinking decree a drinking age of twenty-one, which does not, of course, keep students from drinking; subversion of the drinking laws belongs to the college initiatory experience. Survival of freshman year marks a major milestone on the road toward maturity.

Arnold van Gennep was the first scholar who forcefully demonstrated how much young people need initiation rituals. His studies of initiations in Africa, South America, and Australia show the importance of rites of passage for the young (1960). Introducing the concept of liminality, which involves transition and transformation, van Gennep identifies pre-liminal, liminal, and post-liminal stages. Further developing van Gennep's three-part model, Victor Turner explains that standing "betwixt and between" two states of being makes initiates receptive to their elders' instruction. The rite of passage into adulthood has three stages—departure, initiation, and return—with a period of seclusion as the central initiation phase (1967). This sequence parallels Joseph Campbell's outline of the folk narrative hero's progress, outlined in his *Hero with a Thousand Faces* (1967). Like folk heroes of traditional stories, freshmen follow a three-stage pattern of initiation, with a ceremonious departure from home in the late summer or fall, an academic year of relative seclusion, and return home after examinations in the spring.

Simon J. Bronner's analysis of college initiations offers intriguing examples of initiation rituals for freshmen and pledges of Greek organizations. Penn State freshmen getting "tarred and feathered" with feathers and molasses, Vassar freshmen kneeling and singing to seniors, and Michigan State fraternity brothers branding their bodies with Omega symbols are among the examples Bronner offers (1995: 72–73, 79, 136). Alan Dundes's article "The Elephant Walk and Other Amazing Hazing" suggests that fraternities' central strategies for humiliating their initiates are infantilization and feminization. Various versions of the "Elephant Walk" ritual decree that pledges walk or crawl in a circle, in close touch with each other's genitalia (2002: 95–121).

Unfortunately, some fraternity initiation rituals have had tragic results; the college legend "The Fatal Fraternity Initiation" (motif Z 510) reflects shattering losses. Newspaper articles, television features, and web pages about these tragedies have led to nationwide laws against hazing.[13] In some campus legends, the victim of extreme fraternity hazing becomes a ghost, continually reminding others of what happened to him. Two stories of this kind appear in chapter 4.

In comparison to hazing, storytelling seems like a relatively safe form of initiation into college life. How does storytelling initiate students? Three good examples of this process can be found in folklore studies of the late 1960s and 1970s. In "Some Functional Horror Stories on the Kansas University Campus" (1966), Daniel Barnes shows how horror legends warn students against getting into dangerous situations. In "Dormitory Legend-Telling in Progress," Sylvia Grider demonstrates how freshman women in an Indiana University residence hall "'initiate' or scare for fun" fellow students who have not yet heard Hatchet Man legends they know (1973: 8). And Helen Gilbert, in analyzing fifty-eight versions of the legend "The Crack in the Abbey Floor" at Saint John's University in Collegeville, Minnesota, finds that students emphasize the legend's stable core, evidence of a dead person's spirit (1975: 75). Ultimately, Gilbert says, such legends initiate students into a group of believers (1975: 76). I examine two stories related to Gilbert's study in chapter 8.

At both college and camp, legend-telling helps young people adjust to their new surroundings. Residential Life staff members and camp counselors anticipate discomfort, planning games, storytelling or conversation sessions, and get-togethers to make their new residents feel better. Many camps have traditional campfires, where special foods are served and stories are told. Jay Mechling has analyzed the "Magic of the Boy Scout Campfire" (1980) along psychoanalytic lines, finding campfire rituals to be conducive to masculine bonding.

Some of the best-known camp stories describe a menacing figure who returns cyclically to the place where a tragic event took place. As John Widdowson explains in his study *If You Don't Be Good* (1977), parents and others responsible for children's welfare have often used frightening figures as means of social control. "The Cropsey Maniac," for example, tells of a camp custodian losing his wife and children in a fire accidentally set by campers; counselors say he returns each year to kill at least one camper in payment for his terrible loss (Haring and Breslerman 1977). In "The Boondocks Monster of Camp Wapehani" (1973), James P. Leary explains how counselors in an Indiana Boy Scout camp used legends of a returning monster to control campers' behavior over a period of three decades. Bill Ellis's "'Ralph and Rudy': The Audience's Role in Recreating a Camp Legend" (1982) features a drunken wild man named Ralph, who decapitates his brother Rudy and then terrorizes campers and counselors. As Ellis shows, camp legends like this grow and change according to their context, serving the needs of both counselors and campers.

At college as well as at camp, stories of maniacs and supernatural figures frighten those who have recently joined the community. Deep in the woods, away from home's comforts, children listen to counselors and older campers tell stories as they try to cope with feelings of isolation and disorientation. Similarly, college students listen to upperclassmen, resident assistants, and others who seem like expert navigators of unfamiliar terrain. These veterans of college life understand that a shocking story may facilitate adjustment to a new environment better than mildly reassuring words can.

College has a lofty goal: completion of an education that will lead to a productive adult life. While camps encourage children to acquire skills and develop some degree of independence, their primary goal is to provide an enjoyable interlude away from home. After a few weeks or months at camp, children know they will return to their homes, where the proving ground of school awaits them. College is the culmination of all their schooling, from kindergarten through high school. Offering exciting new opportunities, it also introduces a degree of stress that supersedes what has come before. As speakers at colleges' introductory convocations tend to say, what happens in college prefigures the course of adult life and influences one's sense of self-worth.[14] College lays the foundation for a future that may seem, at first, to be hazy, uncertain, and intimidating.

Small wonder, then, that entering freshmen welcome events that make college seem like camp. Some colleges plan orientation events that take students out of the center of campus and into a wooded area, where they can enjoy hearty meals, games, campfires, and storytelling. At Dartmouth College in Hanover, New Hampshire, members of the Dartmouth Outing Club (DOC) have organized a freshman trip to Moosilauke Ravine Lodge since 1935. In the spring of 2005, Kyle, an eighteen-year-old Dartmouth freshman, e-mailed the following story.

The Ghost of Doc Benton

All incoming freshman students at Dartmouth participate in a group outing (about 20 or so kids per trip) to the Moosilauke Ravine Lodge. It's called the DOC trip. It is geared toward getting to know yous and what not, but one of the events is a late night story telling and the premier story is one about the ghost of Doc Benton.

Benton was the apprentice of a fine doctor in the community, and though the doctor was regarded as a leader in his field, he was considered overly eccentric in his work by some. When he died in the late 1700's, he left all of his materials and research to the rather young doctor Benton. Doc Thomas Benton practiced medicine in many different places, but always was forced to flee after being linked to some very mysterious disappearances. He finally settled in a town, not far from the Moosilauke Ravine Lodge, and became well respected.

Over time he began acting strangely and people noticed that he seemed not to age and looked like the same youth he was when he first arrived. Then one day, he aged quite suddenly and fled to a shack in the woods. Pretty soon some strange things started to happen. Several cows, horses and dogs were found dead, all with a white pinprick on the back of their left ears. A group of men went to go visit the deranged Benton in the woods to ask if they could help, but they found him dead in his home, with a white pinprick behind his left ear.

Some years later a girl was abducted by a man in a long black trench coat and those who witnessed it said it was none other than Doc Benton, who had been dead for years. She was later found dead with the same white pinprick.

Many strange things have happened in and around the Moosilauke Ravine Lodge since that day (since the 1800's): things such as cables being mysteriously cut, strange animal deaths, and weird sightings from first-year Dartmouth students.

It is rumored that he waits in the woods at night each summer on the lookout for a young virgin freshman girl. Fortunately, there hasn't been a death of a young girl since the 1980's. No freshmen virgin girls have come to Moosilauke Ravine Lodge since then!

This college orientation narrative fits the pattern of stories told to new campers about ghosts of demented assailants who have killed campers in various horrible ways. On the anniversary of these campers' deaths, storytellers say, the murderers' ghosts come back, eager to kill again. Young listeners are supposed to shiver, fearful that they themselves will become the next victims. The story's central character is supposed to seem real; in this case, he is a "well-respected" member of the community. Although Benton has a good reputation, he goes crazy, as the Cropsey maniac does, retreating to a shack in the woods and attacking innocent victims. The "white pinprick behind his left ear" sounds sinister, inexplicable.

Up to the last paragraph, this story sounds like it is meant to scare the Dartmouth freshmen who are out in the woods together, like first-time campers. However, the mention of "a young virgin freshman girl" reclassifies the text as a comical "If a virgin enters . . ." story. The line "No freshmen virgin girls have come to Moosilauke Ravine Lodge since then!" will probably elicit laughter. Like "funny-scary" stories told by preadolescents at camp and at slumber parties, stories like this one begin with alarming details and end with funny punchlines.[15]

As the story's narrator explains, the Dartmouth Outing Club trip is "geared toward getting to know yous and whatnot." Hearing that no virgins have come to Moosilauke Ravine Lodge for about twenty years, new freshmen can laugh together and begin to make friends. This familiar-sounding and amusing narrative serves an initiatory function, helping students feel at home in their new environment. It also teaches incoming freshmen about some of their college's culture. Simon J. Bronner suggests that most contemporary college orientations are "psychological rather than cultural," focusing on individuals' feelings rather than groups' rites of passage (1995: 86). At colleges like Dartmouth, administrators know the value of scary stories and make sure that incoming students learn them.

Besides initiatory scary stories, other kinds of college lore resemble the folklore of children at camp and at school. Jokes, pranks, nicknames, beliefs about good and bad luck, sports customs, horror stories about authority figures, and other forms of folklore bring excitement to college campuses, camps, and playgrounds. Space constraints make it impossible to examine these parallels in detail. Like children at school and at camp, college students have a heightened awareness of amazing and uncanny events. Selma Fraiberg's *The Magic Years* (1959) and other studies have examined children's sense of wonder; it is also important to recognize the sense of wonder inspired by elements of campus folklore.

Enchanted Landscape

Students enter the ghostly realm more easily because of the entertaining, established traditions that make college campuses enchanted places. In his book *Mapping the Invisible Landscape*, Kent C. Ryden states that all human habitations have "an unseen layer of usage, memory and significance—an invisible landscape, if you will, of imaginative landmarks" (1993: 40). The need for a landscape that goes beyond everyday reality has been documented in different ways. Writing about people who love fantasy literature, Clyde S. Kilby notes that our primary world has become "emptier and emptier" as scientific measurement has reduced mythic images to quantifiable units. Contemporary reality, Kilby says, makes us long for "a world in which myths turn out to be true" (1979: 71). In a different but comparable context, Sabina Magliocco suggests that "Neo-Pagans are reenchanting the world, creating a complement to the mechanistic philosophy of the post-Enlightenment era" (2004: 121). At American colleges, entering freshmen find that students of earlier eras have imaginatively structured the place where they will study and amuse themselves. This landscape involves many rituals: entrances and exits, tasks, prohibitions, and trysts that make lovers' dreams come true.

When students first arrive at college, they walk or drive through gates that symbolize their entrance into a realm separated from the outside world. Some gates have more ritual significance than others. The main gate of Kenyon College in Gambier, Ohio, framing the Main Path, supposedly stands above the mouth of hell. When walking through this gate, students may hold hands or touch each other in some other way, to protect themselves from bad luck. At Brown University in Provincetown, Rhode Island, freshmen learn that they should only walk through Van Wickle Gate twice: the first time as a freshman at the university's opening convocation, the second time as a graduating senior. Anyone who breaks that rule may suffer failure and despair. To protect students from this terrible fate, guards stand by the gate when it opens at any time other than those two ritually safe moments of the college year.

One danger on the enchanted college landscape comes from touching places that are supposed to cause academic failure. Students at the University of Michigan in Ann Arbor who worry about their grades have avoided stepping on a big "M" on a walkway (Newland 1965). In front of the Law School at Louisiana State University in Baton Rouge is a sidewalk that students avoid before final exams; legend has it that a female student was run over at that spot years ago, and the concrete sidewalk was painted green because the blood stains could not be removed (Bordelon 1991: 12). And at Binghamton University, walking all the way across a circle-shaped amphitheater invites academic failure. These dangerous areas remind us of cracks on sidewalks in children's folklore: "Step on a crack, break your mother's back."

At Randolph-Macon College in Lynchburg, Virginia, older students tell younger ones that if they walk in Mary's Garden, they will be cursed forever. They also explain that if a female student enters the Engagement Tower without getting engaged or married, no man will ever ask her to marry him. Similarly, at the College of William and Mary in Williamsburg, Virginia, students who walk across the Crim Dell Bridge must remember certain rules. Kissing a boyfriend or girlfriend on Crim Dell Bridge ensures a long-lasting relationship. If the relationship goes sour, the best way to make things better is to throw the offending boyfriend or girlfriend off the bridge.

Some traditional tasks on college campuses resemble quests undertaken by a folktale's hero. At the College of William and Mary, students challenge themselves to complete three tasks before graduating. The first task in this "triathlon" is jumping the wall of the Governor's Palace in colonial Williamsburg. The second is streaking through the sunken gardens in the middle of Old Campus, and the third is jumping into the Crim Dell pond. While most institutions of higher learning do not have such triathlons, many have at least one task that students hope to complete.

During the early days of coeducation, women learned that by performing a certain ritual, they could become "coeds." One female student who attended Michigan State University in East Lansing in the early 1960s learned that she could become a coed by being kissed under Beaumont Tower at midnight; another female student at the University of Michigan in the mid-1960s heard that she would be a coed if kissed under the Engineering Arch at midnight, and a third female student at Indiana University in Bloomington in the mid-1960s said, "We have a marble Gazebo (garden house) with a chiming clock nearby. A girl isn't a coed until she's kissed there when the clock is chiming" (Newland 1965). Through such rituals students show their awareness of the transformative power of kissing, which provides happy endings in such well-known folktales as "Sleeping Beauty" (AT410) and "The Frog King or Iron Henry" (AT 440). Until the late 1960s, kisses at certain times and places assured female students at American colleges that they had entered the exciting realm of college courtship, but no such rituals changed male students' status. Chapter 5 examines male and female students' courtship roles from the nineteenth century to the present.

In the enchanted landscape of the college campus, statues that walk, talk, and test students' purity seem to fit right in. Most legends about statues address the ever-popular virginity test: who is still a virgin, and who has become sexually active? Sexual prohibitions for young adults have become

Statue of Andrew Dickson White (1832–1918), whose ghost will walk across Cornell's courtyard if a virgin graduates. Photograph by Geoffrey Gould.

less stringent since the 1950s, but who has had sex and who hasn't remain questions of interest. Freshmen who have not yet become sexually active may do so in college; those who have already crossed the "great divide" may find that they have more freedom for sexual experimentation than they had while living at home.

Two of the most famous "virgin-testing" statues are the ones at Cornell University in Ithaca, New York. On the oldest part of campus, statues of Ezra Cornell (1807–1874) and Andrew Dickson White (1832–1918) face each other across a courtyard. Freshmen learn that if a virgin walks through the courtyard, Cornell and White will step off their pedestals and walk to the center of the space, shaking hands to celebrate their astonishing discovery. Each academic year, students or custodial staff members repaint the red and white footprints between the two statues. These footprints keep the legend fresh in students' minds; in red and white, the university's colors, they reinforce student spirit. This is one of many cases in which uncanny spirits and school spirit intersect: double-edged entertainment that adds depth to students' life on campus.

At Randolph-Macon College, a statue of General Jones brandishes a sword. Freshmen learn that if a student who is not a virgin stands in front of General Jones, he will lift his sword and cut off her head. Few students seem to take this statue seriously. One Randolph-Macon student wrote in the fall of 2004, "I've done that, and I've still got a head."[16] Even though the statue provokes laughter, it reminds students of sexual taboos of the past and present.

Other virginity-testing statues include Willie the Silent at Rutgers University in New Brunswick, New Jersey, who is supposed to start talking if a virgin passes, and a sculpture of Pegasus at Binghamton University, which is expected to take wing if a virgin goes by. At Boston University, a sculpture in front of Manning Chapel is supposed to represent "swords beaten into plowshares," but students say that it looks like a flock of birds rising up into the air. Supposedly, if a virgin ever graduates from Boston University, the whole flock of birds will fly away. There are so many statues and sculptures connected to students' virginity that it is impossible to list them all here.

Checking students' virginity is not the only job for campus statues. Giving students good luck, especially before exams, also ranks high. At Brown University in Provincetown, Rhode Island, students say that rubbing the nose of the bust of John Hay will bring them good luck. John Hay, a Brown alumnus, served as an advisor to President Lincoln. Now, he has a different job: helping students through tests and exams. Another good-luck bringer is the statue of Benigna von Zinzendorf that stands on the south side of Moravian College in Bethlehem, Pennsylvania. This life-sized figure of a serious-looking woman sits in a small garden behind Main Hall. Founded in 1742 by the Moravian Church, Moravian College is the sixth-oldest college in the United States. The statue in Benigna von Zinzendorf's memory reflects the college's focus on early founders, as she established one of the first boarding schools for girls in America. Students say they will have good luck if they pat Benigna's head three times or sit on her lap. Sitting on her lap does not feel right to some students, who worry about how mysterious she looks at night.

On some college campuses, cemeteries remind students of the boundary between life and death. Students at Ohio University in Athens say their university stands at the center of a pentagram, with cemeteries at each of the star's points (Brown 2006). Mound Cemetery in Marietta, Ohio, is on the same street where Marietta College stands. Conus Mound, thirty feet fall, is one of the oldest Indian mounds in the Northwest Territory. Students who choose to climb the mound must go up a staircase, framed by signs warning people not to step on the mound itself. In this cemetery lie the bodies of veterans of the French and Indian War, the American Revolution, the War of 1812, and the Civil War. Few cemeteries provide such an impressive cross-section of American history, including a thirty-foot mound built by the area's oldest inhabitants.

At Mount Holyoke College in South Hadley, Massachusetts, students eat ice cream at the grave of their founder, Mary Lyon, at dawn on the anniversary of the day she was born, February 28, 1797. Strangely enough, Mary Lyon's body does not lie in this grave, because she was interred in Buckland, Massachusetts. Why do the college's administrators ask students to consume ice cream at a grave at dawn on a freezing winter day? Coldness inside and outside of the body give students an unforgettable *memento mori*. This festive ritual entertains students in a quirky way while reminding them to honor their college's founder.

On many American college campuses, freshmen and pre-freshmen hear legends about mysterious tunnels. Tour guides at MIT in Cambridge, Massachusetts, proudly tell prospective freshmen that MIT has the world's third-largest tunnel system, next to the Pentagon and the Kremlin (Corsbie-Massay 2005). On the website "College Tunnels" (1996), students have posted messages about explorations of their campuses' steam tunnel systems, describing hidden doors, labyrinthine underground passages, encounters with strange characters, and busts by campus police. University officials seldom speak of underground tunnels; why would they encourage students to consider an underground zone that is off-limits, filled with potential danger? Some students delight in pushing past these officials' rules, exploring a forbidden part of their campus.

Forbidden tunnels have inspired many legends about murder, accidental death, and suicide. Some stories are based on past mysteries, such as the disappearance of James Dallas Egbert III from Michigan State University on August 15, 1979. Students said that James had gotten hopelessly lost in the tunnels underneath Michigan State while playing Dungeons and Dragons. Investigators proved that, while he had spent some time in the tunnels, James then left the campus to go somewhere else. Unfortunately, he committed suicide a year later. In the years after his disappearance, students told legends saying that he had vanished into an underground labyrinth because of the role-playing game Dungeons and Dragons. Simon J. Bronner includes a story about Egbert's ghost in *Piled Higher and Deeper* (1995: 152).

Other stories tell of fatal fraternity initiations. Students at Johns Hopkins University in Baltimore, Maryland, say that Bloomberg Hall has eleven floors underground where fraternity initiates have died and ghosts have appeared. Students at Florida Southern College in Lakeland recall that during a fraternity initiation underground, an overweight student died because he could not get out. Similarly, at the United States Naval Academy in Annapolis, first-year students learn that first-year students have died in campus tunnels, which can be entered through manholes. In the 1980s, drawing a parallel between campus initiation and wartime Vietnam, students called the Naval Academy's tunnel system the Ho Chi Minh Trail (Burke 2005).

Tunnel legends at the University of California at Irvine focus on student protests of the 1960s. One story explains that UCI, built in the 1960s, got its system of underground passageways so that if students held a violent demonstration, faculty could escape through the tunnels. A second version of the same legend explains that the tunnels' construction had two purposes. The first was to provide an evacuation route for the university's president, and the second was to bring in the National Guard. Students say that administrators created hills in Aldrich Park so that students could not demonstrate there (Burke 2005).

Haunted Places

Some campus buildings are more likely than others to be haunted. High on the "most-haunted" list are residence halls, where students spend much of their time; libraries and theaters also have a strong traditional connection with haunting. In many cases, ghosts haunt a campus's oldest buildings, reminding students of their institution's beginnings. Ghosts that haunt buildings of more recent vintage may help students remember periods of stress and change, such as World War II and the turbulent 1960s and early 1970s. Buildings that resemble castles or mansions may make members of the campus community think about Gothic and nineteenth-century novels, in which supernatural events frequently take place.

One famous residence hall ghost is Condie Cunningham, a student who died in a Main Hall fire at the University of Montevallo in Alabama in 1908. According to the University of Montevallo's "Ghost Stories" website, Condie started the fire herself while making fudge with friends over a Bunsen burner; for almost a hundred years, her spirit has "run through the halls of the west wing in her flaming flannel nightgown" (2006). Condie's story warns students against doing anything that might start a fire; it also takes listeners back to the early days of their university, which was founded as Alabama Girls' Industrial

School in 1896. Main Hall, the campus's first residence hall, opened in 1897 ("Brief History" 2006; Tipton 1996). In recent years, ghost-hunting teams such as Rick and Bubba Ghostbusters have used technological equipment to seek traces of Condie's ghost. Even without advanced technology, it is possible to see Condie's image by looking closely at her room's door, kept in a small, dark area of Main Hall by university officials ("Condie Cunningham's Door" 2004). This image on wood has drawn many student visitors, just as relics draw religious pilgrims to shrines.

At Ball State University in Muncie, Indiana, students talk about the ghost of William Schamberg, who hanged himself in Elliott Hall on January 26, 1947, soon after the end of World War II. An editorial in the *Ball State Daily News* explains that Schamberg, disabled and disfigured after fighting in the war, committed suicide because other students shunned him ("Ghost" 1986: 4). Unlike Condie Cunningham, Schamberg does not seem to have been an actual university student. The story about his death and subsequent haunting of the hall makes the World War II period seem real and frightening; it also emphasizes how hard it can be to make friends in a new environment. As the oldest residence hall on the Ball State campus, Elliott Hall seems to be the right place for a historically significant haunting. Students take pride in their hall's ghost, not appearing to mind that university officials deny Schamberg's existence (1986: 5).

Similarly, students at Ohio University recall a tumultuous historical period while narrating legends about Wilson Hall. Built in 1965, Wilson was originally known as Crook Hall; later it took the name of a chemistry professor who had made a substantial bequest to Ohio University. A former Residential Life staff member at Ohio University told me in the winter of 2003 that Wilson Hall held the spirit of a witch who had committed suicide there in the early 1970s. Dead animals appeared in hall closets; doors locked and unlocked themselves; furniture moved itself around; and lights turned themselves on and off. When students tried to verify the witch's suicide, relevant documents disappeared from the university's archives. Another version of this story published in Ohio University's online newspaper *The Post* states that the resident who committed suicide had "drawn symbols and signs on the walls with her own blood before she died" and that current students can identify her haunted room through "a demonic face seen in the wood grain of the door" (Schonhardt 2001). Like Condie Cunningham's face, this image on the door of a residence hall room recalls past danger and suggests the possibility of a visit to confirm a campus legend's authenticity.

North and South Mandelle Halls, Mount Holyoke College. Photograph by Geoffrey Gould.

It is not difficult to see the connection between this legend about a student witch and fears of student rebellions in the 1960s and early 1970s. When the hippie movement began in the mid-1960s, some adults worried about students running wild. Later, when the war in Vietnam and Cambodia motivated students to go on strike, fears of students getting out of control increased. Rebellion against traditional religions also caused parental alarm. As early as the mid-1960s, some students rejected their families' religions in favor of studying Wicca. Not knowing that Wicca was a nature-oriented religion, some people feared that it involved animal sacrifices, demonic symbols, and flirtation with death. The legend about the suicidal witch of Wilson Hall encapsulates society's fears of rebellion, wildness, and rejection of safe, conventional worship.

If a campus building looks old, creepy, and mysterious, it probably has a ghost. At Mount Holyoke College, for example, the twin residence halls North and South Mandelle, built in 1923, stand on a hill to one side of the campus. Like Thornfield, the home of Mr. Rochester in Charlotte Brontë's *Jane Eyre*, they seem isolated and enigmatic. With gables, tower rooms, and tall chimneys, these four-story buildings have an air of the past. Since the late 1970s, Mount Holyoke students have told stories about a student living in South Mandelle's tower room who committed suicide by jumping off the building's roof. Since then, students say, her room stays locked, and she cries late at night. One version of the story explains that a girl named Jane had visits from the suicide's shadow in the mid-1970s (Birkrem 2001). Like Jane Eyre, who hears the cries and laughter of the insane Mrs. Rochester, this Jane cannot escape from the pall of the past.

Libraries also remind students of past eras. Their shelves of old books bring to mind wondrous, little-known stories. Usually open until late at night on weekdays, campus libraries give students the chance to study for long periods of time in a quiet place. While solitary study sometimes seems peaceful, it frequently involves stress, especially before tests and exams. The quietness of library "stacks" makes small noises seem louder; similarly, the exclusion of activities other than reading foregrounds unexpected sights. For many years, students on college campuses have spoken about encounters with ghosts in their libraries (Motif E338.8, "Ghost haunts library"). One such ghost is Mary Reed, who donated a generous amount of money to the University of Denver, which opened in 1932. The University of Denver's library is located in Mary Reed Hall. Students and library staff members have seen Mary reading in the dark in the library's Renaissance Room and DuPont Room ("Haunted Denver" 2005). Similarly, at the University of Rochester, students have gotten to know the ghost of a construction worker who helped to make the library beautiful. Eleanor, a twenty-year-old student at the University of Rochester, told this memorate in April 2001.

Ghost in the Library

I've told you about the ghost in the library. Okay, I think I saw him, right? He's supposedly a construction worker who fell off the scaffolding while building Rush Rhees Library (the big pretty one here). It was the early 30's, but I don't know which year. So . . . he's like a middle-aged man dressed like a construction worker from the 30's, and he wanders around the library, especially at night. People studying there at night catch glimpses of him once in a while.

I saw him walking around the corner in the stacks (that's where we keep all the books . . . it's the bookshelves, basically). Some people, though no cases have been reported lately, have actually talked to him, and he tells them his story about how he died and stuff. I forget his name, though. Even though I think I saw him, I don't really believe in ghosts; but it's cool, and I am still scared to go into the stacks alone at night, even though he's supposed to be nice.

Eleanor's story expresses ambivalence; she *thinks* she saw the ghost but isn't sure, and she doesn't really believe in ghosts—or does she? What she knows for certain is that "it's cool" to see this ghost and that Rush Rhees Library, the "big pretty one" on campus, deserves to have its own ghost story. Rush Rhees, built in the 1920s, is an elaborate, beautiful building that any ghost would be proud to haunt. Websites about the University of Rochester reveal that the construction worker is Pete Nicosia, a Sicilian mason's helper who died in 1929 (Bultrago 2005). Library ghosts like Pete add excitement to long periods of study. Freshmen making their first visits to the stacks alone may shiver with anticipatory dread, wondering whether a ghost will give them a sudden glimpse of a past tragedy.[17]

Campus theaters also invite ghostly visitations. Like libraries, they usually stay open late at night and serve as focal points for intense, sometimes stressful activity. Unlike libraries, however, campus theaters benefit from a well-established set of customs and beliefs. Members of a theatrical troupe never wish an actor good luck; instead, they say "Break a leg!" Anyone who mentions or quotes lines from Shakespeare's *Macbeth* risks invoking the "Scottish curse." In many theaters, a "ghost light" keeps potentially resentful spirits from causing mischief (Steppenwolf Theatre Company 2004–2005). Many legends suggest that actors, directors, and stagehands haunt theaters after death because they cannot bear to leave their beloved workplaces. At Rutgers University, for example, flickering lights and toppling musical instruments reveal the presence of the Little Theater's deceased director (Amato 2005). Similarly, in Phi Beta Kappa Hall of the College of William and Mary, a young actress who died before her play opened places her costume—a white dress—on a seat in the auditorium during rehearsals (Taylor 1999: 56). With so much folklore of this kind in active circulation, it is no wonder that theaters have some of the most vibrant ghosts on college campuses.

At Utah State University in Logan, the Lyric Theatre has had visits from a spectral actor dressed in Shakespearean garb; rumors suggest that he died at the hands of a fellow actor, who buried his victim in the theater's basement.[18] At Montana State University in Missoula, students and staff members have seen the apparition of a young female ghost, heard her footsteps, and felt fabric from her costume touch their arms (Munn 1994: 55). Sometimes such stories become part of initiation for freshmen and pre-freshmen. At the University of Redlands in California, for example, tour guides have told stories about their theater's ghost. This text came from Barbara Popadak, a junior at the University of Redlands who took pre-freshmen on tours in the summer of 1972.[19]

Opening Night

In about 1925 the University of Redlands had just completed their new Little Theater and it was opening night for the first dramatic production to be performed there. The director of this play, who was a teacher in the drama department, was on her way to the production when she was killed in a terrible automobile accident.

The play went on anyway, and it was reported that the director's ghost attended the production and has actually attended many of the other programs held in that theater. The ghost of this woman has reportedly been seen on several occasions after performances, and very late at night.

According to notes kept by this story's collector, Brigham Young University student Emily Howard, upperclassmen often tell the story of Redlands Theater's ghost to frightened freshmen. "Opening Night" serves as a good example of tour guides' representation of college mysteries, explicated by Kimberly Lau in "On the Rhetorical Use of Legend" (1998). Although a number of folklorists have studied college initiation in the context of freshman year, what happens during tours for pre-freshmen has received less scholarly attention.

Liminal Spaces

Within haunted campus buildings, certain spaces become focal points for a ghost's presence. Many of these spaces fit Victor Turner's definition of liminality: the state of being "betwixt and between" (1967). Entering freshmen have moved from home to college, from relative dependence as children to relative independence as young adults. When they start living in college residence halls, these new students must recalibrate familiar categories. While the residence hall is their new home, it also belongs to an educational institution, so it is partly private and partly public. As freshmen get accustomed to living in this hybrid realm, they learn which parts of the building best express the "betweenness" that they feel as new students.

Some residence hall spaces, such as attics and basements, fall outside the domain where students spend most of their time; they seem remote from everyday life's main routines. Neither uninhabitable nor fully inhabited, they eloquently express liminality. In adolescents' folklore and in horror films, attics have become well-known sources of assault from the supernatural. Since most

American high school graduates are well versed in folklore and popular culture, it is not surprising that they expect attics to hold ghostly dangers. Here is a brief memorate told by Fanchon Carey, a resident of Penobscot Hall at the University of Maine at Orono, in December 1966.

Spirits in the Attic

There was a dorm at Westbrook Junior College that no one would sign up for—voluntarily. It started about three years ago when one girl in the dorm had fantastic powers over the Ouija board. She'd get so excited that she'd even roll on the floor. All the kids thought that there were spirits in the attic that caused her powers, and no one wanted to live in the dorm. (Johnson 1966)

The only explanation for this residence hall's alleged danger is one short phrase: "spirits in the attic." Because attics are such well-known sources of trouble, this brief description suffices (Motif E402(b), "Noise of ghost heard in garret"). The storyteller also says very little about the Ouija board, a popular means of communication with spirits. The student who rolls on the floor seems to be a medium, channeling boisterous spirits. All we know about these spirits is that they come from the grim, shadowy realm of the attic. No further explanation seems necessary.

Similarly, basements function as liminal spaces where ghosts can easily appear. Students tend to visit basements more often than attics, as laundry rooms are often located below the building's main floors. Relatively isolated and quiet, basements provide a favorable environment for encounters with the supernatural. I have collected numerous legends about laundry-room ghosts that turn lights off and on, steal clothes, and appear on the surface of glass dryer doors. These legends depict the basement as an underground realm where students should watch their step.

Like attics and basements, elevators serve as prime liminal spaces. Moving between one floor and the next, they belong to neither one place nor another. Movies and popular television shows have endlessly exploited elevators' potential as places of horror and sudden, unexpected change. Legends told in college residence halls bring mass-media images to mind, as well as introducing warnings for the sake of students' safety.

Leslie, a nineteen-year-old female student at the University of Massachusetts at Amherst, told this admonitory legend in November 2001.

Elevator Surfing

Have you heard of "elevator surfing?" Well, according to my psychology professor, it used to be a common form of entertainment at the University of Massachusetts several years back. Kids in the Southwest residence area used to press the button to catch the elevator and run upstairs one floor. When they heard the doors slide open down below, they'd quickly pry open the doors on their level and hop on top of the car. Someone else would press buttons on several of the other 22 floors. They'd ride up and down. It seemed like a harmless activity at the time. In fact, it was all fun and games until someone got hurt.

Classes had just let out for the weekend. A group of guys began taking turns elevator surfing. Unaware of what was going on, someone on the 22nd floor waited for the elevator. As the elevator approached, the person heard a guy screaming. The screaming abruptly stopped once the elevator had arrived. The surfer had been squished in between the ceiling of the building and the top of the elevator. He was killed instantaneously.

Rumor has it that the elevator breaks down continuously because of the surfer who had died. That it is his spirit haunting the elevator. Whether or not the ghost is true, the incident really did happen!

Leslie's story tells us about a grisly conclusion to a game of danger: one of many forms of the traditional game of "chicken" that puts young people at risk. At the beginning, elevator surfing seems like fun, but soon the story's tone changes. The poor surfer dies horribly, "squished in between the ceiling of the building and the top of the elevator": a painful representation of being "betwixt and between." Leslie does not want her listeners to forget that this incident "really did happen." Lest anyone forget, the elevator's ghost reminds everyone of the tragedy. In chapter 4, I examine a broad range of such narratives of warning.

In a different way, bathrooms express liminality. As Jeannie B. Thomas notes in her essay "The Barfing Ghost of Burford Hall," a residence hall bathroom is "a public, cold, and impersonal place" where students perform private bodily functions (1991: 33–34). Novels such as *Harry Potter and the Chamber of Secrets* (1999), in which the ghost Moaning Myrtle leads Harry to an underground passageway, emphasize the ghostly potential of schools' bathrooms.

I have discovered that "haunted faucet" stories are relatively common in college residence halls. The following story was sent on e-mail by Lindsey, a twenty-five-year-old resident of Cornell University's Dickson Hall, in March 2004.

Haunted Faucet

When I was a sophomore, I lived in Dickson Hall on the 2nd floor. One of my friends lived on the 1st floor where the bathroom was supposedly haunted . . . Whenever my friend Lara would go to the bathroom, she claimed to hear the faucet turning on and off by itself. But when she stepped out of the stall to wash her hands, the water would mysteriously shut off.

When she told me of this, I went downstairs to check it out, but nothing strange happened. I tried this on several occasions, but nothing ever happened. The weird thing was that the faucet only acted up when she was alone in the bathroom. Lara was so freaked out that she began using the 2nd floor bathroom for the remainder of the year.

While I doubted her and attributed the running water to some faulty plumbing, she always swore to me that a ghost was responsible. For a long time, my other friends and I assumed she was a little crazy, but occasionally we would wonder if perhaps a ghost was actually responsible for the mystifying faucet.

Lindsey's story shows how much fun it can be to find a mystery in such a mundane space as a residence hall bathroom. Because the faucet only seems haunted when Lara is present, others can never know if her story is true or false. Lara's friends suspect that she is "a little crazy," but they wonder if the faucet has a supernatural explanation.

While I have never seen the haunted faucet of Dickson Hall, I have become familiar with an unusual faucet in Sullivan Hall at Binghamton University. Students say that this faucet is haunted, because it turns itself on and off. I have seen the Sullivan Hall faucet in action a number of times. This faucet never starts turning itself off and on until water has been running for a while. Does faulty water pressure explain the faucet, or is something stranger going on? Although some of my students have eagerly sought an answer to this question, I have been glad to think of the Sullivan faucet as an unsolved mystery.

Untold Stories

Other mysteries arise from crimes on college campuses and in their surrounding local communities. In the protected realm of the American college campus, narratives about violent crimes, including sexual assaults and attacks based on hate or race, shock and horrify listeners. College officials make campus crime figures available to the public, but when speaking to prospective students and their parents, they do not emphasize crimes. Instead, they talk about provisions for students' safety: "Safe Ride" schedules, "blue light" phones, and keycard systems that are supposed to keep intruders from entering residence halls. Knowing that the college has made provisions for students' safety, parents and their pre-freshmen can relax, feeling fairly confident that nothing terrible will happen.

Students' own techniques for staying safe involve sticking together and staying alert. Freshman women on several campuses have told me that they watch out for their friends at bars and parties, making sure that nobody leaves the public area for socializing. They also warn one another about dangerous scenarios by telling legends about terrible things that have happened in the recent past. Andrea Greenberg's article "Drugged and Seduced" (1973) shows how this kind of storytelling works: female pre-freshmen hear legends about extreme events from older friends, sisters, mothers, and other relatives and friends. Once they get to college, they share the stories they know with other students and learn new ones that are specific to their campus's landscape.

One such story was collected by June Baskett from her fellow student Pat Norville at the University of Western Kentucky in Bowling Green in January 1965.[20]

> One very dark and dreary night, a young girl was chased and raped by three boys in Lover's Lane. Eventually, two of the boys were caught by the police and tried. However, one of the boys was never found or seen again.
>
> Now every night at the time of the horrible incident a white form of a girl comes out and walks around looking in the windows of the cars for the boy that was never caught. Also, the dogs will begin to bark as they did on the night that she was raped.

This narrative is immediately recognizable as a legend. Its setting is "Lover's Lane," familiar to anyone who has heard the horror legend of the hook-handed murderer who tries to get into young people's parked cars. Here the assailant is not a hook-handed human, but the ghost of a victim of sexual assault. Although the narrator says that she was "chased and raped," we have to assume that she was also murdered, because her ghost pursues the only man who got away. Horrifically, she has been assaulted not just by one man, but by three, the European folktale's most common formulaic number.

This female ghost's "white form" reminds listeners of her innocence and purity. She has suffered a terrible crime and will not rest until all three of her assailants have been punished (Motif E415, "Dead cannot rest until certain work is finished"). As she "walks around looking in the windows of the cars," she warns current male students to behave themselves. Dogs bark, recognizing the seriousness of what has happened to the young woman.[21] The story's main message is that students must remember her rape and keep future tragedies from happening. Like the ghost who demands justice, they must do what they can to prevent future sexual assaults. Other ghost stories about rapes and murders are discussed in chapter 6.

Another painful subject is the history of racial discrimination that haunts many college towns and cities. This is, of course, not a subject that college officials enjoy discussing. On an ideal college campus in a pleasant college town, there would be no history of discrimination. In ghost stories, such histories come to the surface. Here is another text collected by June Baskett at the University of Western Kentucky, told by Donna Keith in January 1965.

The Ghost of Eighth Street

As a boy was walking his girl back to the dorm one night, they saw a woman walk by them in a long flowered gown, her eyes sunk far back in her head and no shoes on her feet. The boy remarked that it seemed strange that a woman should be out walking at such an hour by herself. The girl told him that it was not a lady, but the ghost of Eighth Street. As they turned to watch her, she walked right through the tall iron fence surrounding a nearby yard.

Several years before, a Negro woman had been burned to death and her body never recovered. Since that night, she has appeared often, just walking and eventually going through the wall, to return at some other time.

This riveting story does not specify the woman's ethnicity at first; it simply explains that she wears a "long flowered gown" and has "no shoes on her feet." With no shoes, she seems trapped, unable to leave the place where she walks. Her eyes are horribly "sunk far back in her head," showing that she has died and suggesting that she looks back at past injustice.

What injustice does this story describe? In its second paragraph, we learn that the woman "had been burned to death" and that her body had never been recovered. Why was she burned to death? We do not know; there is a mystery here that haunts us. It seems likely that her burning has something to do with her race. The woman's body has disappeared, just as the evidence of other racially motivated murders has vanished in the past. The woman, "just walking," goes right through an iron fence, giving students dramatic proof that she exists. As Jeffrey Weinstock suggests, ghosts like this one "problematize dichotomous thinking"; the spirit of someone who has suffered an unjust death is dead but not gone, absent but also disturbingly present (2004: 4). This legend preserves the memory of the woman's terrible death, educating students through storytelling.

Most campus ghost stories, including the story of the ghost of Eighth Street, entertain and scare students through shocking sensory images. When someone has seen, heard, felt, or smelled something extraordinary, others listen closely to that person's narrative, weighing its believability. In chapter 2 I will closely examine a number of narratives that stress sensory evidence, exploring how such narratives teach students to respond to the supernatural.

Chapter Two

SENSORY EVIDENCE

How do college students learn about the supernatural? In many cases, something that happens late at night demands attention and interpretation. All alone (or at least without anyone else nearby to verify what happens), a student hears, sees, feels, or smells something unusual. The next day, this student shares what happened with friends, either in person or on e-mail or Instant Messenger. Some friends support the idea of a ghost's presence, while others insist on a rational explanation. Both kinds of responses fuel further storytelling. Sensory evidence has a powerful impact.

Linda Dégh, whose study *Legend and Belief* explicates the legend's dynamics in detail, explains that "legends appear as products of conflicting opinions, expressed in conversation" (2001: 2). In court cases, Dégh says, comments such as "I've heard of it" have some impact, while "the eyewitness confession, 'I saw it with my own eyes' or 'it happened to me,' which is most typical in memorate-shaped legends, carries much more weight" (3). Dégh emphasizes the importance of sight, while acknowledging that sound and other sensory stimuli have meaning for legend-tellers.

Americans' emphasis on visual evidence emerges in Alan Dundes's important essay "Seeing Is Believing." Dundes explains that this well-known proverb originally had two parts: "Seeing's believing, but feeling's the truth" (1972: 11). While the disappearance of the proverb's second half reflects what Dundes calls Americans' "penchant for the visual," it also reminds us that tactile sensations have had a significant place in American culture (11). Ashley Montagu's cross-cultural study *Touching* notes that the skin is "the most sensitive of our organs, our first medium of communication, and our most efficient of protectors" (1971: 2). One kind of protection that the skin offers is a warning of something dangerous approaching. In the fourth act of Shakespeare's *Macbeth*, the second witch declares, "By the pricking of my thumbs, something wicked this way comes." Belief that a prickling sensation in the thumb reveals an evil presence originated in ancient Rome and still influences titles of popular books (Christie 2000).

Simon J. Bronner, the author of *Grasping Things*, makes the important point that touch "implies the grip of possession" (1986: 5). Bronner observes that Americans associate themselves closely with their property, expressing this connection through the proverb "Touch my property, touch my life" (5). If a ghost comes close to a person or touches his or her property, the ghost may threaten to possess or dominate that person's soul. Such a threat has increased the fearfulness of many ghost stories, both on college campuses and elsewhere.

Building upon others' observations, I want to examine how perceptions of supernatural activity affect legend-telling on college campuses. How do entering freshmen learn to interpret strange events in the context of their residential communities and the enchanted landscape of the campus as a whole? And how do conversations about brushes with the supernatural encourage students to believe or not believe that their experiences go beyond rational understanding? Close examination of students' narratives, especially those told during their first few months on campus, help us understand how this process works.

New students respond sensitively to stimuli of various kinds. Autobiographies and memoirs about the author's introduction to college life often stress colors and other visual images. For example, Lori Arviso Alvord's memoir *The Scalpel and the Silver Bear* describes her arrival at Dartmouth College in Hanover, New Hampshire, after growing up on a Navajo reservation in New Mexico in terms of greenness: "Green cloaked the hillsides, crawled up the ivied walls, and was reflected in the river where the Dartmouth crew students sculled. For a girl who had never been far from Crownpoint, New Mexico, the green felt incredibly lush, beautiful, and threatening" (2000: 26–27). Having grown up in the aridity of the New Mexico desert, Alvord found Dartmouth's profusion of green both exciting and strange, a constant reminder of being in a new environment far from home.

Other authors have also relied on visual images to convey the otherworldliness of their introduction to college. Molly Peacock, a well known poet, college professor, and performance artist, eloquently describes her introduction to Binghamton University in her memoir *Paradise, Piece by Piece* (1998). Peacock recalls meeting the "Sheet Angel," who distributes "angelic wrappings" for students' beds: "a benign, doughy lady in a flowered housedress who looked as though she went right home and made peanut butter cookies for her grandchildren" (1998: 79). Both a mother surrogate and an angelic presence, this woman offers comfort to homesick freshmen. Fully human but oddly angelic, she accentuates the strangeness of life at college.

Some authors' descriptions focus more on campus architecture than on individuals. Hubert Humphrey, who taught at two colleges in addition to serving as a United States senator and vice president, devotes part of his memoir, *The Education of a Public Man*, to his first days at the University of Minnesota in Minneapolis. Humphrey exuberantly describes Folwell Hall as "a massive, block-long classroom building of four or five stories, red brick, with little turrets and false chimneys" (1976: 37). Like a mansion that holds many secrets, Folwell Hall suggests the possibility of upcoming adventures. Humphrey identifies Folwell's architectural style as "Beer Barrel Renaissance": a name that promises both fun and a sense of the past (37).

Sensory images provide the foundation for exciting campus legend cycles. For example, students at Texas Tech University in Lubbock, Texas, tell stories about a biology student who sneaked into his professor's office to try to steal an exam. When a cleaning lady caught the student, he killed her. In 1995, a cell biology tutor told his students that he looked up while taking a midterm and saw the ghost of the murdered cleaning woman on a glass door (Motif E532(a), "Ghost-like portrait etched in glass"). This startling sight convinced him that the murder had really happened. After hearing the story of their tutor's experience, several students told their friends about what had happened to him.[1] If these students had heard about the murder with no overlay of personal testimony, they probably would not have been as impressed by their tutor's narrative.

Another ghost story with intriguing visual elements has circulated during the past several years at Fordham University in the Bronx, New York. Students say that one night, when a resident assistant was filling out damage reports for student rooms, he found mattresses standing upright against the walls. Around 2:30 in the morning, a Jesuit priest knocked on the RA's door to say he had taken care of the evil spirit that had upended the mattresses. The next day, the RA learned that the priest was a ghost. Both the eerily tilting mattresses and the spectral priest make this story easy to visualize and hard to forget.[2]

However, vision is not the only sense that gets students' attention. In his illuminating book *The Taste of Ethnographic Things* (1989), the anthropologist Paul Stoller argues that scholars should pay close attention to sensory perceptions, particularly those that go beyond vision. Explaining why Western culture gives priority to sight, Stoller notes that the Enlightenment "raised sight to a privileged position, soon replacing the bias of the 'lower senses' (especially smell and touch)." He suggests that visualism can be a "Eurocentric mistake" for ethnographers studying societies where taste and smell matter more than vision (1989: 8–9). I agree that most Western ethnographers have focused more on sight than on other sensory stimuli. In both Western and non-Western communities, it is important for researchers to go beyond visual evidence to discover what the other senses convey.

Within the field of folklore, some scholars have taken an interest in complex sensory perceptions. Gillian Bennett has persuasively demonstrated the importance of more than one sense in the narration of ghost stories. Her study of elderly women in Manchester, England, lists perceptions in their order of frequency: first sight, then touch, hearing, smell, and "experience" (1999: 196). The term "experience" seems especially noteworthy here. Even if a storyteller does not identify specific sensory input, the intensity of a collision with something supernatural can remain in that storyteller's memory. Bennett's examples of ghosts' visual impressions include smiling faces, shadows, and lights. She shows that ghosts can reveal themselves through the sounds of murmurs, moans, and sighs. Less frequently, ghosts emerge through scents of flowers and perfume.

Because vision often takes priority in American culture, Americans tend to believe what they can see. Reading about something that has happened gives an event credibility, as indicated by the proverb "I know this is true, because I read it in the paper." In *Orality and Literacy* (1982), Walter Ong traces folk societies' shift from reliance on the spoken word to faith in words that can be written and read. Gradually, print became canonical and word-of-mouth transmission lost much of its authority. Alan Dundes suggests that "radio and television have created postliterate man, whose world is once more primarily oral-aural" (1972: 12). Although American society has not lost its reliance on reading, it has become more and more devoted to audiovisual technology during the past forty years. Since the 1990s, the Internet's popularity has given us new ways to communicate and new reasons to believe or not believe what others tell or show us. Jan Harold Brunvand's recent article, "The Vanishing Urban Legend" (2004), suggests that Internet sites provide the most likely spots for legend circulation in today's complex world. Internet users read one another's messages and forward messages from people they do not know, wondering whether those messages are true. Webcam users see one another's faces and hear one another's voices. Now YouTube participants can send short videos to millions of viewers. Many of the stories in this book came by e-mail and Instant Messenger, illustrating Brunvand's point about the popularity of electronic communication.

Nonetheless, oral storytelling continues on college campuses. Around Halloween, when interest in the supernatural rises, student storytellers take pride in telling stories that conjure up vivid images of supernatural phenomena they have heard, seen, felt, and smelled. Some stories come up in casual conversation, but others are told more formally in programs planned by resident assistants. Sitting in darkened rooms, watching friends talk about chilling personal experiences, students may feel inspired to tell stories of their own.

Sight

Of all the human senses—sight, hearing, smell, touch, taste, and a possible sixth sense in which some people believe—sight tends to be the most persuasive. If something appears in front of you, how can you deny its reality? Shakespeare's *Hamlet* gives us one of Renaissance literature's most impressive ghosts: a regal father who, materializing outside the family's castle, warns his son to beware of an unexpected murderer. Seeing his father and hearing his voice, Hamlet must believe that his father has come back from the grave. He tells his incredulous college friend, "There are more things in heaven and earth, Horatio, than are dreamt of in your philosophy."[3]

When experiencing something that doesn't fit into a rational/scientific view of today's world, some college students say that what has happened cannot be true. They may explain the unusual experience by saying, "I was close to falling asleep" or "It was only a dream." So many supernatural experiences happen between the states of sleep and wakefulness that it seems natural to seek an explanation related to sleep and dreams. David Hufford's studies of the physiological aspects of the "Old Hag" dream (1982, 1995) have helped people understand how falling asleep, feeling pressure on the chest, and dreaming certain dreams affect legend-telling. Sigmund Freud and D. E. Oppenheim have analyzed encounters with ghosts during dreams in their book *Dreams in Folklore* (1958).[4] No matter how we interpret such encounters, we can conclude that ghosts shock and impress people who hover on the edge of sleep. In some instances, American history provides an explanation of a spectral scene. This story from Jon, a student at Gettysburg College, reminds us of soldiers who died during the Civil War. Jon told his story to student collector Matthew Steward in April 2003.

Soldiers in the Basement

You know how everyone here has their own ghost story, like during everyone's time that they are here, as in students and teachers, they have some kind of an experience with a ghost or some weird occurrence like that. So last semester, I worked in the accounting office, like as a secretary. More like did bitch work I guess, I made copies, carried stuff, put together pamphlets and addressed envelopes. Anyway, the building supposedly was used as a hospital during the battle, so all throughout the basement it was a military hospital, and upstairs I don't know what it was used for.

So I had to take a stack of folders or something down to the basement; they had a lot of filing cabinets and stuff there. I took the elevator, and when it opened, there was a full working civil war hospital in the basement, with like lights, people walking around working, soldiers. I swear to God, I just looked at it like it was in a movie, and I just stared. The elevator door shut.

I stood there for a minute and hit the "open" button, and when the doors opened, it was just the regular basement. I was just there, sounds and everything, and then not when the door opened again. Nobody ever heard of anything like that or saw it too. I swear, though, that this happened.

This story's imagery excites the imagination. In my analysis of the "Elevator Surfing" story in chapter 1, I suggest that elevators function as liminal spaces between one floor and another. Here, the elevator not only moves from our everyday world to the realm of the supernatural; it also brings back the Civil War era, with all of its suffering. Since the Battle of Gettysburg in 1863, memories of soldiers' and townspeople's sufferings have remained strong in the South. Jon's story suggests that Civil War suffering still exists; it has just moved to a realm where most people cannot see it (Motif E334.5, "Ghost of soldier haunts battlefield").

How does Jon react to the shocking sight of a Civil War hospital? He belongs to a generation of American students that frequently watches television and movies, so it seems natural that he says, "I swear to God, I just looked at it like it was in a movie, and I just stared." Like the viewer of a movie, he watches the unexpected Civil War scene quietly, but he also takes the role of a traveler through time and space. Watchers of "The Twilight Zone" and other supernaturally oriented television programs and movies know that elevator doors may open to reveal surprising scenes.[5] Through our knowledge of the media, we can understand much of this story's appeal.

Another dimension of the story's meaning comes from Gettysburg's ghost tours. Billed as the "most haunted" city in the United States, Gettysburg offers nightly tours of haunted places, including Gettysburg College. One story frequently told by tour guides concerns the administrator or professor who, when taking the elevator down to the basement of Pennsylvania Hall, unexpectedly sees bloody patients and doctors in the hospital there. This story also appears in Mark V. Nesbitt's *Ghosts of Gettysburg* (1991: 54–58), which many tourists have purchased while visiting the town and its battlefields. One illustration in Nesbitt's book shows a shadowy apparition photographed in Pennsylvania Hall (57). *Ghosts of Gettysburg* has sold so many copies that its author has published four other volumes in a series about Civil War ghosts.

Knowing about this story's popularity might make some listeners skeptical of Jon's belief, but he vehemently upholds his narrative's truth: "I swear, though, that this happened." Matthew Steward, who collected the story, told me that Jon was a "Civil War buff" who enjoyed participating in reenactments of battles; he had never believed in ghosts before but became a believer after his experience in the elevator. Whether this story is told as a memorate or as a legend, its impact tends to be strong. Several students have told me that this story of a Civil War hospital is one of their favorite ghost stories.

Another famous campus ghost story recounts a secretary's startling experience in the C. C. White Building of the University of Nebraska in Lincoln. According to Gardner Murphy and Herbert L. Klemme, authors of the article "Unfinished Business" in the *Journal of the American Society for Psychical Research*, Mrs. Coleen Buterbaugh smelled a musty odor and then saw a tall, black-haired woman trying to reach the top of an old music cabinet's shelves (1966: 306). When Mrs. Buterbaugh looked out the window, she saw a scene from the past. Her own words describe the scene best: "The street (Madison Street), which is less than a half block away from the building, was not even there and neither was the new Willard House. That was when I *realized that these people were not in my time, but that I was back in their time*"(307). As in Jon's story, this completely unexpected scene has a powerful impact. Investigators from the American Society for Psychical Research listened to Mrs. Buterbaugh's story and concluded that she might have been visited by a ghost.

Many ghost stories with strong visual images mark the beginning of freshman year. At orientation and during the first few weeks of the semester, students make their way through the maze of campus buildings, find routes to their classes, learn to recognize their professors, and get to know fellow students and staff members in their residence halls. In the midst of all these new stimuli, some students see spectral images. Here is a text from Amy, a Binghamton University student who e-mailed her recollections of orientation weekend in November 2003.

A White Figure Going around the Corner

I think it was a Saturday night. It was orientation weekend, and I was in my residence hall. I went down to the basement to have privacy to talk to my boyfriend. I went down there; I was sitting in the basement quiet study room, by a window. As I was talking, I saw a white figure going around the corner out the door. It was maybe 5′10″ with holes in it. The lights were on.

I mentioned to my boyfriend that I saw something and he said, "What did you see?" Then I explained what it looked like. Then we ended the conversation. But this was not the only time. It happened again a few days later. I came down to talk on the phone again, and I saw it basically in the same place, and I told my boyfriend that I saw it again.

That's it. I haven't seen it since. I've never been afraid of it.

According to Victor Turner, someone going through the liminal period of initiation occupies an ambiguous state; the realm through which the initiate passes has "few or none of the attributes of the past or coming state" (1967: 94). Such a state of liminality seems evident in Amy's story. Turner notes that in Ndembu ritual in northwestern Zambia, monsters "teach neophytes to distinguish clearly between the different factors of reality, as it is conceived in their culture" (1967: 105). Do ghosts have similar didactic value in American culture? Looking at Amy's story and others, I would say that they do. Scrutiny of something that does not fit reality's usual parameters helps the initiate understand a new environment and a new stage of life.

When Amy sees her ghost, she is sitting in her residence hall's basement: one of the spaces where supernatural activity most often happens in college ghost stories. Another significant factor is the period of time when the experience takes place: orientation weekend, when freshmen are just beginning to adjust to their new environment. Amy expects to see new things, but the ghost startles her. She describes the ghost carefully: "maybe 5′10″ with holes in it." When she adds "The lights were on," she confirms that no dim light-ing or shadow accounts for what she has seen. This ghost looks *real*, but Amy does not fear it. Like the hero of "The Youth Who Wanted to Learn What Fear Is," as well as the brave contestants on television's *Fear* and *Fear Factor*, she has enough courage to handle startling sights.[6]

The color of the ghost in Amy's story also has meaning. Because the fig-ure is white, it seems like a pale shade of a human figure. Perhaps it reminds her of her boyfriend, whose absence bothers her during the first few days of orientation. The ghost appears twice, and at both times she is talking with her boyfriend on the telephone. It would be wrong, however, to suggest that the ghost just expresses sadness about her boyfriend's being far away. Its white-ness and incompleteness have meaning because orientation weekend has just started; everything seems new, and little seems certain. Those of us who have survived the discomfort of college orientation can understand part of what Amy feels as she sits alone in her residence hall's brightly lighted basement, talking with the person she misses most.

The last text that I want to include in this section describes the death and return of one of my own professors at Indiana University in Bloomington. Richard M. Dorson, chair of the Folklore Institute from 1962 to 1981, impressed his students with his energy, his many publications, and his heart-felt dedication to the field of folklore. Professor Nancy C. McEntire, who entered Indiana's graduate program several years later than I did, shared this moving narrative with several other Indiana University alumni and me on May 28, 2005, at the end of the annual meeting of the International Society for Contemporary Legend Research in Athens, Georgia.

Dorson's Ghost

This was the summer of 1981. Dorson was playing tennis with his son. He collapsed on the tennis court and fell into a coma. He lay in a coma all through the summer. They put him in the Bloomington Convalescent Hospital. I remember going one time to visit. His color was good. He looked like he was just taking a nap, and that you could call out his name and he would wake up. That was what was so wrenching. I don't think I even spoke, I was so upset. Then I went in again and played a jig for him on the penny whistle. He passed away in the fall. It was a severe stroke; he never regained consciousness. There was a huge memorial service in Whittenberger Auditorium. They asked me to play some music, and I played the whistle. His son said his father's daily lists said things like "Read four dissertations and get proofs off to press." Anyway, that was in the fall.

In the spring, I was rushing around, taking classes. The weather had turned for the best; people were full of energy. At that point the secretaries' offices looked out on one point of North Fess or another. I was sitting at Sid Grant's desk looking out on the courtyard. We were chatting, not about anything significant, and I did not have Richard Dorson on my mind. I looked out into the courtyard, and I saw him. You know how he walked. He had on a tweed jacket with elbow patches, everything. I said, "Oh my God, Sid! That's Richard Dorson!" We were the only ones there. We rushed out the door, into the courtyard and there was nobody there. I was quite shaken. Sid asked if it could have been another IU professor who resembled Dr. Dorson, but I knew who she was talking about and I knew this wasn't him. The gait wasn't the same. Nobody else walked like Dorson. It happened *fast*, but it was very memorable.

As I listened to McEntire's richly detailed story, I could picture Dorson walking. While other academics wore similar tweed jackets with elbow patches, "Nobody else walked like Dorson." He moved swiftly, clutching books and papers, eager to accomplish his next task. His energy was extraordinary. Since his dedication to folklore was so strong, it seems fitting that his ghost has appeared at Indiana's Folklore Institute (more commonly known now as the Department of Folklore).

This story's motivating principle is the idea that unfinished business draws a ghost back to a familiar location (Motif E415, "Dead cannot rest until certain work is finished"). If a long "to do" list can bring someone back from the "other side," Dorson's list seems lengthy enough. As McEntire explains, his typical list of daily tasks said "Read four dissertations and get proofs off to press." With an endless succession of things to do, he was not ready to pass on, and his students were not ready to lose him. Those of us who studied with Dorson can find comfort in knowing that his ghost haunts the Folklore Institute, which he loved wholeheartedly. As McEntire told me a week after the narration of her story, the Folklore Institute was Dorson's "true home." Ghosts who feel deeply attached to their homes never want to leave them (Motif E545.18, "Ghost asks to be taken to former home").

Another story about Dorson's ghost describes his delivery of an important message to a horde of eager listeners at an auditorium at Indiana University.

At a recent meeting of the American Folklore Society, Henry Glassie told me that he had seen Dorson's ghost in a dream five years after his death. Wearing tennis shorts, tennis shoes, and a long raincoat, the ghost asked Glassie to gather people together so that they could learn how to solve the world's problems. On the day of the gathering, Dorson's ghost appeared, still wearing tennis shorts, tennis shoes, and a long raincoat. While press photographers snapped his picture, he delivered his important message: "When recording legend texts, never conflate versions, but report each text as it was given by the informant" (Glassie 2006). While this message does not offer a solution to the whole world's problems, it gives advice that fieldworkers should follow (Motif E363.3, "Ghost warns the living") and makes listeners laugh.

Sound

In an unfamiliar place, unexpected sounds shock the listener. Children at camp for the first time must get accustomed to hearing small animals crawl over their tent-tops and rustle through underbrush in the woods. Few animals invade college residence halls, but freshmen may hear furniture moving and small objects dropping and rolling. In ghost stories, these sounds encapsulate the strangeness of finding oneself in a new room, far from home.

While various sounds come up in campus ghost stories, I want to take a close look at a kind of legend that has recently perplexed and excited students across the United States: the marble ghost story. Marbles are well-known childhood playthings, but students do not expect to see or hear them at college. If dropped all at once, marbles roll and ricochet with a sharp, jarring impact. It is hard to predict where they will roll. Even in the daytime, falling marbles may disconcert listeners. At night, they sound inexplicable. If marbles fall above residence hall rooms and students know there is a thick rug above their ceiling, they may start to shudder, wondering if something spectral is trying to get their attention (Motif E 338.1, "Occupants hear ghost fall on floor of room above them"). Like the hero of "The Youth Who Wanted to Learn What Fear Is," they may feel a need to test their courage by investigating the source of these peculiar sounds.

What kind of ghost sounds like a marble falling? Such phenomena fit motif E402, "Mysterious ghostlike noises heard." So far folklorists have shown little interest in narratives about spectral marbles, which seem to have flown under the radar of such legend-tracking websites as Barbara and David

Mikkelson's Urban Legend Reference Pages (http://www.snopes.com). In recent years, the cycle of marble ghost legends has grown rapidly.[5]

Students have told stories about ghostly marbles at a number of different American colleges, including Brown University, the University of Northern Colorado, Rhode Island School of Design, Trumansburg State University in Missouri, East Tennessee State University, and Binghamton University.[7] Most of these narratives are memorates that describe personal reactions to the sound of marbles overhead late at night, but some stories explain the sounds' origin. Here is a memorate from Simon, who was a senior at Brown University in March 2004.

Pencils or Marbles?

Our building had five floors all together, a basement, an attic, and three residence floors. I lived on the second floor with only the third floor and attic above me. Lying in bed at night I was in that comfy almost asleep phase when my upstairs neighbors dropped something that sounded like pencils or marbles. Angry but not angry enough to do anything about it, I rolled over and tried to go back to sleep.

Suddenly they started to move furniture, at about two o'clock in the morning! No way was I going to stand for that, so I called up there. No answer and no change, but I figured they just weren't answering because they knew it was a noise complaint. So I pulled myself up out of bed and went to check it out. When I got to the landing I found my upstairs neighbors and the girls that lived right next to them just getting in. I didn't tell them what had happened, instead I made up a story about missing a movie of mine and wanting to check their suite for it so I went up with them and watched them unlock their rooms, nothing moved and nothing spilled.

Simon's story begins, as many other college ghost stories do, with precise architectural details. Because he lives below the third floor and the attic, we might expect that something unusual will happen. The number three has magical resonance in folktales, and attics have reputations for being dangerous, liminal spaces.

Simon is in "that comfy almost asleep phase" when he hears something falling, so it seems natural enough that he feels some confusion about what is hitting his ceiling. Is it marbles or pencils?[8] Curious, but not curious enough to get out of bed, he rolls over and tries to go back to sleep. Then a more irritating noise, the sound of moving furniture, ruins his repose. Moving furniture traditionally indicates ghostly activity (Motif E599.6, "Ghosts move furniture"), so Simon needs to investigate the source of this sound. Running upstairs, he finds that his friends have dropped no objects: "nothing moved and nothing spilled." It is interesting that he cannot tell his friends what he is really seeking. We can assume that he hesitates to tell them what has happened because he does not want them to think he is strange or abnormal. He never finds out whether he has heard pencils or marbles falling, so his story ends on a note of mystery.

A more detailed memorate came to me from Casey, a female student at Rhode Island School of Design, in November 2001. While Simon's story questions one strange sound, Casey's includes a wide range of unusual phenomena.

Dropping, Swirling, Bouncing

I think it all started with the marbles dropping. At night we would hear marbles dropping on our ceiling. As if the people above us were playing a game of marbles. I mean it wasn't just a dropping sound, that you could pass off as maybe the pipes dripping. It was one marble, or some times, two or three, dropping, swirling, bouncing. Sometimes it would sound like a whole bag, other times just one. And as soon as you started to talk about the marbles dropping out loud, they would start dropping more and more. So my roommate and I went upstairs to talk to the people above us, but they weren't dropping marbles, they didn't own any balls or marbles. We soon found out that everyone on our floor was hearing them drop at night. Then when I'd come home for lunch, and work in my room, my light would turn off and on. Sometimes it would blink, other times it would turn off and I had to switch it back on. It would do this until I yelled at it to stop.

This story's narrator seems to have entered a magical world in which marbles fall without human involvement. These marbles seem playful and defiant; if someone mentions their falling, they start to make even more noise than they had before. Like other tricky, playful ghosts, they like to surprise and annoy the perplexed human occupants of the building where they roll around late at night.

Linda Dégh has called the recent proliferation of legends about inexplicable events an "irrationality explosion" (2001: 8). College ghost stories like the one above reveal a deep desire to understand things that cannot be explained through rational means. The last line of Casey's e-mail message, too long to include here in its entirety, was "I don't know if it was a ghost, but whatever it was, it was *not normal*" (italics mine). In addition to describing marbles falling, she wrote about a weirdly malfunctioning light, telephone, clock, and CD player. This focus on strangely animated machines brings to mind Leo Marx's *The Machine in the Garden* (1964), which explores how strange machines seem in the context of the pastoral ideal in America. What constitutes normalcy, and how much can college students rely on reason to explicate their world? These difficult questions emerge forcefully in campus ghost stories.

At the University of Northern Colorado, students tell stories about Edith, the ghost of a resident assistant who tries to scare female students by rolling marbles. Two 20-year-old students, Jackie and Lisa, combine their own recollections of personal experiences with Edith's story.

Tricks on Edith

Jackie: So anyway, none of her girls liked her, I guess she was really strict. So they played tricks on Edith. They'd roll marbles across the attic floor above her room to freak her out. On April Fool's Day they took all her furniture and stuff and messed it up, pushing the bed against the wall. So Edith comes home and doesn't say anything. No one sees her for a couple of days until a weird smell starts to come out of her room. So the police came and found that she's hung herself from the bed that was propped up against the wall. She had this note on her that said that the girls were mean and nasty. So now the legend is that she rolls marbles in the attic to scare the girls. I've heard the marbles many times, especially in the morning.

Lisa: I heard them too! But I had my own experiences with Edith. There were lots of times when I would be in our dorm room by myself and I would hear our beads moving in the vanity. I'd get up to check and they would stop. When I would sit back down I'd hear what sounded like drawers opening in the vanity. I would check to see if our suitemates were home, but no one was ever there. (Nellsch and Tinnin 1999)

This is a good example of the kind of legend that explains spectral phenomena through a coherent story based on the tensions of college life. Some students have enjoyed playing elaborate, creative pranks on each other. The consequences of such pranks can be harmful, even fatal.[9] This story teaches freshmen to respect their RA and to think twice before doing something that will hurt someone's feelings. Because Edith's residents have rolled marbles above the ceiling of her room, she plays the same prank on students who live in the building after her death (Motif Q280, "Unkindness punished"). Besides rolling marbles, she moves beads and opens drawers. Like other ghosts associated with marbles, she likes to play tricks (Motif E599.10, "Playful revenant").

Both in Edith's story and in other texts, the sound of marbles falling has a strong connection to suicide. For example, in a text sent by AOL Instant Messenger in the spring of 2003 to the student fieldworker Justin Phillips, Sean, a student at the State University of New York at Oneonta, described the sound of marbles overhead in two halls. In this transcript of their conversation, Sean's screenname (changed to protect his privacy) is Galway9, and Justin's is Matrix 72 (also changed):

Galway9 (12:21:48 AM): theres one where u will hear a jar of marbles fall on the floor above you

Galway9 (12:21:54 AM): even if you are on the top floor

Matrix72(12:22:07 AM): sweet

Galway9 (12:22:14 AM): its supposed to be a girl that hung herself and when she did her foot knocked over a jar of marbles off her desk

Matrix72 (12:45:03 AM): what building is this in?

Galway9 (12:45:17 AM): any I think

Galway9 (12:45:25 AM): ive heard it in hulbert and in huntington

Matrix72 (12:46:08 AM): you mean you've heard the marbles?

Matrix72 (12:46:27 AM): or you heard the story

Galway9 (12:46:29 AM): yea

Matrix72 (12:46:31 AM): whoa

Galway9 (12:46:35 AM): a few times

Matrix72 (12:46:37 AM): tell me about the time you heard them

Galway9 (12:47:04 AM): I would just hear it sometimes in Hulbert, but that was before I knew the story

Galway9 (12:47:09 AM): so I didn't think much of it

Matrix72 (12:47:14 AM): oh

Galway9 (12:47:28 AM): one time this year me and the 2 other quadmates heard it pretty loud

Matrix72 (12:47:36 AM): where?

Galway9 (12:47:37 AM): but it sounded like one marble at a time

Galway9 (12:47:47 AM): it was repeated

Galway9 (12:48:09 AM): I heard it right over my head in my room, and Steve was in the other room and he heard it right above his head too

Matrix72 (12:49:13 AM): that's cool

Matrix72 (12:49:17 AM): what building are you in?

Galway9 (12:49:38 AM): Huntington

The transcript of Sean's and Justin's conversation demonstrates the relationship between the sound of marbles and the legend that explains it. Hearing the marbles *before* hearing the story proves that the sounds aren't just the result of an overactive imagination. Sean describes the sounds he heard very precisely: "it sounded like one marble at a time/it was repeated/I heard it right over my head in my room, and Steve was in the other room and he heard it right above his head too." Notice the repeated focus on the marbles being right above a person's *head*. Does this emphasis give us a clue to the meaning of the marble experience?

After hearing many such stories, I have come to the conclusion that marbles overhead have metaphoric meaning. Like bats in the belfry of the typical American haunted house, marbles rolling around on an upper floor give us the message that there is "something wrong upstairs." As a signifier for insanity, "losing marbles" has flourished in American slang since 1907 (*Oxford English Dictionary*). This metaphoric meaning seems to be present both in reports of hearing marble sounds and in the explanatory legends that sometimes accompany them. In Sean's story, we find this explanation: "its supposed to be a girl that hung herself and when she did her foot knocked over a jar of marbles off her desk." The female student in the story seems to be both "losing her marbles" and "kicking the bucket" (or jar). After her death, the sound of marbles overhead reminds students that what happened to her could also happen to them.

In college, where students feel pressure to be rational, controlled, and successful in getting good grades, metaphors of madness represent just the opposite of a desired future: irrationality, lack of control, and failure. Many college legends mention insane asylums, insanity, and suicide that results from mental instability. Although college ghost stories vary greatly, the themes of insanity and suicide tie many of them together.

Besides evoking the specters of insanity and suicide, marble ghost stories illustrate the relationship between legends and death omens. Death omens and ghosts are different, yet closely related. According to Avery Gordon, author of *Ghostly Matters*, a ghost is a presence that marks an absence (1997: 6). While a death omen shows that someone will soon become spectral, a ghost enacts the death omen's prediction, confirming physical absence with a supernatural presence.

Harry M. Hyatt's *Folklore from Adams County Illinois* (1965) offers an intriguing range of death omens. Glass breaking and objects falling make sudden sounds that startle the listener, suggesting an imminent death. The closest cognate to marble sounds in Hyatt's collection is a "spirit noise" that a husband and wife heard around 1920, when their baby was sick with the croup. The baby's mother recalled that it sounded like "someone was rolling a ball across the porch." She said, "My husband went out, but nothing was there. We heard it three times that night and every time we went out, but could find nothing. It was a warning, for my baby died the next day with the croup" (731). Of course, the repeated word "nothing" signifies that something *is* there: not a visible supernatural presence, but a presence that people can hear. This focus on invisible intrusions reminds us of the Puritans' alertness to signs from God's "invisible world" (Tracy 2004: 23). During health crises or other difficult times, such signs can become very important.

Frank C. Brown, the intrepid collector of North Carolina folklore, does not mention marbles in college buildings but lists a death omen specifically related to colleges: "If the plastering in a college building falls, someone intimately connected with it will soon die" (1964: 26). This death omen parallels the folk belief that plaster falling in a family's house means the death of one of its members (26). It is only natural that beliefs learned at home emerge in groups of students living in residence halls. Margaret Mead has described how groups of friends at college create bonds of kinship among themselves (1972: 106) In this quasi-familial setting, traditional beliefs flourish and take new forms.

College students' stories of the twentieth and twenty-first centuries seem less concerned with forewarnings than with signs of spectrality. A paper on "The Ghost of Colvin Hall" written at the University of Maine in 1992 includes descriptions of a variety of spectral phenomena in one residence hall room: "things rolling across the floor," something knocking on the door, a light going on above a dresser, a hand running across window blinds, and a finger poking through a mattress (Meiklejohn 1992). This blend of sound, sight, and touch convinced the roommates that something spectral was sharing their space. Just what it was they didn't know, but they wondered if the ghost might be Caroline Colvin, rumored to have committed suicide in the building some years ago. Several versions of the Caroline Colvin legend had given these two roommates and other students in Colvin Hall the message that Caroline was responsible for spooky events. The allegation that Caroline had killed herself made these events more frightening than they might have been otherwise. If Caroline had lost control of her life and died, others might do the same. I discuss Colvin Hall's legends in more detail in chapter 6.

Recently, in my Folklore of the Supernatural class at Binghamton University, I saw dramatic proof that the sounds of marbles can start a quest for meaning. Courtney Kelly and Lauren Moscowitch, two advanced undergraduate students, decided to investigate why students in several halls on campus had been hearing marbles falling. Two years before, in the spring of 2003, Lauren had collected narratives about marble ghosts from her resident director in Cleveland Hall at Binghamton University. When she signed up for my Folklore of the Supernatural class, she was eager to learn more about this phenomenon. With Courtney's help, she interviewed her former resident director, who had moved to another campus, as well as other Residential Life staff members. Both interviewers gave most of their attention to students living in Suite 325A, who said that they had seen ghostly images. Lauren and Courtney finished their project several days early. Smiling, they brought me an envelope containing two documents that I expected: papers about the stories they had collected (Kelly and Moscowitch 2005). The third document, which I had *not* expected, was a CD labeled "Cleveland Ghost Evidence." I put this CD into my computer right away and saw two pictures: one of footprints on a rug, another of a young woman bouncing on a bed. It took me a few days to learn the meaning of these pictures, which became clear when the two students gave their oral report.

In reporting their findings to the class, Lauren and Courtney first spoke about the stories they had collected: narratives about marbles falling above ceilings with loud plinking noises, even though there were carpets on the floors above. They explained that there was a wide range of responses, from apparent belief to complete skepticism. Then the two students began to talk about some discoveries that had surprised them. One former RA had said she had heard a child singing in a Cleveland Hall stairwell. When she went to investigate with another RA, no child was there. The former resident director of the hall had said she had seen so many lights going on when the building was empty that she had called the police, but the police had found nobody. Her supposition was that Cleveland Hall had been built on a hillside where Indians once conducted rituals, so this past history could explain the presence of supernatural phenomena.

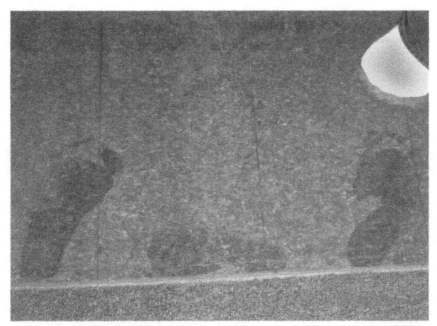

Tiny footprints left by the ghost of Cleveland Hall, with a student's normal-sized foot on the right. Photograph by Courtney Kelly and Lauren Moscowitch.

However, Lauren and Courtney were not very excited about those inter-view results. The best evidence of supernatural activity in Cleveland, they said, came from students in suite 325A. One of the suitemates had told them, "When my roommate and I came back from Winter break, . . . the next morning, out of nowhere, there were footprints on our floor, that didn't match any of our feet (they were smaller) and that we tried to wash off over and over, but they never came off. They are still here today." These child-sized footprints seemed to match the image of a little girl that one suitemate had seen on the wall. When this suitemate blinked, the image of a little girl changed into a poster of the actress Sarah Jessica Parker. Since the little girl and Parker had different stances, the suitemate believed the little girl was truly a ghost. She said that the little girl was very pale and wore a white dress. A friend of hers in the suite had seen a slightly different visual image of the ghost: "a girl, very pale, but with rosy cheeks, and brown hair."

While both of these ghost sightings seemed exciting, the clincher was a video of one suitemate bouncing on a bed. While she was bouncing, an image appeared by one of the desks. One suitemate described the image as a "black blurb" that was "sort of shaped like a person, but wasn't clear at all."

Ghostly face in the window of a bedroom in Cleveland Hall, observed by a jumping student. Photograph by Courtney Kelly and Lauren Moscowitch.

She said that she could "clearly see, in the reflection of the window, a young girl, sitting at [the] desk, just facing forward." Is there any better proof of ghosts' existence than a video image? When my class saw the video (which was playing in almost total darkness), many of them screamed. This was our class's pivotal event: the moment, on the last day of class, when the "spectral evidence" we had been discussing all semester suddenly seemed real—and it was all because of two students' outstanding investigation of the sound of marbles on the ceiling. Lauren and Courtney have considered sending this video to the TV show *Unsolved Mysteries*. Even if it never appears on TV, it has already served an initiatory purpose for one group of college students.

Touch

Some of the creepiest college ghost stories involve the sensation of touch. While visual images and sounds offer persuasive evidence, a ghost's touch confirms its uncanny presence. During the Salem witch trials in the 1690s, witnesses described various kinds of spectral evidence, including dramatic instances of touch by the spirits of those who had been accused of witchcraft. John Cook, who testified at Bridget Bishop's trial in 1692, asserted that a "Shape" of Bishop's had "Look'd on him, grin'd at him, and very much hurt him with a Blow on the side of the Head" (Burr 1914: 224). Another speaker, Samuel Shattock, explained that Bishop had, in the form of an "Invisible Hand," thrown his eldest child against stones and bruised him badly (Burr 226). Now, more than three centuries after the conclusion of the Salem trials, Americans still fear spectral touch, featured in such popular films as *The Haunting* (1963), *Ghost* (1990), and *The Sixth Sense* (1999).

Mark Twain's classic essay "How to Tell a Story" explains that a storyteller's well-timed touch can give the story an exciting conclusion. "The Golden Arm," a campfire story about a woman's ghost coming back from the grave to find her arm, often ends with the teller grabbing someone nearby while shouting, "You've got it!" If the grab comes after a suspenseful pause, there is a good chance that the person who has been touched unexpectedly will scream (1900). "The Golden Arm" (Aarne-Thompson tale type 366) has circulated actively at summer camps, giving children a sense of a ghost's tactile presence.

Ghostly touches in college students' stories range from simple taps on the shoulder to pokes, chokes, pushes, and pressure on the chest. The most dramatic stories come from personal experience, but legends from a "friend of a friend" can evoke a shiver too. Here is such a legend, told by a male student at Mount Saint Mary's College in Emmitsburg, Maryland, in the spring of 1992.

Not Buried Deep

As the soldiers were retreating from Gettysburg, they were burying the dead. This one young fellow was buried on campus, either in the woods or by the towers. He was not buried deep, but upside down. Today, students feel a tap on the shoulder, and it is a Confederate soldier looking for his buddies. (Babula 1992: 7)

Several versions of this story have circulated at Mount Saint Mary's during the past five decades. One of the most popular versions, told by both upperclassmen and faculty members, explains that the Confederate soldier and his girlfriend had agreed to look at a certain star while the Civil War kept them apart. When the soldier went into his grave upside-down, he could no longer see the star, so his ghost started touching students' shoulders and begging "Turn me over" (Babula 1992: 7).

This legend teaches new students about the traumatic Civil War years in a memorable, somewhat disturbing way. Since Civil War soldiers occupied Emmitsburg for a period of time and hasty burials sometimes happened, the young soldier's story seems relatively reasonable. Both folklore and literature have favored stories about young soldiers on hopeless quests to find their lady loves; Charles Frazier's *Cold Mountain* (2003) is one appealing novel of that kind. Mount Saint Mary's freshmen who hear about the upside-down soldier may understand how he feels. As Simon J. Bronner observes, college students often tell legends about campus buildings, bridges, and other landmarks that were built backward (1995: 147–48). Freshmen's confusion takes various symbolic forms, including legends about people and things that are all mixed up.

An especially important part of "Not Buried Deep" is the soldier's touch. When he taps students' shoulders, saying "Turn me over," he offers chilling proof that ghosts exist (Motif E542, "Dead man touches living"). This reminder not only subverts Western culture's scientific view of the world but also offers a pathway toward otherworldly experience. At Yale University, "Tap Night" is the night on which students receive invitations to join campus secret societies. In a ghost story, a tap also suggests initiation: in this case, initiation into the realm of the supernatural. Students who take the story of the Confederate soldier seriously may worry about feeling a tap on the shoulder late at night, as they walk their campus's pathways. However, the story is so well known that it seems to have lost its potential to startle.

A similar legend at Clarkson University in Potsdam, New York, says that Elizabeth Clarkson, wife of the university's first president, roams the halls of the admissions building. Matt, a twenty-year-old student at Clarkson in the spring of 2005, noted that "Cleaning ladies have seen images of a woman on the third floor and they claim, every once in a while, someone will tap their shoulder." Is the "someone" Elizabeth Clarkson? We don't know for sure, but the implication is that she haunts the admissions building, reminding cleaning ladies of her presence. The cleaning ladies then tell students about their experience, encouraging the students to take ghosts seriously. For a more detailed discussion of cleaning staff members' roles in college ghost stories, see chapter 4.

While legends about shoulder-tapping ghosts sound somewhat scary, memorates about spirits pushing or choking someone in bed can cause real alarm. Bed is supposed to be a place of safety and peace; ghosts turn that expectation around. In *Obake Files* (1996), a collection of ghost stories from Hawaii, Glen Grant summarizes the experience of a female student at the University of Hawaii at Manoa in 1935. While living in Ikeda Dorm, run by "a wizened old witch," this student hears that an older student has been attacked by a choking ghost: "two hairy, big hands pushed down and choked her, yet no one person was there . . . just huge, hairy hands" (1996: 136). Her description evokes a paradox: presence and absence, two hands but no body (Motif E422.1.11.3, Ghost as hand or hands).

This "choking ghost" story fits David J. Hufford's explanation of sleep paralysis and strangulation in *The Terror That Comes in the Night: An Experience-Centered Study of Supernatural Assault Traditions* (1982). Hufford has persuasively shown that stories of nocturnal assaults by supernatural beings constitute a cross-cultural pattern of experience. In Newfoundland, people have complained of being attacked by the "Old Hag"; in China, the attacker bears the name of *bei Guai chaak* (Hufford 1995: 13). One interesting example of an assault that follows Hufford's pattern is Maxine Hong Kingston's story of her mother's fight with a "Sitting Ghost" at the To Keung School of Midwifery in China. Kingston's mother stays up all night in a haunted residence hall room, chanting her lessons until she vanquishes the ghost (1976: 68–71).

Among Hufford's narratives from the United States are several told by college students. One especially dramatic text came from a twenty-two-year-old medical student who felt and saw a "grayish, brownish murky presence" that he struggled to overcome; after a while, the presence went away (1982: 59). Showing how well he had mastered the technique of scientific observation, the student said that the presence "was almost kind of gaseous—but *not* gaseous in that it didn't have the transparency that a gaseous kind of thing would have" (1982: 62). His description of the feeling of pressure sounds more youthful: "It was very much as if somebody put me in one of those, those junkyard things that are made to crunch cars. You know, they make little squares out of a two-ton mass? And there's the process where the big thing comes slamming down on you, OK? Bam! To flatten the whole thing out. That's what I felt like I had on top of me" (1982: 61). This graphic description helps the reader understand how oppressive such an experience can be.

During my years of teaching and fieldwork, I have heard many students explain how terrifying it is to feel pressure on the chest while sleeping. These students have different ethnic backgrounds and have attended college in various parts of the United States. Although I have heard especially vivid sleep paralysis stories from Asian American students, I have also heard some lively ones from students of other ethnicities. Here is a memorate about a shocking freshman-year experience from Linda, a Penn State student of Chicano heritage, told in the spring of 2003.

George

My first year at PSU, I went to a smaller campus in a tiny town called Schuylkill Haven, PA. The campus didn't have more than seven or eight buildings including all housing buildings. It was said that the entire campus was built over old hospital grounds.

There were four housing buildings and one was completely secluded from the other three. This building, known as "Phase 1," was on a small hill. I happen to live in that building. Behind Phase 1 there was yet another smaller hill and at the top an abandoned insane asylum. The hill below Phase 1 was the section of the hospital where the dead bodies were kept. We knew because there were still incinerators in the wall that led down the stairs.

One night I was feeling really tired and decided to take a nap. I was dozing off when I realized that my roommate came into the room and turned the lights off for me because I was too lazy to get up and turn them off. She immediately left after doing so; I knew when she left because I heard her closing our squeaky door. But the damn thing didn't close all the way! My other apartment mate was on the phone with her friend and was being extremely loud. I couldn't sleep with all the noise, but I was also too lazy to get up and close the door.

I began to feel very weak. Again, I felt someone in the room, but my roommate had not come back in. I was lying down in my bed facing the wall and suddenly I felt the other side of my bed lower, as if someone had just sat down next to me. I tried to turn around but was paralyzed! I tried to scream, but no sound came out. I could still hear my apartment mate on the phone, and my roommate in the kitchen making dinner, but I was unable to move, or make a single sound. The feeling of trying to scream and not being able to is the worst feeling in the world. I finally "broke" out of it, ran out of the room with almost no breath, and said, "Help!"

Startled, my apartment mates asked me what was wrong, and as I finished telling them, my roommate replied with, "Oh, you didn't know George lived here." She then told me about the history of the land, and mentioned that a lot of crazy stuff goes down, and they decided to name this ghost George. "He comes all the time," she said. "Opening and closing cabinets, turning lights on and off." It was hard to believe, but whenever I noticed the shower light on and random cabinets open in the morning after closing them at night . . . I would just think . . . oh, George.

Linda's story paints an unusually vivid portrait of a college campus's spooky landscape. The name of Linda's residence hall, "Phase 1," represents the new stage of life in which freshmen must figure out how to manage day-to-day life on their own. Intriguingly, Phase 1 is situated between two potentially frightening places. Above and behind the hall is an abandoned insane asylum; below the hall is "the section of the hospital where the dead bodies were kept." The basis for both of these landscape features is the rumor that the campus was built over an old hospital. Like references to Indian burial grounds, which I discuss in chapter 7, such rumors make a campus seem both exciting and slightly sinister.

When Linda feels pressure on her bed, tries to move or scream, and can't, she struggles to escape. Finally she bursts into the room where her friends are making dinner, shouting "Help!" Her horror at being overwhelmed by an inexplicable presence changes to relief when her friends explain that all the "crazy stuff" in their apartment comes from a ghost named George. Opening and closing cabinets, turning lights on and off, George has become a familiar presence in the women's living space, proving Simon J. Bronner's assertion that campus ghosts "both personalize the place and underscore its strangeness" (1995: 148). With the help of her more experienced friends, Linda gains knowledge of both the realm of the supernatural and the complexity of freshman year.

Smell

Smell is less prominent than some other senses in college ghost stories, but its presence can be unforgettable. When I was studying folklore at Indiana University, I took the exorcist BarBara Lee on a tour of my dormitory, Eigenmann Hall.[10] Halfway down the hallway of the fourteenth floor, BarBara stopped and pointed to one of the doors. "I smell funeral flowers here," she told me. "It's a funeral wreath." This wreath, BarBara said, marked the room of a student who had committed suicide by jumping out of a window. She led me to a window in the stairwell, then flattened herself against a wall as she struggled with the student's ghost. "He's trying to make me jump out too," she explained. After pushing the ghost away, she followed me out of the stairwell. Never having seen anyone fight off a ghost before, I felt shocked and surprised, but BarBara quickly recovered from the attack; finding ghosts and persuading them to go to heaven was her life's work. Smell had revealed the student's death; touch had made his presence both real and dangerous.

Many legends suggest that the smell of death, like an ineradicable blood-stain (Motif E422.1.11.5.1), never disappears completely. This insistence on an everlasting smell reminds listeners of death's inevitability. Since the turn of the twentieth century, American culture has kept bodies of the dead separated from the living (Mitford 1998: 148). Jan Harold Brunvand has analyzed the legend of "The Death Car," in which, because someone has died in a car, the smell of death will never go away (1981: 20–22). Citing Richard M. Dorson's study of this legend (1959), Brunvand mentions that many college students have found the story to be credible (1981: 22, 41). A death smell contaminates and frightens perceivers, reminding them that no matter how hygienically dead bodies are separated from living ones, death is the inescapable endpoint of human life.

Students in some college residence halls have reported everlasting death smells. In the late 1970s, a student at Smith College in Northampton, Massachusetts, told me that one of Smith's residence halls at 150 Elm Street had a third-floor room in which students noticed a strong smell of death. Supposedly, this smell had filled the room ever since a female student had hanged herself in the attic. Some residents refused to believe that a death smell existed, while others said that they had smelled it themselves, so it must be real.

For many of us, a smell's truth is difficult to deny. If we smell something oursevles, how can we say the smell does not exist? When the sense of smell becomes linked to a legend, that legend may become more persuasive. The legend of a suicide in Smith's Elm Street residence concerns a nameless young woman who supposedly hanged herself in one of the third-floor rooms of this old house, which was built in the late 1800s. Often, campus ghost stories say very little about why a female student decided to kill herself. The reader or listener has to fill in the blanks, imagining what went wrong. This subject receives more attention in chapter 5.

In another interesting legend-telling situation, students at the University of Georgia in Athens reported that the suicide of a male student in Joseph E. Brown Hall left a death smell that could not be removed. Charles Greg Kelley's study "Joseph E. Brown Hall: A Case Study of One University Legend" (1992) presents a number of legend texts that explicate the student's death by hanging in 1972. Some accounts of what happened suggest that the student died because of autoerotic asphyxiation. Since nobody found the student's body until several days had gone by, the smell that filled the room in Joe Brown Hall—and ultimately led to the body's discovery—became

Joseph E. Brown Hall at the University of Georgia, where people said the smell of death was difficult to remove after a student's suicide. Photograph by Elizabeth Tucker.

dominant in some legends about the suicide. Version "E" in Kelley's article, narrated by a University of Georgia senior named Julie, ends with these words:

> *And apparently, when they found him, something about, he was all bloated up and all his bodily fluids were, like, on the floor, which was, like, part of why it stunk so bad, and that it didn't even look human. It just was hugely swollen and everything. The smell was so bad that they never could get it out, and they ended up just bricking up or closing off that wing or section. (1992: 143)*

This focus on disgusting details shows how hard it is for Julie to think about the student's death. She distances herself from the "hugely swollen" body by saying that "it didn't even look human." At the end of her story, she explains that because the smell of death was so bad, university administrators had to close off the whole wing where the suicide took place. As a metaphor for Americans keeping their distance from death, this closing of a "death wing" works extremely well. Even though the wing has closed, students at the University of Georgia know that the smell of death will not go away. They also suspect, as students on other campuses do, that their university's administration wants to suppress the truth about ghosts' revelation of students' deaths. As I mention in chapter 1, students at Mount Saint Mary's College believe that administrators keep their campus's ghost stories in a locked room. Legends about college administrators giving the roommate of a student who commits suicide a 4.0 average also support the contention that administrators will do whatever they can to make bad situations seem better (Fox 1990). Such legends also suggest that students care more about truth than do administrators who want to protect their institution's public image.

Not all stories about spectral smells repel or frighten the listener; some combine shock value with humor. A good example of this kind of story comes from a fieldwork collection made by Doug Shoback, a student at the University of Northern Colorado at Greeley, in the spring of 1999. Doug's main informant was Kurt, a theater major who enjoyed telling ghost stories. This was one of Kurt's favorites, and it is one of my own favorites as well.

Stoney Ghosty

Stoney Ghosty is apparently a ghost who lives in the walls on the 11th floor. I think it's like, room 1104-1105. But apparently some guy died in that room or something like that. But now the Ghost, like, comes in the room and smokes pot—and there's always like a pot smell coming from the room and there's always like a guy's voice even though there's just like four girls living there and none of them smoke pot and just like, all the time they smell this pot smell and there's just this Stoney Ghosty.

Like many other college ghost stories, this one focuses on numbers. Kurt identifies both the haunted floor and two rooms that seem haunted: 1104 and 1105. Although he explains that "some guy died in that room," the death seems incidental to the story: just a reason for a ghost to be hiding in the walls. Of course, we can speculate that Stoney Ghosty died because of smoking marijuana, leaving a moral message for the room's later occupants—but that hardly seems to be the legend's point.

What gets our attention here is the interaction among four non-pot-smoking women and the ghost's smell and voice. With his silly, stereotypical name, Stoney Ghosty parodies the concept of a hippie drug dealer, but the smell of marijuana and the sound of his voice fill the young women's room. Although none of the four young women smoke marijuana, its smell and the sound of Stoney's voice make them think of the drug all the time. Will they cave in to Stoney's pressure? The legend doesn't say what happens later but suggests that they may have trouble resisting. The women, wanting to avoid marijuana, are undergoing initiatory pressure. Whether or not they decide to give up and start smoking, they are not having an easy time.

Another source of conflict here is male/female tension. Stoney is a male ghost, and the room's four residents are female. Does this story suggest that one persistent male voice, accompanied by an overwhelming smell, can overpower four women at once? I do not think this interpretation is too farfetched, given the number of legends college women have told about men offering them drugs and then taking advantage of them. Andrea Greenberg's article "Drugged and Seduced" (1976) offers examples of this kind of story from the era when drugs were starting to become common on college campuses. More recently, contemporary legends about dangerous "club drugs," including roofies (Rohypnol), have frightened both college students and their parents. Fearful of being overpowered by drugs without their knowledge or consent, some female college students have taken such legends seriously. "Stoney Ghosty" temporarily relieves tension, giving its listeners a chance to laugh at a serious subject.

And the subject of marijuana is certainly serious. Judicial sanctions vary, but students who get caught smoking marijuana on a college campus usually have to pay a fine in their college town's court. If formally charged with a drug offense in local records, they will have a blot on their records that may keep them from attending law school or medical school. If they work as resident assistants, they will lose their jobs. Such consequences cast long shadows. However, many students on college campuses have tried marijuana, and illicit sales continue.[11]

Stoney Ghosty's smell pollutes the women's space, disturbing their sense of order. In *Purity and Danger*, Mary Douglas suggests that disorder destroys existing patterns, but because order is restrictive, disorder offers positive potential and power (1966: 94). For some students, recreational drug use is appealing because it subverts their parents' restrictive order and gives them new experiences. It would be wrong to view Stoney Ghosty as an entirely negative force, because he represents the excitement of risk-based discovery that belongs to many forms of initiation in college.

Also along positive lines, we can compare Stoney Ghosty to certain medieval saints whose bodies emit a powerful smell. In Jacobus de Voragine's *Golden Legend*, Saint Alexis spends many years serving God, then dies. The bearers of his cortege work for seven days to build a monument covered with gold and precious jewels. From Saint Alexis's monument comes "a fragrance so powerful that everyone [thinks] the tomb [is] filled with perfumes" (1993: 374). This miraculously strong smell, sometimes called an odor of sanctity, reveals the saint's power (Motif V222.4.1, "Aromatic smell of saint's body"). While no one would call Stoney Ghosty a saint, his overwhelming smell verges on the miraculous, at least in a comic sense. He is one of the funniest spirits in the annals of college ghostlore.

Chapter Three

GHOSTLY WARNINGS

W hen freshmen arrive on campus, they learn to handle everyday life without parents nearby to guide, warn, and help with crises. Conversations by telephone, e-mail, and Instant Messenger give parents some opportunities to advise their children, but friends, resident assistants, and other peer-group members take over as day-to-day advisors. During the first weeks of their freshman year, students must figure out how to conduct their lives safely and independently: a big change from living at home as a member of a family.

Learning how to stay safe is a complex process in which ghost stories play a part. Some ghost stories emphasize excitement and intrigue, but others primarily warn students to take care (Motif E363.3, "Ghost warns the living"). Since ghosts have lost their lives, they can teach students about problems and dangers of college life. Ghosts of students who came to grief warn living students to take more care than they did themselves. Their message is the Latin *memento mori*: "As you are, I once was. As I am, you will be."

Ghostly warnings take the form of words and visual images. Visualizing dead students who could have stayed alive by avoiding certain dangers both horrifies and educates the person who is listening to the story. The cautionary nature of these images brings to mind the medieval morality play, which offered viewers abstractions of desirable and undesirable qualities.[1] By putting vices and virtues into human form, authors of morality plays offered audience members guidelines for their own lives. Similarly, ghost stories give college students frightening examples of consequences that they should avoid. These examples develop so dramatically that they seem like morality plays for our contemporary era.

For the sake of cultural congruity, this chapter will focus on ghostly warnings in students' early twenty-first-century stories, which emphasize the dangers of overindulgence in alcohol and recreational drugs. These stories characterize college life as "binge living": not just mass consumption of alcohol and drugs, but also intermittent, intense focus on studying. This portrayal reflects some of Barrett Seaman's observations in his study *Binge: What Your College Student Won't Tell You; Campus Life in an Age of Disconnection and*

Excess (2005). Seaman, a graduate of Hamilton College in Clinton, New York, decided to visit twelve institutions of higher learning to learn about the perils and pleasures of modern college life. His book expresses concern about excessive alcohol use, drugs, and date rape. These subjects also emerge in campus ghost stories. This chapter primarily examines stories about alcohol and drug consumption. Another painful subject, sexual assault, is addressed in chapter 6.

Drinking

Dangers related to binge drinking have become prominent in the national media during the past decade. According to a study by Ralph W. Hingson and others, fourteen hundred college students die every year from injuries related to alcohol use, both in car crashes and in other situations (2002). This study served as one of the main databases for the report issued by the National Institute on Alcohol Abuse and Alcoholism in 2002.

Alarmed by these frightening statistics, college administrators have planned special events where no drinking can take place. Residential Life staff members have organized alcohol education programs, punished students charged with alcohol policy violations, and moved some of the students with the biggest drinking problems out of their residence halls. Still, drinking remains deeply entrenched in college culture. With humorous exaggeration, student author Aaron Karo suggests that for many students, drinking is a point of pride: "No one can funnel, chug, or rip shots like a college kid can. Because when you get down to it, college is really all about drinking—excessively, frequently, and irresponsibly" (2001: 97). Karo's comment reminds us of the "up" side of drinking: excitement, exuberance, and freedom from adults' rules. The "down" side, however, involves danger and untimely death.

Ghost stories dramatize the worst outcomes of binge drinking on campus. Often the central character is an innocent victim of alcohol poisoning. Ashley, a student at Susquehanna University in Selinsgrove, Pennsylvania, sent this story on AOL Instant Messenger in April 2005.[2]

Footsteps in the Attic

i know one ghost story
apparently the Kappa Delta house is haunted because
a boy died in the attic from alcohol poisoning a long time ago

when the house was a frat house
that frat got kicked off campus
and it became the kappa delta house
when the boy passed out his brothers put him in the attic
they forgot about him and he died
and now apparently the girls that live there hear footsteps

This story's line-by-line form and lack of punctuation make it a typical text sent by AOL Instant Messenger, one of the most popular forms of communication for twenty-first-century college students. Ashley gives a concise summary of this ghost story situated in a local fraternity house. She explains that the tragic event happened "a long time ago," comfortably removed from the present. "A long time ago," like the "once upon a time" of the folktale, makes a distressing legend easier to hear. What happens in this story is tragic and horrifying: after a fraternity member passes out from alcohol poisoning, his brothers put him in the attic and forget all about him. As a result of their neglect, he dies.

Ashley's story has a two-pronged warning: don't drink to excess, and take care of friends who have drunk too much. Although this legend is about fraternity brothers, its message applies equally well to friends who do not belong to Greek organizations. Kathleen Raftery, the author of an undergraduate paper on the "chunk lore" (folklore of vomiting) that follows binge drinking, explains how some students learn to help others who have drunk too much. Through a "chunk list" on the wall, friends keep track of who has drunk too much (1989). Without such safeguards, tragedy can ensue.

Why did the fraternity brothers put their inebriated friend in the attic? While this choice may seem absurd, it fits the ghost story's focus on liminal spaces. In the attic, above the realm of day-to-day activities, a dying person might not be discovered until it is too late. The attic is also a good place to haunt, a place from which spectral footsteps might well be heard. The sounds of footfalls overhead remind the house's residents that the ghost will never forget his brothers' negligence. Interestingly enough, the house's current occupants are *women*, not men. The presence of a male fraternity ghost in females' living space suggests that women should watch out for problems at fraternity parties. If fraternity brothers get each other so drunk that they come close to death, their female guests may also be at risk.

Whether or not Ashley believes this story is debatable. She says "apparently" twice, indicating that she questions the story's credibility. That is not surprising, considering the story's simple plot and lack of authenticating details. Nonetheless, the double warning comes through clearly.

Some ghost stories combine binge drinking with the sobering theme of suicide. This e-mailed text came from twenty-year-old Alyssa, whose brother was attending Endicott College in Beverly, Massachusetts.

Totally Creeped Out

At Endicott College a couple of years ago, the Dean's son committed suicide by drowning himself in a dorm bathroom. After the incident, the school thought it best if they boarded up the bathroom and stairwell on that side of the hall, and closed off the hall so no one could get into the bathroom.

A couple of years later, two of Endicott's star football players were dicking around drunk one night and decided to find a way into the bathroom after hearing the story earlier that day. After searching for a while they found a vent that led from the study lounge on their floor directly into the bathroom.

The two players found the tub and lied [*sic*] down in it one after the other, each claiming that they got the chills the second they laid into the tub. The two were totally creeped out and crawled back through the vent as fast as they could. Within the next two weeks, both players suffered critical injuries and were out for the rest of the season. No one admits to going in the bathroom since.

This story follows the classic pattern of rule-breaking that the Russian folklorist Vladimir Propp identified in his book *Morphology of the Folktale*: interdiction, violation, and consequence (1968). The star football players who are "dicking around" not only act foolishly, but also disobey their college's rules, making their way through a vent to enter a forbidden bathroom. As noted before, bathrooms are liminal spaces representing danger and emotional turmoil. Anyone with an awareness of what bathrooms symbolize knows that these two football players are "cruising for a bruising." And that is exactly what happens: the players receive critical injuries and miss an entire season of play with their team.

Alyssa's story raises a couple of interesting questions. Why do the two football players feel such a strong compulsion to break into the bathroom where the dean's son committed suicide? Do they have a morbid fascination with suicide, or do they just want to break the rules? Although their break-in could be interpreted in different ways, I see it as a quest to investigate the suicide legend's validity. Note that the two students lie down in the bathtub, waiting to see if something will happen. Not immediately but later, after their return to their team, they discover that reclining in the bathtub had a pernicious effect. Perhaps the dean's son wanted to hurt these two students, or perhaps he wanted to punish them (as his father, the dean, might do), for entering a place made dangerous by death. In any case, the ghost of the dean's son is a malevolent spirit who wants to inflict punishment on the two intruders who rudely enter the room where he died (Motif E230, "Return from dead to inflict punishment").

Students who hear this story learn to respect the dead and to think twice before drinking, then going on quests to investigate places where people died. If they had not been drinking, would the football players have still been willing to break into the haunted bathroom? Although they might have done it anyway, Alyssa's story leaves us with the impression that drinking and rule-breaking make a dangerous combination.

Drinking before swimming or boating can also lead to tragedy. On campuses near lakes, streams, and oceans, deaths by drowning sometimes occur. The tragic loss of a student who has gone swimming or boating after drinking alcohol can become the subject of an enduring campus legend. This story came on e-mail from Ingrid, a sophomore at the University of Miami in Coral Gables, Florida, in April 2003.

Reflection Off the Top of the Lake

Last year on the night of the big hurricane and Ludicrous [sic] concert, a guy pledging a fraternity drowned in the lake on campus. No one knows exactly how it happened, except that a few guys were swimming in the lake and one drowned.

Many of the students on campus say that late at night you can see a reflection off the top of the lake that resembles a man's face. I have yet to see it because I'm afraid to walk around the lake late at night since this tragic event.

According to Hank Nuwer's "Unofficial Clearinghouse to Track Hazing Deaths and Incidents," a number of students have drowned on college campuses while pledging their chosen fraternities. In the fall of 2001, a fatal accident occurred at the University of Miami: an eighteen-year-old male student drowned in Lake Osceola while swimming with two friends from the fraternity that he was pledging. Investigators determined that all three of the students had been drinking before they died. Allegations of hazing made the loss of this student's life seem more mysterious and frightening than it might have seemed otherwise. Ingrid does not fully explain the student's death, saying "no one knows exactly how it happened," but she connects "pledging a fraternity" to the tragedy.

In the second paragraph of Ingrid's story, we see the process of spectralization at work. A student who has died in a terrible accident turns into a ghost: a face reflected from the top of the lake (Motif E334.2.2(c), "Ghost of Drowned Person"). Many college ghost stories introduce ghostly faces through the medium of window glass. Here, the reflecting surface is lake water, in which the student drowned. Ingrid's story shows us how shattering such a loss is for other members of a campus community. Through spectralization, the lost student remains with his or her friends and teachers, delivering a warning that may prevent them from risking their own lives.

Several years ago, a senior who had taken my introductory folklore class drowned while swimming in the Susquehanna River during a night out drinking with friends. His friends, his other professors, and I were deeply saddened by this terrible loss. Struggling to find meaning, we talked about the lost student's kindness and enjoyment of life. A few years later, a male student who was under intense academic pressure told me he had sensed the presence of the "drowned senior" in a basement bathroom of Sullivan Hall. The senior's ghost had comforted him, he said, offering "friendly feeling" and "sympathetic energy." It seemed fitting that the lost student, who had been such a kind friend, was still helping others who felt desperate. His gentle presence made fellow students feel safe. In a basement bathroom where other ghosts had appeared, he offered support and sympathy. Like some of the wailing female ghosts discussed in chapter 6, he had become a guardian of students who needed help. His name, "the drowned senior," warned students not to take the same kinds of risks that he had taken himself.

The next story warns students to be careful about another notoriously perilous combination of activities: drinking and driving. Monica, an eighteen-year-old freshman at the University of Rochester, e-mailed this story in November 2004. Before telling the story, Monica mentioned that it was well known among students on her campus.

The Vanishing Info Booth Attendant

The strangest thing happened to a guy friend of mine (whose name is Jeff) this one night when he went out partying with his friends. He was the one that was designated to drive when everyone got wasted, and as he was driving back, he stopped by the information booth because it was late at night.

There was this beautiful girl . . . Jeff was really surprised because he had never heard of a female working so late at night in the info booth. He started flirting with her and asking what her name was, but she wouldn't reply. The rest of Jeff's friends were too drunk to notice, so he figured he'd come back to the info booth once he dropped off his friends to their dorms.

It was around 2 AM now, and when he came back to the info booth, there was the old geezer instead. Jeff asked him where the pretty lady went, and the old guy replied, "What pretty lady? I've been working here all night, son."

The incident more or less escaped Jeff's mind for a few weeks, as he attributed it to his crazy imagination. However, the other day, the school newspaper printed the picture of a girl who died a year ago being the victim of a drunken-driving incident. It was the exact same girl as the info booth girl!

Jeff swears that he's not joking . . . he still worries on some nights when he drives home after having some beer . . . worried that the girl will do something truly horrible to him.

Monica's story belongs to the well-known "Vanishing Hitchhiker" legend cycle, which Jan Harold Brunvand explicated in his book by that name in 1981. As Brunvand says, "The Vanishing Hitchhiker" is the only legend that has its own motif number (E332.3.3.1). I have not seen other variants of this legend cycle in which the vanishing young woman is a campus information booth attendant, but there may well be others. In Lydia Fish's article "Jesus on the Thruway," one phantom hitchhiker appears at a thruway entrance (1976: 5–13). Toll booths, entrance gates, and information booths on college campuses all have liminal status, since they serve as passageways between one domain and another.

"The Vanishing Info Booth Attendant" has many details that fit our contemporary campus drinking culture: a designated driver, a group of partying friends who want to get "wasted," and an information booth that marks the border between the safe, familiar campus and the wilder terrain where bars exist. There are also other authenticating details that might make listeners believe in the story more: the name of the "guy friend," the time of his arrival on campus, his discovery of the girl's picture in the campus newspaper, and his oath that he is "not joking." With so many pieces of credible-sounding information, it is no wonder that many students on the University of Rochester campus have passed the story along to their friends.

This story also gets students' attention because of its focus on a vengeful female ghost. As a victim of drunk driving, why does she want to "do something truly horrible" to the male student who has been flirting with her? Is she so repelled by the presence of drinkers in Jeff's car that she wants to punish him, even though he is a designated driver who is driving safely? One possible answer to this question comes from Asian folklore. Monica, the story's narrator, is Korean American. In many Korean stories about female ghosts, a man gets killed in a strange accident because he has been hypnotized by a female ghost's beauty. The beautiful, vengeful female ghost of the horror movie *The Ring* (2002), based on the Japanese movie *Ringu* (1998), is one example of the kind of spectral figure that appears in Monica's story. In Brunvand's *The Vanishing Hitchhiker*, the teller of variant J explains that a Korean taxi driver becomes "fatally ill" after a young woman in his vehicle disappears (1981: 33). It seems natural, then, for the vanishing info booth attendant to inflict some kind of punishment on the male student who sees her.

Is the toll booth attendant a malevolent spirit or simply a ghost who wants to scare people who are not obeying drunk-driving laws? Does she want vengeance against her killer or against drivers in general? Since we cannot know the answer to these questions, Monica's story has a strangely disturbing ambiguity.

A more lighthearted legend about drinking came from Nathan, a nineteen-year-old student at Brandeis University in Waltham, Massachusetts, in April 2005.

The Beer Duck

My friends from down the hall think their fridge is haunted because they claim whenever they want a beer their fridge gets jammed and it's hard to open. And it happens for no other drinks.

The beer duck's refrigerator. Photograph by Geoffrey Gould.

There is a pond just outside our building which has littered beer cans in it and every so often a duck will die from cutting itself or getting stuck on the cans. So they believe that one of these ducks, which they call the beer duck, has possessed their fridge to try to stop them from drinking beer or something. Weirdly enough, it did happen once when I was over.

When I first saw Nathan's "Beer Duck" story, I thought it was just a joke. A haunted refrigerator possessed by the ghost of a duck? That seemed like a parody of a college ghost story, as *Scary Movie* (2000), *Scary Movie 2* (2001), and other films have parodied horror movies. I was not sure whether this story belonged in a collection of "serious" ghost stories.

However, as I thought about the beer duck's refrigerator, I realized that this memorate is both funny and serious. While parodying more weighty possession scenarios, it introduces a dimension of magic that enchants the listener. Stith Thompson's *Motif-Index* lists a motif for the "Revenant as duck": E423.3.10. In the folktale "Hansel and Gretel" (AT 327A), a little white duck guides the two children home. Although Nathan's story is a memorate, not a folktale, it introduces a duck that protects a group of students by keeping them away from beer. Like a parent, it limits their alcohol consumption, jamming the refrigerator when one of the students wants to get a can of beer. Since the fridge jams "for no other reason," the students know this phenomenon must be real. As the old proverb says, "Seeing is believing." Nathan, who has seen the fridge jam, seeks a supernatural explanation for his observation.

Certainly one serious message of this legend is for people to be more careful about littering around lakes, where animals can get hurt. It is sad that ducks have died because of people's carelessness. This ghost story serves a twofold educational purpose, reminding students to be careful about littering and to hesitate before drinking too much beer.

Drugs

Since the late 1960s, when recreational drug usage started to become common on college campuses, stories about drug-related tragedies have multiplied. These stories' central characters have no names; they represent every student who worries about having a hard time in college. Some drug legends begin by describing academic pressure for which pills promise a magical solution. Others describe social situations where marijuana and other drugs offer the temptation of an alternative state of mind in which relaxation and freedom from restraint make exciting new discoveries possible.

Bill Ellis has suggested that legend trips, like recreational drug use, are "escapes into altered states of being where conventional laws do not operate" (2001: 189). We can apply that helpful insight to drug-related scenarios within the legend itself.[3] Most campus drug legends begin with students' desire to escape from academic pressure, social discomfort, restrictive rules, or a combination of all three. In the legend, such a wish usually leads to disaster. The wish to get away from conventional restraints results in a consequence worse than anything the students have encountered before: premature death, which may result from taking too many risks. The campus drug legend begins with excitement and ends with tragedy. Highly moral and admonitory, it teaches students to think twice before indulging in "quick fix" drugs.

Of all the drugs available on college campuses, the best known is marijuana. According to the National Institute on Drug Abuse, marijuana is "the most commonly abused illicit drug in the United States." Folk names for marijuana include "weed," "pot," "grass," "ganja," "hash," "mary jane," and more specific terms referring to brands: "Bubble Gum," "Northern Lights," and

"Fruity Juice," among others (InfoFacts-Marijuana 2006). Marijuana appeals to college students because it seems to be a relaxing, consciousness-expanding drug that does not cost much money. Students' opinions on marijuana's negative effects vary. Does marijuana cause car accidents, heart problems, birth defects, other health difficulties? While the National Institute on Drug Abuse has provided answers to those questions, some students are better informed than others.

In ghost stories, the danger of using marijuana comes through clearly. Nancy, a twenty-two-year-old student at the University of Rochester, told this story in November 2003.

Trapped under the Ice

When I first came to the University of Rochester, the first thing that my suitemates told me about was the lake. It's really more of a pond actually, but it's right off the side of Tiernan Hall, which is where I was my first year. It's always frozen over during the school year because it's so cold up here.

Anyway, supposedly there were these two students back in the sixties who lived in Tiernan Hall. They were boyfriend and girlfriend. The wood behind the lake is where all the hippies used to go to smoke pot and stuff. So one night, these two kids go off into the woods with all of their other friends. Anyway, it gets really late and the two of them start to walk back to the dorm. Except that it's so cold and there was a blizzard the day before so they couldn't really see where they were going very well.

They were also really stoned and without realizing it, they walked right onto the frozen lake. The ice cracked under them and they went under. It was so cold that the ice froze back over where they fell in right away.

The next day when everyone realized they were missing, they sent out a search party. When they walked out near the lake, they stared down and saw the faces of the two missing students frozen in the ice looking back up at them.

If you walk out near the lake at night on the coldest night of winter, their faces will appear frozen and trapped under the ice.

Nancy heard this story during her freshman-year initiation, when her suitemates warned her about the lake. As on other college campuses with bodies of water, University of Rochester students scare new students with legends about the past. This story's protagonists, "two students back in the sixties," represent a period in American collegiate history when students were experimenting with drugs and insisting on having more freedom. Jan Harold Brunvand describes one of the most upsetting legends of the 1960s as follows: "Supposedly, a group of college students, high on acid, sat on a hillside and stared straight into the sun until they were blind" (1993: 109). Drug-induced obliviousness to peril comes through strongly here, as it does in Nancy's story. The point, of course, is that students should not enter this dangerous territory.

Beyond delivering a warning, Nancy's story hints at the possibility of an exciting discovery: "If you walk out near the lake at night on the coldest night of winter, their faces will appear frozen and trapped under the ice." This vivid visual image reminds me of the scene in the movie version of Stephen King's *The Dead Zone* (1983) where child hockey players fall through the ice of a pond, looking desperately up at the ice above them. Would students at the University of Rochester really want to see such a horrifying image? Apparently they would; Nancy and a friend of hers had considered going out on the lake to look for the faces but decided that the legend might not "work" if the weather was too warm. Potential for magic exists here. Under ideal conditions, two students' faces appear under the ice, proving that amazing things can happen.

Some of the most dramatic drug legends explore what can happen if a student experiments with performance-enhancing drugs. Adderall, a stimulant prescribed for patients with ADHD and narcolepsy, has become a popular "study drug" on many college campuses. Lori Whitten's article about the abuse of Adderall and other prescription drugs notes that, based on a survey in April 2006, highly competitive colleges have a 5.9 percent Adderall abuse rate, while less competitive colleges have a much lower rate of 1.3 percent (2006: 6). Folk names for Adderall have proliferated on the easily accessible *Wikipedia* website, demonstrating the drug's popularity: "study buddies," "smart pills," "smurphs," "orange tic-tacs," "amps," "a-bombs," "addies," "diet cokes," and "team blue," among other terms. Students joke about "taking the A train," jocularly referring to Duke Ellington's famous song; they also call Adderall "A+," pairing it with "A−," the popular sedative Ambien.[4] As Ethan A. Kolek has noted, many college students find prescription drugs like Adderall to be more familiar and acceptable than drugs that doctors do not prescribe (2006). It is not unusual for students with Adderall prescriptions to share pills with fellow students, either gratis or for a small or larger fee.

Ariana, a Binghamton University freshman, told this Adderall story in April 2003.

Still There Trying to Study

See years ago there was this kid who went to Bing and his parents put all this pressure on him to do well and become a successful doctor but no matter how hard he tried he just wasn't able to do well. So he'd spend all his time studying and his roommate and everyone would call him a geek.

So around finals time he was in the library studying. He had been there for a couple of days and wasn't able to stay awake. Well, this kid passed by trying to sell Adderall to people in the library and he figured there was another way he'd pass his orgo final, so he took some Adderall.

Only he didn't know that it was really speed, and he started going crazy. He thought he was invincible. So he snuck up to the top of the library tower and jumped. Now his ghost haunts the library tower. He is still there trying to study for his orgo final.

The central character of Ariana's story is so desperate to pass Organic Chemistry that he will try anything. Since someone else has made some extra money selling Adderall to friends, he figures there will be no harm in trying Adderall himself. Tragically, the medication he has taken turns out to be not Adderall but speed, the fabled "study drug" of the sixties. After taking the drug, the poor student goes crazy and jumps off the library tower. Because of his rash action, he becomes trapped in a never-ending cycle of work. Like Sisyphus, the hero of the ancient Greek myth who must always push his rock uphill, he will never stop studying for his orgo exam—and he will never take the exam or pass it.

This story delivers two warnings. The first is that drugs can make you crazy and prematurely end your life. How can you be sure about the contents of a bottle of illegally purchased Adderall? The bottle may contain something else altogether, such as speed. When this poor student swallows speed, thinking it is Adderall, he feels "invincible" and jumps off the top of the library tower. Obviously, this story's main lesson is to avoid taking drugs and to stay safe.

There is, however, another important message here. Why is the student studying so desperately? His parents relentlessly pressure him to study, hoping that he will become a doctor, and his friends shun him, calling him a "geek."

If his parents were not so unyielding in their insistence on studying, their son would have more fun and more friends. The message, then, is that a well-balanced life matters more than a push toward perfection. Excessive studying can ruin a student's life, dooming him to study in a library's tower forever as a shade of his former self.

Another drug, the pain-reliever OxyContin, has endangered students' health on college campuses in the twenty-first century. OxyContin has become fairly well known, as its folk names—"oxycotton," "kicker," "blue," and "hillbilly heroin"—indicate. According to a study at the University of Michigan, 2.2 percent of college students reported using OxyContin in 2003: significantly more than the 1.5 percent of college students who used the drug in the previous year. Although the proportion of students using OxyContin may seem small compared to the proportion of students using other drugs, the frightening consequences of taking too many pills—respiratory depression, stupor, and coma, followed, if no intervention occurs, by death—have made OxyContin notorious on college campuses and elsewhere (OxyContin 2005).

This OxyContin story came from Mitchell, a student at Northeastern University in Boston, in April 2005.[5]

Sleeping at the Same Table

> There is apparently a ghost in the library of a deceased Engineering student. He allegedly OD'ed on OxyContin, passed out in the third floor library, and never woke up. Some kids say they see him still sleeping at the same table. I don't know any other details.

This short, minimally developed ghost story relies on one central image: the student "still sleeping at the same table." Like Sleeping Beauty (AT 410), this student sleeps forever, making his presence known to others who might feel tempted to take OxyContin. Quiet though this character is, his message is a powerful one. His eternal slumber reminds students that if they dare to take this drug, they may never awaken again.

A much more elaborate story about the danger of drug use came from Emma, a freshman at Binghamton University, in mid-November 2004, two weeks after Halloween. Emma sent her story over IM late at night; since she had to go out in the middle, she sent the story in two parts.[6]

"!! Em Pleh"

My friend, Julie, lived in the last room on Broome's first floor when she was a freshman. Then, strange things started to occur in the room, and Julie and her roommate began to believe that there was a ghost in their room. Julie's roommate used to be so freaked out that she would NEVER stay overnight in the room. She always stayed at a friend's room, especially if she didn't go home during the weekend. Julie, however, was a Watson engineering major and had to study all the time with her textbooks. She didn't want to deal with moving her books all the time, so she just tried to ignore what was going on in her room. But the ghost refused to be ignored . . .

Julie began to notice weird things more often. For example, Julie has an optical computer mouse that has a red light that turns on whenever it's moved. If you leave it alone, the red light will turn off. When Julie was studying at her desk, the mouse's light would be turned off, but then all of a sudden, the red light would turn on by itself. This happened all the time, and Julie would have just brushed it aside if other things did not happen. Things used to always fall off Julie's desk. Her wallet would be sitting on her desk, but then it'd just fall to the ground, as if something or someone pushed it off. Also, Julie's physics textbook would ALWAYS fall to the floor and open to the same exact chapter every time: Thermodynamics.

Additionally, every night at 3:17 AM, Julie's door would unlock, slide open a little, close, and then lock itself. Julie thought that maybe it was her roommate or her RA playing a trick on her the first couple of times. However, when her RA and her roommate weren't in the building one night, there was nobody left that had the ability to unlock her door. This just freaked Julie out even more.

Furthermore, Julie's computer began to act bizarrely. One night when she was IM-ing her close friend Mike, her computer started to flash on and off over and over again. Mike called her up and told her to stop. Jen said, "I'm not doing anything!"

Mike said, "Uh, you do realize that you signed on and off for every second for the past minute?"

"Yeah, right."

"No. Honestly." Mike copied and pasted the IM notices back to her (at 8:01:00 signed on, 8:01:01 signed off, 8:01:02 signed on, etc etc)

Also, Julie would leave her AIM on, with an away message, whenever she went to class. One day, Julie was at classes all day and her close friend Mike approached her, telling her to stop changing her away messages. He said that they were freaking him out. Julie didn't understand what he was talking about, considering she hadn't been in her room since morning. When she got back to her room, her away message read, "!!EM PLEH NAC OHW ENO YLNO EHT ERA OUY !!EM PLEH !!EM PLEH ("HELP ME!! HELP ME!! YOU ARE THE ONLY ONE WHO CAN HELP ME!!" written backwards).

Whenever she went home on the weekend, she'd turn off her comp and leave. When she came back on Sunday, her computer would be turned on with a document open. (you needed a password to open her computer). The document would say "!!EM PLEH NAC OHW ENO YLNO EHT ERA OUY !!EM PLEH !!EM PLEH"

She got freaked out, and started to change her password every time she went home, but somehow the password was always decoded and there would be the same message on her computer.

She decided to take a stance and wrote back to the ghost before leaving her dorm:

"Why are you doing this to me?"

ghost: written backwards: "you are the only one who can help me"

Julie: How can i help you?

ghost: everybody's wrong. it was all a mistake!

Julie: what was a mistake?

ghost: it was just an accident

After communicating with the ghost for a while, Julie discovered that the ghost's name was Brian and he used to live in her dorm room.

Julie went to the library's microfilms to find out who this Brian was and discovered that Brian apparently committed suicide the night before his last final, thermochemistry.

His body was found in the morning next to the stream that runs behind broome hall.

Julie decided to investigate. One night, Julie and Mike walked out of her dorm room and began walking through the woods towards the stream.

Before Julie reached the stream, she blanked out and lost consciousness. She awoke back in her room with Mike trying to revive her.

Julie: what happened?

Mike: are u kidding me? you mean to tell me you don't remember what happened?

Julie: all i know is that we were walking to the stream, i blacked out, and i ended up back in my bed . . . and my head hurts.

Mike stares at her and says: as we were walking, you started to sway and couldn't walk straight, you began flailing your arms around and started to crash into trees. finally, you crashed into the tree near the stream, slid your face down the tree, and collapsed right next to the stream.

i had to bring you back to the dorm, and i was about to call an ambulance.

After that, julie was determined to get to the bottom of this.

she continued writing to the ghost, and when she got enough information, she decided to visit brian's parents, who just happened to live nearby.

Julie walked up to the door and rang the doorbell.

a woman answered the door and asked her why julie was here.

Julie: Hi. you don't know me, but i'm a student at BU. I was wondering if you had a son named Brian.

Woman was shocked and introduced herself as brian's mother

she invited julie into the house

Julie and brian's mother and father sat in the living room

julie explained how she thinks that brian's spirit is still occupying her room and that he wanted his parents to know something

julie asked them if they knew how brian died

they replied that the investigation concluded that brian committed suicide by overdosing on pills the night before his last final but that they never believed it bc brian was such a good, moral kid and would never do such a deed.

julie said that she believed that brian didn't commit suicide but died by accident

julie discovered that brian was up studying for four days straight before his thermo final

he was taking caffeine pills to stay up

the night before his exam, he was popping pills like crazy to stay up just a couple of more hours for the exam

brian started to feel woozy and lightheaded and decided he needed a breath of fresh air he left his room at 3:17 am, locking the door behind him, and walked behind his building

Julie emphasized that Brian didn't die bc he committed suicide, but bc
he accidentally overdosed on caffeine pills

brian's mother started to weep and said: i knew brian would never do
such a thing. thank you so much for telling us this. for telling us the truth

from the moment julie left brian's home, nothing ever happened again
in her room

tadaaa! the end

Of all the college ghost stories I have collected, this is the one that most
deserves the title of *magnum opus*. Emma devoted much more time to telling
her story on Instant Messenger than most students would spend and added
some wonderful creative touches, such as the backward spelling. The story's
punctuation breaks down in its last third, showing the strain of maintaining
creative concentration for so long. The "Tadaa!" at the end proclaims pride
in composition, as well as happiness that the long story is finally done.

Emma's story is based on an incident that took place in Broome Hall in
February 2003. During a Halloween storytelling program in late October
2003, a female Broome Hall student told a story about what had happened
the previous winter. Her narrative emphasized a mysteriously repeated time,
a computer mouse that moved, a message on a computer screen, and a door
that inexplicably opened, as well as a book that strangely opened to a certain
section. At that time there was no mention of an engineering student's death.
But later on, students speculated about the possibility that a tragic death had
caused the spectral activity in Broome Hall.

Campus ghost stories rely on central metaphors. Falling marbles suggest
madness; rearranged furniture reveals disorder, and construction represents
new beginnings. In Emma's story, the self-starting mouse expresses a dead
metaphor. Most of us who live in today's technological society are so accustomed to the term "mouse" that we hardly give it a thought, recognizing the
mouse as a device for clicking our way toward information and communication. However, a clicking tool is not the same as a living mouse. Emma's
story brings the computer mouse to life, reminding us of its metaphoric
name. When the mouse turns itself on, it suggests, as many other ghost stories
do, that machines have lives of their own. If we don't keep an eye on our
computerized creatures, we may be shocked by what they do.

We should not be surprised to see ghosts communicating through televisions and computers, since horror movies like *Poltergeist* (1982) and *The Ring*
(2002) have repeatedly shown spirits reaching humans through television

screens. The widely circulated Internet legend of the "Excite Chat Ghost" describes an asthmatic thirteen-year-old girl named Mandy who seems "allergic to modern life." After her death, Mandy communicates with her friends and mother, using the screenname "Belvedere_13." Told as true, this legend suggests that Mandy's ghost still cruises chat rooms. Brian's ghost communicates somewhat differently, by putting backward messages on Julie's "away" message. Inversion of the usual order of things works well as a sign of spectral activity. The MIT scholar Sherry Turkle, whose *Life on the Screen* explores the relationship between the computer culture of simulation and identity, says that we are "dwellers on the threshold between the real and the virtual, unsure of our footing, inventing ourselves as we go along" (1995: 10). Ghosts, which thrive on and express ambiguity, fit smoothly into the cyberspace realm that characterizes much of our communication today.

We should also note that a ghost that communicates by writing hearkens back to Americans' preoccupation with spiritualism in the second half of the nineteenth century. In 1882, John Newbrough, a New York dentist, published his *New Bible in the Words of Jehovih and His Angel Embassadors*, which, he said, had come to him through automatic writing on a typewriter (Newbrough 1998). At that point in time, the typewriter was a relatively recent invention. Now Americans turn to the Internet for signs of spirits' communication. In her article "Technologies of Vision: Spiritualism and Science in Nineteenth-Century America," Sheri Weinstein suggests that spiritualism has generated "new types of vision, new terms for vision and, overall, new conceptions of visuality" (2004: 125). Her emphasis on new types, terms, and conceptions shows how much innovation matters to Americans. Rapid changes in technology have not altered spirit communication's main point: bridging the gap between the realms of the living and the dead.

Supernatural legends that have circulated for many years have dramatized people's hopes to stay in touch with lost loved ones. Julie's visit to Brian's mother reminds the reader of the "Vanishing Hitchhiker" legend subtype in which a young man gives a ride to a young woman, lends her his sweater or jacket, and drops her off at her home. When he goes back to get his sweater or jacket, he asks the girl's parents about her and learns that she died years ago; he finds the lost piece of clothing on her grave (Brunvand 1981: 24–25). Here there is no vanishing hitchhiker or lost piece of clothing, but the visit to Brian's parents confirms that Brian died after swallowing too many caffeine pills and collapsing next to a stream. Later, Julie can reassure Brian's parents that he died accidentally, not by design.

Emma's story conveys several compelling messages, not the least of which is Brian's desire to comfort his grief-stricken parents (Motif E361.2, "Return from dead to give consoling message"). His determination to haunt Julie's room until he completes all unfinished business shows how much he loves his parents, who have felt very sad about his apparent suicide. Certainly two perils that the story emphasizes are the dangers of studying too much and of taking too many caffeine pills. Drug overdose, collapse, and sudden death are all frightening expressions of the pressure students feel while studying for their exams. Brian's ghost, who wants to tell the truth and console loved ones, represents the strength of familial love, which can outlast death.

Most ghost stories about drugs describe substance abuse, but some remind students how important it is to take prescribed medication. The following text came from Stacy, a sophomore at the University of Scranton, in April 2001.

Chomping Down Sweets

There was a girl who was found dead in my dorm. The story goes that she was lonely and had moved to my dorm mid-semester. My dorm is all single rooms. She was diabetic and took daily insulin shots. Many people would see her in the cafeteria chomping down sweets even though she knew that they were bad for her.

Well, she stopped taking her shots one day and was found slumped over her desk in her room. The maintenance people who would get rid of her garbage daily noticed that she would be in the same position every time they entered her room. So they asked my friend to go check on her since she was a nursing student. She confirmed that she was dead.

Well, my friend says that the RA from the first dorm that she lived in sees the dead girl all the time there. The ghost walks around at night around the doors of the people who gave her the most trouble when she was there. Things are always missing from their rooms as well.

Like many other college ghost stories, this one begins with architectural details. Stacy explains that her residence hall has "all single rooms," so listeners know that the lonely young woman has no chance to live with a roommate, although she desperately needs company and supervision. We do not know why she is lonely; all we know is that she keeps "chomping down sweets." She seems to be seeking comfort in food, even though having diabetes makes it dangerous for her to eat sugar. Of course, discontinuing prescribed insulin shots also imperils her life. When the lonely young woman stops taking her shots, she dies.

Although this legend is about a young woman who lives alone, its structure has some similarity to the structure of "The Roommate's Death." Linda Dégh makes the point that when one roommate dies tragically with a knife in her back, unaided by the other roommate who fears to open the door, the discovery of her body takes center stage (1969b). Here also, the discovery of the diabetic student's body is described in detail. The people who express alarm are the maintenance staff members who empty her garbage each day (an unrealistic detail, as most students empty their own wastebaskets themselves).

When the maintenance staff see that the student's position never changes, they ask a nursing student to check whether she is alive or dead. At this point, we might wonder why students and custodians are the ones who are checking on this poor student. Where are the resident assistants, other staff members, and college health personnel? While it may seem unrealistic that students and custodians take charge of a crisis, this pattern fits the campus legend's hierarchy very well. Students often discover truths that others on campus do not understand, and custodians, who belong to the local community, have access to information that others lack.

What happens after the diabetic student's death helps us understand why she ate too many sweets and stopped taking her insulin shots. The resident assistant from her original dorm sees the girl's ghost walking by the doors of "the people who gave her the most trouble when she was there." What kind of trouble is this? While Stacy does not give us any details, we can imagine that other students teased the diabetic student, making her feel lonely and isolated. Like the "Red Lady" of Huntingdon College in Montgomery, Alabama, this student haunts her residence hall because of the unkindness of other women (Windham and Figh 1983: 97–104). And like Edith, who drops marbles above students' rooms to pay them back for goading her into an untimely death, she finds that revenge is sweet. She not only appears in the corridors, frightening students who bothered her, but also takes things from the offending students' rooms. Her story reminds students to follow doctors' orders and asks them to treat fellow students with kindness and sensitivity.

Students' residential communities have long memories. After a tragedy takes place, the story of what happened can meander through a community for many years. Consolation, guidance, and fellow-feeling can emerge from tragedy through storytelling, providing positive messages for students who are struggling to make their way through college.

Chapter Four

TROUBLING ENCOUNTERS

While warnings comprise one important aspect of college storytelling, students' stories have other kinds of meaning. One of these is recognition, through confrontation with a supernatural figure, of growing self-awareness. By telling legends about gender transformations, ghostly lovers, suicide, and violent death, college students undergo a quasi-initiatory experience that facilitates their development of a more complex sense of self.

Students' supernatural experiences tend to focus sharply on one kind of sensory input: sight, sound, touch, or smell. This sudden influx of sensory data shows the perceiver that he or she is not alone. Someone else—the ghost of a student who died tragically—has come into the room to demand attention. Like a lover, this ghost may try to come close and initiate physical contact. Alternatively, like an "evil twin," it may frighten and annoy the living person, suggesting dismal and dangerous possibilities. Because this process involves complex insights, I have chosen to apply a modified form of Jungian analysis, which makes it possible to identify key patterns of self-discovery. Another choice would have been to trace cultural transitions in college, from the initiatory first year to the final phase of a four-year maturation process. The nature of the stories, however, makes psychological analysis more suitable. Encounters with a spectral "other" evoke intense feelings that raise questions about identity, sexuality, safety, and belief.

The first part of this chapter presents a series of encounters with visual images of ghosts in mirrors or on other reflecting surfaces. The narratives examined here come from five years of study of one residence hall. In the second part of the chapter, I examine several narratives in which other kinds of sensory images—sound and touch—proclaim a ghost's presence.

Reflections

Seven years ago, I was surprised to discover that students at Binghamton University were telling stories about ghosts in mirrors. A few students spoke of deliberately summoning apparitions; others said that frightening figures had inexplicably appeared.[1] As I listened to their stories, I realized that these college students were actively pursuing a ritual primarily identified by folklorists, including myself, as a preadolescent phenomenon known by the name "Bloody Mary."[2] In late adolescence, these students were discovering a mode of self-expression that paralleled, but went beyond, the fear test favored by younger individuals. Having learned about mirror magic as children, they found themselves standing in front of a mirror again, seeing something new reflected in its shimmering surface.

A flashback to my graduate-school days reminded me of the first time I saw preadolescents performing a ritual in front of a mirror. In 1976, while I was doing my dissertation fieldwork, something unexpected happened. Alison, a ten-year-old member of my Girl Scout troop, asked permission to go to the bathroom during circle time and did not come back. Gradually, three other girls excused themselves and joined Alison in the bathroom. None of them returned. Knowing that good Scout leaders didn't let their troops disappear, I hurried into the bathroom to retrieve the errant girls.

No lights were on in the bathroom; as my eyes adjusted, I could see that a ritual was taking place. Alison and the three other girls were standing in front of the mirror, chanting a name I didn't recognize: "Mary Wolf, Mary Wolf, Mary Wolf, Mary Wolf, Mary Wolf."

"What on earth are you doing?" I asked impatiently.

Alison replied, "It's Mary Wolf! And you go in the bathroom at night, uh, not at night, but you turn off the light. And then you say 'I believe in Mary Wolf' either ten or fifteen times, and, uh, you'll see a wolf dressed in a burnoose with scratches all over her face, and you'll get a scratch on your arm" (Tucker 1977: 408).

In *Legend and Belief*, Linda Dégh devotes part of her "Legend-Tellers" chapter to "Calling Back Mary Worth," bringing together "Vanishing Hitchhiker" texts, ritual elements, and insights into cultural acquisition (2001: 243–46). Viewing the slumber party as the main setting for invocations of a mirror witch, she closely examines a "Mary Worth" text from an eighteen-year-old boy who, at the age when many students enter college, vividly remembers rituals from his elementary-school years (243–44). Dégh's analysis of this text and others supports her assertion that the "mirror witch" legend has evolved from stories of innocent victims, such as "Resurrection Mary," to stories of aggressive women who burst out of mirrors to hurt the young. She describes Mary Worth as a "phantom heroine" who is, with some self-contradiction, "victim, witch, mother, avenger, child abuser, and protector." According to Dégh, the key to Mary Worth legends is "believing and trusting"; children who are willing to take the risk of summoning her are rewarded with a glimpse of her face, while non-believers are punished (2001: 244). Although I agree that believing and trusting are important, I find the process of daring and testing—an initiation of sorts—to be even more significant. An older woman, a mirror witch, puts children through a fear test that may result in a painful scratch. Like the women in charge of certain girls' initiation ceremonies in Africa, the mirror witch inflicts pain when it is appropriate to do so.[3]

Examining the texts I had collected from college students after reading *Legend and Belief* in the fall of 2002, I realized that my stories differed from Dégh's in one intriguing way: all of the figures in mirrors were male, not female, and most of them were young, approximately the age of college students. Their faces were compelling and disturbing, suggesting a challenge. What challenge were the students seeking? Almost all of the storytellers were freshmen; some were sophomores, and a few were junior and senior resident assistants. Some of the freshmen told me how much they enjoyed staying up later than they had in high school, eating whatever food they wanted, playing computer games for hours, and telling ghost stories. To some extent, fresh-men experiencing this kind of freedom are like preadolescents at a slumber party; however, they must adjust to living away from home while coming to terms with academic and social pressures. As students become accustomed to their college environment, the supernatural becomes one area where bound-aries can be probed and stretched.

Narratives about apparitions in mirrors help students to explore a more mature sense of self; both gender and sexuality are part of this exploration. Many works of literature, from Carroll's *Through the Looking-Glass* (1946) to Hesse's *Steppenwolf* (1961) and Rowling's *Harry Potter and the Sorcerer's Stone* (1997), show how looking into a mirror reveals a new dimension of oneself: a little girl becomes a heroine in a world on the other side of a mirror; a man sees himself struggling with a wolf; and a boy sees himself with the parents whose presence he deeply desires. Mirrors tell the truth about aspects of the maturing self that are difficult to acknowledge. In "Mary Whales, I Believe in You," Janet Langlois explains that the mirror "literally reflects the identifica-tion of the participants with the revenant. In normal situations, when any of the girls looks in the mirror, she sees herself; in reports of the game-playing, she sees Mary Whales, or at least, expects to. In a sense, Mary Whales becomes the girl's own reflection" (1978: 11).

Commenting on this point, Alan Dundes, in his illuminating psychoanalytic essay "Bloody Mary in the Mirror," states that Langlois is "absolutely correct" (2002: 79). Enthusiastically seconding his statement, I further suggest that college students' stories of apparitions in mirrors reflect a search for affirmation of a complex, sometimes contradictory self. These apparitions differ radically from what the viewer expects; instead of seeing her own face, a female student may see the face of a young man. Instead of seeing his own full-length reflection, a male student may see the image of a grim young man wearing black clothes. Seeing the opposite of what one expects is startling and frightening; it is the stimulus for telling stories that make it possible to understand perceived experience.

The intricacies of college storytelling, embedded within the matrix of campus life, suggest a need for analysis with both a social and a psychological orientation. Finding that study of archetypes can illuminate subtleties of college students' legends, I use Jungian analysis in combination with studies that emphasize social context, gender, and folk tradition. C. G. Jung explained archetypes by comparing them to the axial system of a crystal: invisible and inherited, this system determines a crystal's structure, although it has "no material existence of its own." An archetype, like the crystal's axial system, is "a possibility of representation"; an archetypal image, on the other hand, comes from the archetypes being "filled out with the material of conscious experience" (Jung 1970: 13). This explicit metaphor of the crystal's axial system applies to college legends in two ways: both as an explanation of how archetypal images can be perceived and as an indication of how storytelling works in a college residence hall. When freshmen arrive at their new home-away-from-home, they enter a domain where a communication pattern for storytelling already exists. This pattern is invisible (not readily apparent) and inherited (passed along by older students). Stories that spring from this underlying pattern come to the surface with subtle variations.

Intriguing characterizations arise from Jung's animus and anima archetypes, which represent male/female complementarity. The anima is the "female element in every male," while the animus is the male element in the female (Jung 1968: 14–17). A woman's animus is always male, while a man's anima is always female. Both the anima and the animus often seem dangerous. To some extent they resemble the shadow archetype, which represents negative aspects of the psyche.

In *Feminist Archetypal Theory: Interdisciplinary Re-Visions of Jungian Thought*, Estella Lauter and Carol Schreier Rupprecht praise the "remarkable range, complexity, and fluidity" of Jung's archetypes but decry their "rigid oppositions" (1985: 5–6). With regard to the anima and animus archetypes, Lauter and Schreier Rupprecht agree that "the most important implication of this line of thought is that culturally defined masculine and feminine qualities are equally available for development by either sex" (5). Naomi Goldenberg and other feminist scholars have further explored the need to reinterpret uses of the animus and anima archetypes (1976: 443–49). I agree that these archetypes should be interpreted flexibly, with a focus on re-vision.

Most of my material for the study of ghosts in mirrors consists of forty-two narratives collected from students in Sullivan Hall, a residence hall at Binghamton University, between 1999 and 2003.[4] Because I served for eight years as Faculty Master of the residential area where Sullivan Hall is located, I spent many hours there getting to know its folk traditions very well.[5] Sullivan is known as a haunted hall where supernatural experiences are quite likely to happen. Some of the narratives tell of ghosts appearing in mirrors; others describe related supernatural events.

The first text I examine came from Christie, a freshman who lived on Sullivan's "Chem-Free" floor with her roommate, Jessica. Students on the Chem-Free floors at Binghamton University sign a contract stating that they will avoid drugs and alcohol; instead, they engage in activities that promote a healthful lifestyle. Ghost-hunting has become one of those activities, especially on or before Halloween. In the spring of 2001, a female student in my folklore class told me, "It is already known that Sullivan Hall is said to have a ghost, but what is probably not known is that Chem-Free is one of the places it likes to haunt." Whether the "no drugs, no alcohol" policy encourages students to explore supernatural phenomena is beyond my ken, but Christie's story, the first of its kind that I collected in Sullivan, marked the beginning of a series of dramatic encounters with ghosts in mirrors. Christie wrote her story around midnight on Saturday, May 6, 1999, then slipped it under the door of my office, where I discovered it Monday morning.

Man in the Mirror

Jessica (room 207) was meditating in front of the mirror when the face shimmered and changed to the face of an unfamiliar male. Jessica, a tad frightened, left the room for a few minutes, returning with Jason (room 201), who felt a "presence" of some sort in the room. (Jason is versed in shamanism and has felt something before in 207). They went downstairs to the sub-basement, determining that the "presence" was also noticeable in the far corner by the outside exit.

Jason's conclusion is that the "ghost" is probably the spirit of a student here, that either lived or had extremely close friends in rooms 207 and 208. The presence in the sub-basement which had malignant overtones lacking in the other locations is most likely where the event that led to the ghost's coming into being took place. Based on what he and Jessica felt, Jason concluded this was probably in the 1970s.

When I first saw Christie's story, I wondered what the word "meditating" meant. Was Jessica just staring into her mirror, contemplating her own image, or was she trying to summon a spirit? Friends of Jessica's described her as "psychic," "sensitive," and intrigued by the supernatural. Although none of her friends thought she had tried to raise a ghost, they were not surprised that she wanted to figure out why the ghost had appeared. Her trip with Jason to the sub-basement was part of a serious investigation that a student with less interest in the supernatural might not have chosen to pursue.

Another question that demanded an answer was why Christie described Jessica's apparition as an "unfamiliar male." Superficial application of Jung's animus archetype would suggest that Jessica saw an image of her animus, the masculine side of her psyche. Certainly the tension between female mirror-gazer and male apparition is important, but a close look at the text shows that unfamiliarity is another cause of discomfort. Seeing the face of an unfamiliar male, Jessica goes to look for her friend Jason, a *familiar* male who leads her down to the sub-basement. Because Jason is a friend, he offers a more comfortable version of her masculine side than that which appeared in her mirror.

The importance of unfamiliarity is made clear by Emma Jung, C. G. Jung's wife, whose explanation of the animus begins with its meaning in Latin: "spirit" (1981: 9). According to Emma Jung, the animus is "a lightning-change artist who can assume any form and makes extensive use of this ability" (1981: 27). One of these forms is that of the ghostly lover, which seems to be related to the large corpus of marriage divination rituals practiced by college students over a long period of time. Ohio college women's rituals for summoning lovers' faces in 1925 included placing candles on either side of a mirror and walking downstairs backward while holding a small mirror (Puckett 1981: 525). Many other summoning rituals on college campuses and elsewhere have sought to create a ghost-like image.[6] But in Christie's story, the main thing we know about Jessica's ghost is the fact that his face has taken the place of hers. This substitution suggests the possibility of subversion: what Judith Butler calls "a failure to repeat, a de-formity" that undermines gender binaries (1999: 179). Suggesting that the gendered body is performative, Butler looks closely at acts that occur "*on the surface* of the body" (173). While the mirror provides a different surface, its close connection with identity makes it appropriate for enactment of complex self-perceptions.

Further information comes from Jason, whose familiarity reassures the ghost's viewer. "Versed in shamanism," Jason quickly concludes that the face Jessica saw belongs to a male student who died in the sub-basement. Why does he come to this conclusion so quickly? Christie says he senses "malignant overtones" that indicate evil and death. While Emma Jung's view of the animus emphasizes power, Estella Lauter's analysis of the animus in visual images by women focuses on male frailty (1985: 71–72). Both power and vulnerability are traditionally associated with images of the animus.

Could previously told legends about Sullivan's sub-basement have something to do with self-destruction? Jason thinks the male student died in the 1970s. College ghost stories about students who died in the 1960s and 1970s often emphasize drugs, aberrant behavior, and a propensity for occult activities, as well as suicide.[7] Since many college campuses underwent dramatic changes during the late 1960s and early 1970s, it is not surprising that those changes are preserved within the framework of ghost stories. Folklorists who have studied college students' legends and legend-related behavior include Andrea Greenberg, who wrote "Drugged and Seduced" in 1973, and Bill Ellis, whose "Speak to the Devil: Ouija Board Rituals among American Adolescents" was published in 1994. Jan Harold Brunvand and William S. Fox have analyzed the college legend about a student receiving a 4.0 average after his roommate's suicide (Brunvand 1989; Fox 1990). The popular movie *Dead Man on Campus* (1998) translates this legend into cinematic form. It is no wonder that campus legends express worry about suicide; college life includes both academic and social pressures that can seem daunting and unbearable at times, and suicides do actually occur in this context.

Christie's account of Jessica's and Jason's adventure emphasizes their descent to Sullivan's sub-basement, a place seldom visited by students except for the purpose of doing laundry. College students often tell stories of ghosts in basements; like preadolescent narrators, they tend to find ghosts on the top and bottom floors of dwellings, the liminal spaces (see Tucker 1980). College students, however, approach such spaces differently from preadolescents. Having learned about liminality during their preadolescent and early adolescent years, many college students enjoy expressing their more sophisticated knowledge through ostensive play: ludic enactment of a situation that occurs within the text of a legend. Sometimes this kind of play involves no more than visitation of a spooky site; other times it is more complex. As Linda Dégh explains in *Legend and Belief*, full-fledged ostension involves the enactment of an entire legend scenario in a serious way, sometimes with criminal consequences (422–40).[8]

College residence halls, many of which are large buildings with multiple levels and passageways, make good places for ostensive play. As Jung explains in his autobiography, *Memories, Dreams, Reflections* (1961), dwelling places have symbolic meaning. His own home in Bollingen was, he said, a "representation in stone of (his) innermost thoughts and of the knowledge (he) had acquired" (223). Although college students do not usually live in their residence halls for more than a few years, these edifices take on deep, if transient, meaning as the students move toward adulthood.

Why did Jason go down to the sub-basement to search for the "presence" with Jessica? In Sullivan Hall, focus on the sub-basement developed from a personal experience in 1997. Alice, a member of the cleaning staff, was standing on a stepladder cleaning a light fixture in the sub-basement when she suddenly felt cold, then light-headed. As she slipped from the stepladder to the floor, she decided that a ghost named Michael had overpowered her at that moment. Shortly after that happened, she refused to go back to the sub-basement, telling staff members and students why she would not go there. Intrigued by her story, Residential Life staff members shared it with colleagues on campus. Students who heard Alice's story took it very seriously, wondering who Michael could be. Some of them asked whether a student by the name of Michael had died in the sub-basement, but, to the best of my knowledge, no one has ever checked campus records to verify this possibility. Alice's story was well enough known two years after her fall that it provided an explanation for supernatural activity. Her story had the same kind of tension that Christie's story expressed: a woman, encountering a male ghost, briefly felt overwhelmed and sought an explanation of what had happened to her. The sub-basement, an underworld of sorts, became a locus for supernatural energy that influenced the shape of both narratives.

Two years after Jessica saw the man in the mirror, other students and staff members in Sullivan Hall speculated about what the incident meant. A resident director, Ron, told a student interviewer in April 2001 that Jessica "saw a face of a male figure covering her face" and feared that this was a spirit "trying to make contact with her"; this statement showed that Jessica's memorate had entered oral tradition. The phrase "covering her face," more specific than the description in Christie's story, shows worry about loss of identity. The spirit who appears in the mirror is aggressive, determined to make contact; in his relentless pursuit of the young woman, he resembles the Bluebeard figure that Emma Jung identifies as one representation of the animus (1981: 33–34). The elusive spirit of Christie's story becomes a possessive and threatening presence in the story told by Ron.

Other narratives told in April 2001 describe aggressive spirits, both in room 207 and down in the sub-basement. One story from Jennifer, a sophomore resident of Sullivan, tells of both roommates in 207 feeling someone come up behind them while they study at their desks. While the word "ghost" is not mentioned, the story clearly indicates that the mysterious entity comes from the side of the room with the mirror. A second story told by John, a sophomore, describes what happens when a staff member organizes an "MTV Fear" program in Sullivan's sub-basement: students light candles and use a Ouija board to see if any spirits are present. A freshman woman, feeling "a hand on her back," becomes upset and pulls up her shirt to see if the hand has left an imprint; everyone around her is shocked to see that a red letter "A" extends across her back. With its connection to Nathaniel Hawthorne's *The Scarlet Letter*, this evidence of a spirit's presence strongly suggests a ghostly or demonic lover.[9] In a comparable text analyzed by Bill Ellis, a female adolescent uses a Ouija board to summon a violent spirit identifying itself as a "bondage hooker"; the spirit, which appears to be female, leaves "a red welt" on the young woman's arm (Ellis 1994: 70). This attack's erotic overtones show that a ghostly lover can be of the same gender as the summoner. Butler's concept of "subversive resignification" applies to both situations: a disturbing physical sign in the context of play disrupts familiar categories of sexuality and gender (1999: xxxi).

A story told about the Sullivan ghost in April 2003 reveals a dramatic shift from memorate to legend. Nick, a senior who used to live in the haunted hall, describes a shocking case of ghost-summoning and devil worship.

Pentagram on the Ceiling

I forgot some of the details about the Sullivan ghost, but he's rumored to live in the wing on Sullivan where Chem-free is. Apparently, there was a girl on Chem-free who worshipped the devil and summoned the ghost in

the room where she lived, you can still see to this day a burned pentagram
in the corner of the ceiling.

By the time this story was told, Nick no longer lived in Sullivan; a year had
passed since Christie's and Jessica's graduation. With no personal ties to the
women in room 207, Nick transformed the mirror incident into an episode of
devil worship where a ghost (or the devil) is summoned. The "burned pentagram in the corner of the ceiling" seems to show that the "girl on Chem-
free" was a witch. This physical evidence makes the story's transformation
into a legend complete. A comparable text in Bill Ellis's *Lucifer Ascending*, collected in 1972, tells of a female college student who deliberately summons
evil spirits as she sits alone in front of a mirror in her room. Evidence here
includes the student's face, "scratched all to pieces" (like the faces of Bloody
Mary's victims), and the sudden insanity of the other student who has gone
in to check on her friend (2003: 164–65).

What image of the animus, if any, do we find in Nick's story? It seems to
be the devil or a demon lover. The devil is a powerful figure, well matched
to the witch who confidently summons him. One could say that this is a
strong animus, part of the psyche of a woman who does not hesitate to reach
beyond the borders of the supernatural; it also seems important to recognize
that summoning the devil in a college residence hall is a highly subversive act.
Binghamton University, like other institutions of higher learning, allows students who are Wiccans or Pagans to light candles in their rooms, but devil-
summoning would certainly go beyond the code of acceptable behavior.

Another set of stories from Sullivan Hall tells of a ghost in a window, a
reflecting surface that is analogous to mirrors made of metal and glass. Dan,
a sophomore resident assistant, was checking to make sure all was well on
his floor when he saw the ghost. He told this story many times, when fellow
students asked to hear it. This version was told to a student collector in 2001,
two years after Dan's experience.

Reflection in the Hallway

I was walking out of my room, probably around, you know, two or three
o'clock in the morning, walking down the hallway. At the end of the hallway, there's a window, so I could see my reflection. I was walking down,
I saw a reflection in the hallway of someone walking behind me, wearing

all black. I turned around and there was nobody there, and all the doors were closed.

Dan told his story in a matter-of-fact way, emphasizing its setting: a hall-way. Corridors of all kinds symbolize transition: passage from one place or state of being to another. In children's scary stories and horror movies such as *The Shining* (1980), chases through hallways offer some of the most suspense-ful moments. Here, Dan offers enough details for the listener to picture what happens as if it were a scene in a movie. The sequence of visualizations is sim-ple but clear: first his own image ("I could see my reflection") and then a new perception ("I saw a reflection in the hallway of somebody walking behind me, wearing all black"). Who is this black-garbed follower? All Dan tells us is that "there was nobody there." It is clear that he means no *living* person was present; hence, the reflection in the window must have been that of a ghost.

Although, at first glance, Dan's story seems to fit the classic horror-movie pattern of a sinister supernatural figure sneaking up on an unsuspecting hero, a closer look reveals deeper meaning. When Dan sees the reflection of the man in black, he no longer sees his own image; the man in black replaces his usual perception of himself. This shocking moment of revelation fits Jung's descrip-tion of the shadow, "the imperfect being in you that follows after and does everything which you are loath to do, all the things you are too cowardly or too decent to do" (1984: 76). Unlike the animus or anima, the shadow has the same gender as the person to which it belongs. According to Steven F. Walker, "Acknowledging one's shadow and learning to deal with it honestly is one of life's great, if usually distasteful, psychological tasks" (1995: 35). For each per-son, the shadow's appearance is startling and difficult. A ghost, both insubstan-tial and compelling, is an apt representation of the shadow-self.

The feminist scholar Jolande Jacobi has stated that the archetype has a "dynamism which makes itself felt in the numinosity and fascinating power of the image" (1976: 2). The shadow, embodying all the destructive, negative, and antisocial impulses that people learn to avoid, represents an exciting and dangerous part of the psyche. Jung describes the shadow as "dark aspects of the personality" (1991: 8); Dan briefly describes what he sees in the mirror as a man "wearing all black," like a demonic figure (Motif E422.2.4, "Revenant black"). Startling in its contrast to the self, the shadow fascinates and disturbs its viewers. Telling a story about one's shadow-self is, to some extent, a rebel-lious act that reifies dangerous behavior.

Like Dan, male students on other college campuses have seen ghosts in mirrors or on other reflecting surfaces. A legend narrated by a Hofstra University student in the spring of 2003 tells of a formally dressed man appearing in a bathroom mirror: ". . . my friend Randy was standing in the bathroom and he saw a tall figure of a man with a black coat and hat standing behind him, and when he looked over his shoulder there was no one there."[10] Glimpsed briefly, this man in black clothing seems to represent the shadow: a dark, dangerous-looking analogue of the young man who stands in the bathroom. College bathrooms are well known as sites for spectral appearances; since these bathrooms are usually single-sex, it stands to reason that students would expect to see reflections that match their own gender. In Jeannie B. Thomas's study of the "barfing ghost of Burford Hall" at Indiana State University (1991), female students connect sounds of regurgitation with the presence of a female ghost.

I first collected a version of Dan's story in 1999, a few months after he saw the reflection in the window. During the five years afterward, the crystalline structure of student storytelling yielded some intriguing results. In April 2001, Maria, a junior living in Sullivan, remembered hearing a story about Dan.

Gus

Freshman year, when I lived in Sullivan, I heard this story from someone in my building about an RA named Dan from the previous year. Apparently, he was walking down the hall really late after everyone was sleeping, and in the reflection of the window at the end of the hall, he thought he saw someone walk across the hall behind him. He looked around to see who it was, but all of the doors were closed, and he hadn't heard anyone run across or shut the door real quick or anything. It's really weird. It is said that it was Gus's reflection. Gus is the ghost that haunts Sullivan.

Maria's revelation that the ghost was named Gus startled me, bringing back memories of a student program that had, I thought, been forgotten. In the fall of 1991, when I had just moved into my new office in Sullivan Hall, I helped to plan a program in the adjacent hall, at which students could share stories about the supernatural. At this program, two freshman women decided to use a Ouija board to ask if any spirits were present. The answer they received from the Ouija board was that a spirit was in the room; he had died in the hall many years ago. This spirit's name, spelled out by the Ouija board's pointer, was Gus.

Before hearing Maria's story, I had had no idea that students had retained the memory of summoning Gus; I also had been unaware that Gus had moved to Sullivan. Clearly something about Gus was important enough to have stayed in campus tradition for ten years. I collected more stories, hoping to figure out what made Gus so interesting. Finally, in April 2003, I learned the answer. Describing Gus, Steve, a sophomore, said,

> All I know is that some guy hung himself during finals week. It was in the base-ment of Sullivan. Now it's incredibly cold down there and people say that his ghost haunts Sullivan. One day one of the cleaning ladies went down in the basement and in that very spot where the guy hung himself, the "cold spot," she fainted. The cleaning ladies refuse to go down there anymore.

For Steve and other students, the crux of the Sullivan ghost's meaning was his mode of death: suicide. No one knows whether an actual student hanged himself in Sullivan's basement, but the history of suicides on college campuses makes this ghost seem credible. Like characters in medieval morality plays, Gus represents a typical person: a student who has felt overwhelmed by academic or social pressures. The coldness of Sullivan's basement epitomizes the chilling finality of Gus's self-destruction. What matters about the "Gus" legends is their recognition of self-destructive impulses that might be felt by anyone at times of stress. Gus is the shadow-self that could choose annihilation if not acknowledged and put in its place. Hearing stories of the Sullivan ghost, students can recognize its importance. Coming to terms with this ghost is part of an initiatory process of adjustment to college.

The Jungian psychologist Richard Frankel has pointed out the need for adolescents to undergo rites of passage, some of which are ritualized death experiences followed by symbolic rebirth (1998: 82). His interpretation is supported by Mircea Eliade's observation that the "central moment of every initiation is represented by the ceremony symbolizing death of the novice and his return to the land of the living" (1958: xii). According to Kaspar Kiepenheuer, adolescents, in an "intensive quest for the meaning of life," benefit from a spiritual ordeal involving symbolic death and new birth; while such ordeals are common in traditional cultures, they are harder to find in contemporary society (1990: 11–14). Secret societies such as Skull and Bones at Yale have offered college students a chance to undergo a symbolic death resulting in a new way of life. James Hillman's illuminating study *Suicide and the Soul* explains that the urge to commit suicide can be transformative; a part of the self can die to make way for a new phase of life (1964). Telling ghost stories and translating them into ostensive play, as in Jessica's and Jason's trip to the sub-basement, college students recognize the transformative power of death in the midst of everyday life.

Pressures

Just as reflections of ghosts in mirrors excite and disturb their viewers, other kinds of ghostly signals upset students' equilibrium. Stories about spectral roommates have stayed alive in campus oral tradition for many years, transmitted from older to younger students. When a storyteller explains that an earlier occupant of a certain room committed suicide, the room's current occupant may shiver with trepidation. Suicide legends remind students that academic and social pressures can lead to tragic consequences. However, as noted earlier, legends about suicidal students also have positive connotations. In each text, the blend of positive and negative elements takes its own unique form. The following story, told in January 2003 by Carl, a graduate of Edinboro University of Pennsylvania, illustrates the staying power of stories about suicidal roommates.

Taping Over the Cracks

I was an RA in Rose Hall beginning in September of 1983. Rumor had it that a previous RA in that room had committed suicide by taping over the cracks around the doors, windows, and electrical outlets and lighting a grill in the room. I never attempted to check out this rumor, but many of the residents of the building said that it was true.

While living in the room I heard a few strange noises and I noticed a few objects not being exactly where I thought I put them. But being a scientific kind of person, I was always able to explain away the sounds and misplaced items.

I would attribute the sounds to the wind, the people upstairs, my neighbor playing tricks on me, etcetera. The misplaced items were explained away by my belief that I just didn't remember where I put things.

I graduated from Edinboro University of Pennsylvania in the fall of 1994. I returned to Edinboro for the purpose of continuing my education a year later. When I arrived on campus, I was told that one of the RAs who lived in the room after me asked to be moved out of the room because of the strange goings on in the room. I never checked up on the reasons why the other RA left, but I do know that the rumor mill said it was because of the ghost.

Most narratives about ghostly roommates describe one event from the past linked with a more recent personal experience. Carl's story goes farther than most, tracing the evolution of a legend in Rose Hall from 1983 to 1995. During these twelve years, three 4-year "generations" of students completed their educations at Edinboro University. When I talked with Carl in September 2005, he assured me that students were still telling the legend of the Rose Hall ghost. Minimally, then, this legend cycle is twenty-two years old, and it is probably older.

Carl's spectral roommate, an RA like himself, committed suicide in a bizarre and frightening way: lighting a grill in his room, after putting tape over all the room's doors, windows, and electrical outlets. Why would a student kill himself in this fashion? And what kind of grill would necessitate taping over every possible crack? A grill with an open flame would thrive on oxygen, creating a blaze that would incinerate the room very quickly (and probably burn the rest of the residence hall down as well). We have to assume that this is a gas grill, which would cause death if no fresh air circulated through the room. Since residence hall rules prohibit students from lighting grills and other dangerous appliances in their rooms, this choice of suicide method seems unlikely and strange.

In the context of the resident assistant's job description, however, the choice of a gas grill for a suicide attempt makes perfect sense. Resident assistants not only serve as role models for students; they also enforce rules of appropriate behavior, including those that ban dangerous appliances. An RA who chooses to do away with himself by lighting a gas grill expresses both personal despair and negation of the rules he has promised to follow. The gas grill, which generates both heat and fumes, serves as a metaphor for the "heat" of the RA's job, including prohibitions and disciplinary sanctions. Carl, an RA in Rose Hall, did not hear that a resident of Rose Hall had committed suicide in his room; he heard that it was "another RA". The legend of the RA's suicide functioned (and presumably still functions) as an initiatory scare story for the new RA who was moving into his room, wondering what joys and horrors his new job might entail.

In Jungian terms, Carl's spectral roommate represents his shadow-self: the part of himself that favors danger and destruction as a response to pressure.

Instead of trying to find a way to handle stress, this young man methodically destroys himself, taking care to put tape over every crack in the room. Perhaps he is expressing his fear of "falling through the cracks": failing to succeed as a student and as an RA. He certainly fulfils his own worst fears, killing himself before anyone or anything else can hurt him. Then, as a ghost, he finds it impossible to rest quietly (Motif E411.1.1, "Suicide cannot rest in grave"). He becomes tricky and playful, making strange sounds and moving objects around. No longer vulnerable to stress, he devotes himself to "stressing out" students who move into his room.

In sharp contrast to his shadow-self, Carl takes a positive approach to the eerie things that happen in his room. He describes himself as a "scientific kind of person" who does not worry much about strange noises and inexplicably lost objects. Thinking rationally about his observations, he blames the wind, next-door neighbors, and people upstairs for the peculiar events. Later, however, he hears that another RA has "asked to be moved out of the room because of the strange goings on" and that rumors identify the ghost as the cause of the RA's request. Carl and the later RA, both of whom have had the same spectral roommate, react to their fear tests in different ways. While Carl feels brave and confident, his successor gets scared and insists on leaving: another representation of the shadow-self. Having put both negative figures in their place, Carl can feel good about his unusual experience at Edinboro University.

Another suicide legend from the University of California at Berkeley describes a victim whose ghost takes over his entire building. Joel Rane, a twenty-one-year-old Berkeley student, told this story in October 1986.

The Ghost of Barrington Hall

While many houses claim to have a ghost, our house is the only one in the cooperative system I know of to have a ghost. I learned of the ghost legend from Mr. Spencer, one of the house managers, when I first visited Barrington Hall in 1983, and have heard many residents tell me the tale. I have told the tale myself and in fact believe I saw or rather felt the apparition in the Spring of 1985.

The ghost is supposedly the spirit of a student who committed suicide off the third floor landing of the center stairwell into the well. No one knows for sure who or when, but it must have been after 1943, when the center stairwell was added to the building. The ghost's presence is sometimes felt in the stairwell at night, when it is pitch dark because it is unlit. It also travels along the rooms of the north side of the third floor, probably because it once lived there and is trying to get back. The only way to avoid angering the spirit is to place your bed with the major axis parallel to the hallway, so the spirit can travel through your body rather than being impeded by it. The legend is not so widely believed as earlier, although as recently as 1984 every bed in this part of the building was turned along the major axis of the building, including of course my own.

Like many other campus ghost stories, this one has precise architectural details but less clear description of the student who died. Was this student male or female? Did he or she suffer from academic or personal stress? All we know is that the student jumped down a stairwell and died. We can also infer that this ghost gets angry, since students take great trouble to place their beds parallel to the hallway. Sleeping in that position, students can feel fairly confident that the ghost will keep on moving rather than becoming a permanent guest or roommate. Imagine a ghost controlling the positions of all the beds in a residence hall! It is awe-inspiring to think of a ghost having so much influence. In a general way, this ghost represents the shadow-self of all Barrington Hall students: the self-destructive side that necessitates taking precautions.

Interestingly, the narrator of this story seems unsure about how he perceived the ghost's presence. He explains that he "saw or rather felt the apparition" himself in the spring of 1985; later, he mentions that students can feel the ghost's presence in the hall's stairwell at night. Because the main point of the story is to clarify how the ghost moves through students' bodies, we can assume that the ghost makes itself known through tactile sensations. These sensations were becoming less common in 1986, when Joel told his story, but possessions of entire buildings have continued to worry students and administrators in other residence halls. The "eerie presence" with which I began chapter 1 is one case in point. While many campus ghosts do not cover such a broad area, those that do so can cause widespread alarm.

While some spectral roommates make students think about suicide, others make sexual overtures. I have collected a number of stories about ghosts that appear in bed, frightening the bed's occupant (Motif E338.1, "Ghost haunts bedroom"). Like medieval incubi and succubi, these campus ghosts desire sexual contact. In some stories it is easy to identify the ghost's gender, but in others it is not clear whether the assailant is male or female. Such is the case in the following story told by Alan, a twenty-year-old student in New Rochelle, New York, in November 2004.[11]

"Go to the Light!"

When I tell this story people never believe me, but I'll tell you anyway. When my older cousin Sabrina was in college at Rutgers, she became an RA in her third year. She was sick of having a roommate so she was really excited about living in her own room. She was the RA on the third floor of a girls' dorm, and everything was great for a while.

Three weeks into the semester she started feeling weird things. When she went to bed, she felt stuff rubbing up against her, like someone was touching her under the covers. She thought it was the wind coming from the windows in her room, but the shades weren't moving and when she eventually got up the nerve to check, the window was closed too.

Sabrina only felt things when she slept alone; if her friends would sleep over, she would never feel it. She didn't see or feel anything again for a while, but she told her family about it over Thanksgiving break and we kinda just blew her off and told her to forget about it. She had friends sleep over more often than not after that, but she was still nervous about sleeping alone in her room, so she went to a psychologist. She told her doctor what was going on and the doctor told her to talk to whatever it was, tell it to "Go away! Go to the light!" When she got home she decided she would sleep alone that night and when she felt the thing touching her again she did what the doctor had told her, and she never felt it again.

Like the legend of Barrington Hall, Alan's story describes weird tactile sensations experienced while lying in bed. Sabrina, a new RA, feels excitement about living alone but quickly discovers that she is not alone after all. Her companion, a ghostly lover, immediately begins to pursue her sexually. She not only feels "stuff rubbing up against her," but also feels as if someone is touching her under the sheets and blankets. At first, she wonders if the wind might be to blame, but her window is closed. If it were open, she might imagine Zeus making his way into her room as a shower of gold, as he did to Danae. However, it is impossible to tell what kind of spirit this assailant is and whether it is male or female. We only know that it makes Sabrina very nervous and uncomfortable.

Alan's story follows the formulaic pattern long associated with the American campus legend. Sabrina's encounter with the ghost under the covers takes place during her third year at Rutgers, three weeks into the semester, on the third floor of a women's residence hall. Legends often describe lurid attacks upon women who live alone; as Jan Harold Brunvand has pointed out, such legends highlight single women's vulnerability (1984: 16, 76–77). Since Sabrina is an RA, she has the privilege and danger of occupying a single room. This ghost story represents her initiation into the RA role, with all of its responsibilities and interpersonal pressures.[12]

Because Sabrina fears the ghost's overtures, she consults a psychologist, who urges her to tell it "Go away! Go to the light!" This advice comes from the classic horror movie *Poltergeist* (1982), in which a trained medium banishes a ghost that has abducted a little girl and subjected her family to a series of terrifying attacks. Mentioning the line "Go to the light!" makes us think of the haunted American household, in which good struggles with evil. Like the heroic family members in *Poltergeist* (1982), Sabrina must banish an inexplicable evil force.

It is interesting to see that the person who solves Sabrina's problem is a male doctor who tells her to send the ghost away. Unlike the policeman in "The Boyfriend's Death," which was popular in the 1960s and 1970s, he does not advise the distressed young woman to avoid dangerous confrontations. This story gives its central female character more power than earlier legends did. Only Sabrina herself can banish the ghost, and she does so quickly. Her initiation into living alone has come to a successful conclusion.

In contrast to the narrative about Sabrina's gender-neutral ghost, the next story, told in the first person, presents a ghost that is distinctly male. Unlike most of the other college ghost stories I have collected, it describes a relationship between two male students. Luis, a student at Binghamton University, sent his story on e-mail in July 2005.

Into the Closet

On Saturday, August 9th 2005, my boyfriend and I were sleeping in my room. I dreamed that I was in a hotel, in bed with my boyfriend, just like I was in reality. I dreamed that we were away with some friends, one of which is known to be a serious practical joker. In the dream, I felt someone messing with my shorts in the area between my legs. At first,

I thought it was my boyfriend, so I reached down to touch him. When I reached down it was not my boyfriend's face.

At first, I thought it was my friend the practical joker. This is where I began to wake up. I felt in my hand and partially awake, round steel rimmed glasses. I set up and yelled out, "Who the fuck are you?" A boy, about my age, wearing a track jacket and shorts, got off the foot of the bed, stood up and backed into my open closet. He faded into my woredrobe as he backed away. As soon as I had sat up, my boyfriend woke up and grabbed my arm. He was looking around the room while I saw the boy fade into the closet. He did not see the boy. I have yet to turn the light off when I go to sleep.

This intriguing memorate moves from dream to reality through a series of questions. As Luis dreams about staying in a hotel with friends and lying in bed with his boyfriend, he feels someone touching his shorts. Initially, he thinks it is his boyfriend, but when he reaches down to touch his boyfriend's face, he feels unfamiliar features. Could this be their friend, the "serious practical joker"? No, the round, steel-rimmed glasses are completely unfamiliar, so this must be a ghostly lover of unknown origin. Half-asleep and half-awake, shouting "Who the fuck are you?," Luis demands an explanation for this intruder's presence.

In the story's second half, Luis starts to wake up and tension builds. A young man of about his own age, clothed in a track jacket and shorts, leaves the foot of the bed and backs into the closet, which is open. It seems important that this mysterious young man is the same age as Luis and is similarly dressed in shorts. Like many other ghosts that appear in college students' rooms, this one closely parallels the student himself—but instead of showing strength, he seems hesitant and uncertain. Significantly, the boy backs up into the open closet. "Coming out of the closet" is a well-known metaphor for identifying oneself as gay, lesbian, or bisexual, so backing up into the closet suggests fearful withdrawal from open self-identification. At this point, the ghost becomes a less assertive version of Luis. In a society that privileges heterosexuality, full self-disclosure can be difficult.

It is also interesting to see that Luis uses the word "woredrobe" as a cognate for "closet." "Woredrobe" is a misspelling of the word "wardrobe," not commonly used in the United States in the early twenty-first century. In the summer of 2005, fantasy fans on college campuses and elsewhere were eagerly awaiting the release of the movie *The Lion, the Witch and the Wardrobe*, based upon C. S. Lewis's novel for children (1950). Perhaps awareness of this movie made Luis more sensitive to the possibility that a figure from another world might come to visit him.

Clearly, the spectral young man's appearance and disappearance frighten Luis. After going through this experience, he keeps a light on while sleeping. Is he just afraid of seeing ghosts, or does he fear something more? The fact that the ghost resembles him so closely persuades me that he is worried about his own hesitation. Awake, he knows who he is and what he wants, but in the "twilight zone" of sleep, he loses some of that confidence. The young male ghost reminds Luis of mainstream society's pressures. As long as the light stays on, fear of what the ghost represents stays under control.

For college students, ghostly presences take various roles. Some act as phantom lovers, shadow-selves, or both. These images are evanescent; they serve their purpose, then fade away. College students excel at pushing back the boundaries of what they know, suspending disbelief while exploring new territory. Seeing, hearing, and feeling ghostly presences, they may find they have discovered something more substantial than any ghost: a deeper sense of the complexities that make them fully themselves.

Chapter Five

DESPERATE LOVERS

S ome of the saddest ghosts that roam college buildings are the spirits of young women whose romantic relationships have ended tragically (Motif E334.2.3, "Ghost of tragic lover"). Like most of the ghosts discussed in chapter 4, these miserable lovers have killed themselves in a fit of despair. But unlike those spirits, these are all women who have been rejected, forced into an impossible marriage, or left alone because of a lover's sudden death. Overwhelmed by tumultuous feelings, these ghosts seek current students who will pay attention to their stories. Why are unhappy female lovers' ghosts so prominent at colleges and universities? In *Piled Higher and Deeper*, Simon J. Bronner makes the point that "With courtship such a prevalent distraction for students, it isn't surprising that lovers' ghosts frequently haunt campuses" (1995: 150). Many students seek partners, but the frantic pace of academic and social routines does not encourage calm, stable interaction. Students who have fallen in and out of love can sympathize with a ghost whose death resulted from an ill-fated relationship.

However, the fact that the great majority of unhappy lovers' ghosts are *women* requires more explanation. Why do almost no male ghosts lament the loss of lovers in college residence halls? Both male and female students have felt anguish about losing romantic partners in everyday life, but in ghost stories, women have been the ones who express the horror of lost love. Their sad, pale ghosts suggest that if a relationship suddenly ends, there is no alternative but suicide. In Jungian terms, these ghosts represent a shadow-self: a dependent, self-destructive version of the self that cannot survive independently. This shadow-self reflects nineteenth-and twentieth-century patterns of courtship, which limited women's freedom of choice. Before looking at legends about the ghosts of women who have died for love, we should briefly consider the social circumstances that shaped their stories.

Campus Courtship

American college courtship patterns have changed drastically since women first enrolled as students in the 1830s. Male students of the nineteenth and early twentieth centuries visited their girlfriends under the strict supervision of housemothers and chaperones. College and university officials believed that it was important to protect female students by regulating their interaction with men. The president of the College of Wooster in Ohio, for example, banned public skating, dancing, and theater-going in the mid-1880s; he would unexpectedly visit students' rooms to make sure that the students were behaving themselves (Notestein 1971: 160). At the University of Wisconsin in Madison, a university committee formed in 1905 to "better protect the young women students who room in houses in town." This committee wanted to give women students "parlor privileges" to receive male visitors (Curti and Carstensen 1949: 498). Fifteen years later, young women at the University of Tennessee in Knoxville could only receive callers in dormitory parlors or sororities when two other couples were present. Evening dates in cars or boats required chaperones, as did dinners in town (Montgomery, Folmsbee, and Seifert 1984: 376).

Although college rules limited women's freedom, some female students managed to get around the rules to have more fun. At Syracuse University in the 1920s, for example, rules stated that women could stay out until midnight only once a week. Betty Dumars, who graduated in 1930, cherished the memory of a fellow student who decided to sneak out of her dormitory window by jumping into the arms of her boyfriend. He succeeded in catching her but fell into a clump of barberry bushes. So many barberry thorns pierced his arms and legs that his fraternity brothers had to spend most of the night removing the thorns from his body (Wilson 1984: 335).

In the 1950s, college courtship emphasized laying the foundation for marriage. Jill Ker Conway, president of Smith College from 1975 to 1985, has commented sardonically upon "the 1950s obligation to be paired inextricably with a male partner by one's late teens" (2001: 7). College women of the 1950s joked about getting their "M.R.S." along with their B.A. or B.S. degrees. It was unusual for young women to ask men out on dates except on such special occasions as Sadie Hawkins Day. Men chose which women they would date, while women eagerly anticipated moving toward marriage. This pattern continued into the mid-1960s. At Wellesley College in Massachusetts, an ad in the college newspaper asked, "Taking your M.R.S.? Do your cramming with *Modern Bride*" (Horn 1999: 24).

As recently as the late 1960s, female students at eastern women's colleges waited to see their boyfriends in designated "date parlors," with housemothers hovering nearby. Parietals (designated visiting hours for male guests) strictly limited men's presence in residence halls. But in the last years of the

1960s, a radical change took place. The women's movement gave female students a sense of broader choices, and protests against the war in Vietnam and Cambodia increased students' awareness of their own power. Also significantly, the "sexual revolution" encouraged young people to rebel against parietals and other rules that gave college officials the right to act *in loco parentis*. Resident directors and resident assistants replaced housemothers; men visited women's residence halls freely; and modes of dating began to reflect more equality in gender roles.

Although college courtship patterns have changed, sorority rituals of the twentieth and early twenty-first century have continued to celebrate men's choice of romantic partners and women's hope to be chosen. In "The Folklore of Academe," Barre Toelken describes pinning and engagement rituals that involve elaborate plans and signals. During dinner, the passing of candy indicates that a ritual will take place soon, but the identity of the pinned or engaged person remains secret. After dinner, the young women stand in a circle in a darkened room. Someone passes around a candle surrounded by rosebuds, fruits, cookies, or even vitamin pills. After lighting the candle, the women sing a love song. The third time the candle goes around the circle, the pinned or engaged student blows it out. Toelken notes that the flowers and fruits, which symbolize fertility, serve as "a dramatic and socially acceptable—perhaps expected—way in which to reveal the exciting news of one's engagement" (1968: 328). Such ceremonies make women passive receivers and announcers of invitations to get pinned or engaged. Men deliver these invitations; women accept and celebrate them. Postings on sorority websites show that young women still celebrate such invitations today.[1]

Contemporary student culture combines old traditions with new choices. While male-oriented courtship rituals persist in Greek groups, female students are relatively free to choose romantic partners. Rather than formally planning dates, many students go to parties in groups, joking about "hooking up" (anything from kissing to more intimate activity). Barrett Seaman, the author of *Binge*, makes the point that "in the hanging-out/hooking-up culture, both men and women initiate." He suggests that this wide range of choices causes uncertainty; students sometimes feel confused about what will happen next (2005: 43–45). Social discomfort and lack of clarity can certainly cause problems, especially for first-year students. Ghost stories in which characters take well-defined roles offer a familiar framework for exploring courtship issues. Many of these stories take the teller and listener back to the late nineteenth century, when gender roles were more rigid and clear. In campus ghost stories about the Victorian era, young women eloquently express their anguish at the loss of their lovers. Feeling angry, ashamed, and desperate, they violently destroy themselves. After their deaths, as lively ghosts, they show that they have the power to influence young women who are trying to handle their own romantic relationships.[2]

Brides-Never-to-Be

Among the most poignant ghosts are brides-to-be who lose their chance to become brides. There are two kinds of doomed brides: those who get jilted and those who would rather kill themselves than get married. A bride of the first kind inspires sympathy. Thrilled and expectant, dressed all in white, this young woman learns that her fiancé has jilted her. Her wedding will be cancelled; her parents will pay for a cake that no one will eat; friends and family will know that the man she loves has left her at the altar. Heartbroken and furious, the bride kills herself. Forever afterward, she will haunt the place of her betrayal, dressed in the white clothes that she chose for her wedding.

One famous ghost of a jilted bride-to-be haunts the Alpha Gamma Delta sorority house at the University of Georgia. When I saw this house in the summer of 2005, I immediately noticed its resemblance to a wedding cake. With Ionic columns on stone piers, a recessed central entrance flanked by pilasters, and friezes on both portico and balcony, this beautiful Beaux Arts mansion brings to mind the prosperous 1890s, during which it was built. After a visit to the Columbian Exposition in Chicago in 1892, architect William Winstead Thomas planned and built the house. His widow sold it to the Hulme family in 1909; the next owner was James Yancey Carithers, who bought the house in 1913. Since 1939, the house has belonged to the sisters of Alpha Gamma Delta.

In May 2005, folklorist Elissa Henken, a professor at the University of Georgia, told me this version of the "jilted bride-to-be" legend.

Wedding Cake House

A young woman's father gave this house as a present to the bride and her fiancé. On the day of the wedding, the groom didn't show up, so the young woman went upstairs and hanged herself in the attic. It turned out that the groom had been delayed because a bridge was out.

Wedding Cake House, University of Georgia. Photograph by Elizabeth Tucker.

Now, any girl who lives in the room in which the young woman hanged herself will get lavaliered, pinned, or engaged. So the ghost is looking out for the girls' romantic welfare.

Sorority members and their friends know this legend; so do people who tour the campus.

This legend's most memorable feature is its tragic irony. While the man seems to be jilting his fiancée, he actually does not show up because a bridge is out (or, in other versions, because his carriage overturns). The bride's immediate decision to hang herself in the attic shows how desperate she feels about the blighting of her hopes and dreams. As in "Marbles on the Ceiling" stories, the legend of the jilted bride-to-be uses the attic as a symbol of emotional turmoil. At the top of the house, with a noose around her neck, the bride-to-be makes it clear that without marriage, her life has no value.

Henken explains that female students living in the ghost's room will become romantically involved with men through the ghost's intervention. Three steps lead toward the altar: getting lavaliered (receiving a necklace with a young man's fraternity letters), getting pinned (receiving a fraternity pin), and getting engaged. All of these steps depend upon the man expressing a commitment toward the woman, sometimes with the support of his fraternity brothers. Successful expressions of commitment invoke celebration, but there are no rituals for the breaking of these bonds. To some extent, the telling of ghost stories ritualizes the painful process of getting "disengaged" or giving up pins, lavalieres, and other symbolic representations of romantic bliss.

Students' legends about the Wedding Cake House have identified the jilted student as Susie Caruthers: almost, but not quite, the name of the Carithers family that once owned the house. "College Town Ghost Stories," an essay written by a journalism student at the University of Georgia, explores Alpha Gamma Delta sorority sisters' reactions to their resident ghost at the beginning of the twenty-first century. According to some of the sisters, Susie Caruthers committed suicide early in the twentieth century after her groom failed to show up at her wedding. She hanged herself in the sorority house's attic, right above a room called the "Engagement Suite." Some sisters say that they have seen Susie's face through an attic window, but others doubt that she exists. Odd events like doors opening and closing and lights going on and off have encouraged sisters to believe in Susie's influence. While some of them insist that no ghost haunts the house, others believe that Susie has been there for a long time, helping her protégées to get engaged and married (2001).

This ghost's main function is to encourage marriage. In folk literature, marriage is usually something wonderful; a couple that has just gotten married lives "happily ever after." The ghost of the Wedding Cake House may simply want other women to experience the happiness she could not have herself. However, in light of her tragic history, her actions seem more malicious than altruistic. Her engagement led to her death, not to an idyllic "happily ever after." Ghosts often want to perpetuate the scenarios that led to their own deaths (Motif E337, "Ghost reenacts scene from own lifetime"). In this case, the ghost wants to keep her own drama alive by promoting romance.

Because Susie haunts a nineteenth-century mansion, she has a connection to nineteenth-century literature. Charles Dickens's *Great Expectations* (first published in 1860) offers an intriguing example of a jilted bride-to-be. Miss Havisham, an elderly woman whose fiancé deserted her on her wedding day, always wears her wedding dress and keeps her moldering wedding cake on a table. Although she is not a ghost, she walks "in a ghostly manner" (Dickens 1937: 310) and wears a "shroud of a dress" (242). When her fiancé left, she stopped all the clocks and resolved never to look upon the light of day. For her, interruption of marriage means cessation of hope and pleasure. She has only one desire: to train Estella, her ward, to make men fall in love with her. For Pip, the young hero, falling in love with Estella leads to heartbreak. On two different occasions, Pip sees a vision of Miss Havisham hanging from a beam in her brewery, committing suicide because of her fiancé's disappearance on her wedding day. By training Estella to spurn her own suitors, Miss Havisham can avenge herself for the terrible rejection that she has suffered.

Dressed in bridal attire, constantly evoking the specter of a doomed wedding, Miss Havisham represents what Joseph Andriano calls the "daemonic feminine": a tormenter and destroyer of men (1993: 139). This character fits both C. G. Jung's anima archetype and Erich Neumann's archetype of the Great Mother, who creates and destroys (1972). Although she wears white, a color often associated with marriage and joy in Western culture, Miss Havisham specializes in revenge. Susie, her fellow sufferer of "left at the altar" misery, seems less grim than Miss Havisham does. Nonetheless, these two jilted brides-to-be have similar fates and frustrations, and both of them work on arranging marriages for young women.

The ghostly bride who can never forget her doomed wedding shows the reader, in a dramatic and compelling way, how important it is for young women to get married. Although times have changed since the 1860s, the Wedding Cake House's ghost tells us that marriage still matters intensely. It also suggests that people should never underestimate the power of a rejected woman.

Another legend from Clarkson University in Potsdam, New York, describes a bride-to-be whose family arranges a tragically inappropriate marriage. Joe, a Clarkson student, told this story on Instant Messenger in March 2005.[3]

The White Lady

Joe23: well, one of the stories is there was a girl who was in the Sisson family who owned the house, she was engaged to marry her uncle because families with wealth always married within their families, so this girl ended up the night before her wedding locking herself in her room, dressing up in her wedding dress, and she hung herself in the closet.

Joe23: so now there are people who claim that randomly around the house they will see "the white lady" and also in the room that she hung herself in the closet where she hung herself the door never stays closed. brothers have put crates and things in front of the door and no matter what is there when they go back to the room the door is open.

This story conveys the horror of preparing for a wedding to a close relative. With a wry sense of the peculiarity of the very rich, Joe observes that "families with wealth always married within their families." Rebelling against her family's cruel dictum, the young bride-to-be dresses in her wedding finery and hangs herself in her closet. After her death, she becomes an ever-present "white lady" whose color represents both ghostliness and the blighted hope of a happy marriage.

Trapped in an impossible situation, symbolized by her confinement in the closet, the White Lady chose suicide as a way out. Why does the door keep opening now? Perhaps the door's message is that students should never get stuck in heartbreaking situations dictated by others. The phrase "coming out of the closet," often used for gays' and lesbians' declarations of their sexual preferences, works well for the ghost's revelation of her identity. Determined not to let others forget what happened to her, she keeps the door open, no matter what objects fraternity brothers place in front of it. Conventional morality suggests that scandals, like skeletons, belong in a family's closet, but this ghost wants the brothers to know the truth. While marriage to a relative seems remote from fraternity brothers' concerns, date rape has been a troubling issue for some members of fraternities and sororities.[4] The White Lady, who refuses to forget her own trauma, warns fraternity brothers that they had better behave well in their romances with women.

The "White Lady" legend circulates among the brothers of Tau Epsilon Phi, a fraternity that has owned the old Sisson mansion on Sissonville Road since 1968. Traditionally, these brothers have held haunted houses in their mansion on Halloween to raise money for charities such as the Red Cross. The brothers have also participated in freshman orientation, sharing their ghost stories with the newest members of Clarkson University. They have taken an initiatory role in the Clarkson community, offering new students shocking views of what can happen when people get overwhelmed by tragic events.

Cheri Revai, author of the popular book *Haunted Northern New York* (2002), describes the Tau Epsilon Phi fraternity house's traditions in detail. When she visited the house, a fraternity brother told her about the White Lady's history and recent activities. He explained that the White Lady had killed herself in the "Frying Pan Room," which got its name because of an east-facing bay window that generates heat. Near the closet door, there was "an almost suffocating presence" (2002: 22). In the early 1990s, a brother who was sleeping in the "Tent Room" (so-called because of its small size and sloping walls) awoke to see the White Lady standing at the foot of his bed. She told him the date of his death, scaring him so much that he immediately moved out of the house and left instructions in his will for later fraternity brothers to check his actual death date against the White Lady's prophecy (22–23; Motif M341.1, "Prophecy: Death at certain time"). With all of these legend variants offering grisly details about the White Lady's behavior, it is no wonder that she has frightened freshmen, both at orientation and on Halloween.

Scorned Girlfriends

Many campus ghost stories describe women who have suffered torment because their boyfriends suddenly rejected them. Although "dumped" is a more popular term for rejected girlfriends or boyfriends these days, I have chosen to use the term "scorned" from Stith Thompson's *Motif-Index of Folk Literature*. The motif T81.2.1, "Scorned lover kills self," applies very well to college ghost stories about relationships that go sour. Typically, the boyfriend finds another young woman that he prefers, and his original girlfriend commits suicide. These stories tell of lovelorn, self-destructive young women and callous, fickle young men. In emphasizing suicide, the stories suggest that women need men's affirmation to keep on living: a troubling message that foregrounds the dependent, self-destructive shadow-self.

As I mention in chapter 4, legends about suicide have transformative potential. James Hillman's *Suicide and the Soul* (1964) eloquently suggests that part of the self can die to make a new phase of life possible. If we see a campus community as a group with its own selfhood and identity, we can apply Hillman's thesis to its adaptation of suicide legends. In telling legends about suicidal young women, campus leaders may change the stories' emphasis from a ghost's misery to a joyful expression of school spirit. This happens at an institutional level, with orientation leaders, Residential Life staff members, and members of the faculty telling legends that support school spirit and pride.

Orientation leaders at Mansfield University in Mansfield, Pennsylvania, and Henderson State University in Arkadelphia, Arkansas, have told legends about scorned, suicidal female students since the mid-1970s. Both legend complexes have drawn the attention of local and national media. Close scrutiny of these two legend complexes shows how ghost stories about scorned girlfriends initiate new students into college life.

At Mansfield University, entering freshmen learn that a student named Sara died after falling down the stairwell of North Hall. In most versions of this legend, Sara commits suicide by jumping over the railing of the hall's

Stairwell of North Hall at Mansfield University, where Sara supposedly fell to her death. Photograph by Geoffrey Gould.

central stairwell after her boyfriend rejects her. Shocked and miserable, she enacts his dumping her by throwing herself away.

Several years ago, I began to collect variants of Sara's story in an effort to understand why the legend mattered so much to orientation leaders and students. In the spring of 2003, I briefly interviewed Josh, who had entered Mansfield University in the fall of 2001.

ET: *"Did you hear any ghost stories at Mansfield?"*
J: *"Oh, yeah, they told us a story at orientation. This girl supposedly killed herself by jumping down the stairs, and she comes back to haunt the students who are at Mansfield now."*
ET: *"Did you hear that story from another student?"*
J: *"No, it was a teacher at orientation."*
ET: *"A professor?"*
J: *"Yes! It's Mansfield's urban legend!"*

When Josh said *"urban legend,"* he smiled and rolled his eyes. Clearly, the story of Sara held no horrors for him. It was just a story that he remembered from his freshman orientation: a story told by "a teacher." When teachers tell stories to new students, they convey part of the institution's meaning or values. Even if the story sounds funny or flippant, it comes from someone in an authoritative position. A freshman may shrug the story off, but he or she will probably remember this initiation into college life, as Josh did.

One corollary of Sara's story that has fascinated both students and faculty members is a psychic's visit to North Hall in the early twenty-first century. My friend Tom, the brother of a Mansfield alumna, told me about the psychic's visit in March 2003.

> My sister went to Mansfield University in the mid-1970s. The oldest building there was supposed to be haunted. They said a woman student had thrown herself down from the top of four or five flights of stairs to kill herself.
>
> After a while they glassed in the stairwell, because of the risk, and strange emanations started happening—weird lights, unusual things. They brought in a psychic, and she said the spirit of the student who died didn't like the glass—it blocked her. Maybe it kept her from repeating her death. So they took some of the panes of glass out, and the strange things stopped happening. That was it.

After hearing Tom's story, I wanted to see the glassed-in stairwell where Sara had supposedly leaped to her death, but I had no time to travel to Pennsylvania. Finally, in the spring of 2006, I found an opportunity to visit North Hall, Mansfield University's oldest and most beautiful building, which houses the campus library and administrative offices. A kind librarian gave me a tour of the building.[5] She explained that North Hall, built in 1874, served as a dormitory for women until the mid-1970s, when it fell into decrepitude. For twenty years the building was boarded up and abandoned, with bats and pigeons as its only residents. North Hall underwent a nine-million-dollar renovation in 1996. Its Doric columns, large porches, and staircase underwent thorough restoration.

As I listened to the librarian's account of North Hall's history, I looked up at the building's elegant central stairwell, six stories high. No glass or other material surrounded the open stairwell. "Did anything ever cover this stairwell?" I asked the librarian. She told me that college authorities had insisted on covering the stairwell with wood in the 1930s, because wardens had identified the stairwell as a fire hazard. There was no glass around the stairs, but the building's restoration team covered the porches on the building's sides with sheets of glass. It seems likely that the use of glass in the porches' restoration gradually became part of the legend of Sara's leap to her death.[6]

Seal of Mansfield University, where Sara's body landed; some people say that the imprint of her body still pulsates there. Photograph by Geoffrey Gould.

While I gazed at North Hall's glassless stairwell, the librarian told me her favorite version of Sara's story, which I summarize here. Sara was a beautiful music major who loved to sing. One night, when she and all the other female students in North Hall stood around the stairwell singing Mansfield's alma mater, Sara became so emotional that she lost her balance and fell over the stairwell's highest railing. As she fell, she kept on singing while her fellow students screamed. After her body hit the floor, it pulsed to the alma mater's rhythm. A macabre addition to this story's conclusion appears in the book *Life at Mansfield*, written by the sociology professor Gale Largey: "if one looks closely at the floor of the well one can find the imprint of her body. It moves in the rhythm of the Alma Mater" (1984: 119).

The "music major" version of Sara's story clarifies the connection between this beloved ghost and loyalty to Mansfield University. Sara cares so much about her university that she keeps on singing its song, even while falling to her death. Like saints in the *Legends of Gold*, she dies because of her loyalty and belief (de Voragine 1993). Her devotion to school spirit explains her transformation from living student to spirit or ghost: a meaningful linguistic twist. When pre-freshmen and their parents visit North Hall, they see Mansfield University's round seal at the bottom of the stairwell. If they understand circles' significance as feminine symbols (Dundes 2004: 184), these visitors may sense a connection between school spirit and femininity. Later, entering freshmen learn more about the stairwell's significance through legends told by professors and upperclassmen.

Another reason for the story's tenacity is the fact that North Hall stood empty for twenty years. In 1983, James York Glimm summarized hundreds of variants of Sara legends that had been collected by Amy Kelchner, Mary Claversteine, and John Heim. Some of these summaries mention students sneaking into North Hall through a window, then following a secret passage to catch a glimpse of the ghost's long, white nightgown and candle or lamp (1983: 120–22). Some of the main events of the central legend include Sara going crazy after being jilted by her lover, swinging her leg over the stairway's banister, and then jumping, screaming while hitting each floor. University officials, some students said, "hushed up" the death, but Sara always found a female student who could explain that she just wanted to help other women. Glimm's summary of this large corpus of stories shows that students wanted to find their own truth in the administration's closing of North Hall, rejecting the official account of the building's decrepitude in favor of a more sinister explanation.

Besides giving students a sense of the past, Sara represents the pain and ambiguity of student life, which may bring out an individual's shadow-self. Staircases—passageways from one place to another—provide an ideal setting for legends about difficult transitions.[7] When freshmen enter Mansfield University, they hear about Sara's death: either the "music major" version or the "boyfriend/suicide" version. Several Mansfield students and staff members have told me that the legend about Sara throwing herself down the stairwell after being rejected by her boyfriend circulates more actively than the other version does. Although the administration has actively promoted the more positive "music major" version, students have preferred to tell the version of the story that fits their own needs. Hearing about Sara's death, freshmen can recognize her as a "worst case" character who dramatizes the dangers of courtship and other stressful situations that they may encounter on their college campus.

Another suspenseful legend about a scorned girlfriend concerns the Black Lady at Henderson State University in Arkadelphia, Arkansas. W. K. McNeil, author of *Ghost Stories from the American South* (1985), suggests that the Black Lady "serves to create a feeling of unity and tradition among the student body of Henderson State University" (174). At some universities, school spirit focuses on rivalry with other institutions, usually through athletic competitions. In this case we see a different kind of contest: rivalry for the affections of a male Henderson State student. The "home team," represented by a young woman from Henderson State, wins, while a student from Ouachita Baptist University loses and becomes a ghost.

McNeil's text, collected from a female Henderson State student in December 1974, tells of heartbreak, suicide, and subsequent scare tactics.

The Black Lady

> One year a boy from Henderson fell in love with a girl from OBU. Their friends tried to break them up because they were from different schools and different religions. Finally they succeeded in getting them apart, and while they were dating other people the boy fell in love with someone else. The girl from OBU was upset about this, and she tried to get her lover back, but there was nothing she could do, so she committed suicide during homecoming week.
>
> Every year during homecoming week the ghost of the girl from OBU—she is called the Black Lady—comes back through the girls' dorms at Henderson looking for the girl who stole her lover. Every year during homecoming week the junior and senior girls at Henderson get together and go through the freshman dorms and scare the girls. The freshmen have heard the story of the Black Lady, so they know what is happening (77).

This classic initiatory legend combines past history with current danger. The story of the blighted love affair draws a contrast between colleges based on different religions. Originally, Henderson State University was a Methodist institution known as Henderson Brown. Some variants of the Black Lady legend specify that Jane, the OBU student, is quiet, shy, and possessive, while her competitor at Henderson State is more lively and outgoing. Joshua, the boyfriend, finds that his friends will not accept his choice of a girl from a rival school. The boyfriend's choice to reject Jane not only affirms school loyalty, but also proclaims the superiority of the home college's religion. For those reasons, the "Black Lady" story makes an ideal legend for homecoming, when school spirit runs high.

Looking at the "Black Lady" from a Jungian standpoint, we can observe that she represents the shadow-self's negativity. Quiet, shy, and jealous of competitors, she has no resilience or enthusiasm. When confronted with a rival, she kills herself rather than trying to get her boyfriend back. Her poor self-esteem and lack of social skills make her the obverse of a well-integrated personality. The same observation applies to another college ghost known only by her color: the Red Lady of Huntingdon College in Montgomery, Alabama, whose anger and refusal to make friends culminate in a bloody suicide (Windham and Figh 1983: 97–104)). Both the Red Lady and the Black Lady warn students to keep their shadow-selves from becoming dominant. Like the "Black Man" and other bogeymen delineated in John Widdowson's study *If You Don't Be Good* (1977: 112–16), these female ghosts dramatize negative consequences for bad behavior.

In addition to setting guidelines for behavior and expressing school spirit, the desire to give freshmen a good scare motivates the telling of this legend. Just as children at camp tell each other that a monster, maniac, or ghost will kill a camper on a certain day, students at Henderson State University tell new recruits that they had better watch out for the Black Lady during homecoming celebrations. Juniors and seniors walk through the women's residence halls, making sure that freshmen know about the threat from the Black Lady.

Because of Mary Jo Mann, a popular staff member at Henderson State, entering freshmen do not need to wait for homecoming to learn about the Black Lady; they hear the story when orientation begins. Misty Brown, a student at Henderson State University, described recent storytelling in June 2005:

> They tell the story of the Lady in Black at the Pine Tree Speech every year. Mrs. Mary Jo Mann, former sponsor of Heart and Key, the invitation-only service honor society for HSU, usually gives the speech. I'm sure our site somewhere tells her (the Black Lady's) story . . . Supposedly, she haunts the Smith girls' dormitory around Homecoming each year. I've never stayed the night in that dorm, so I'm not aware of any scary stories from there.

The Pine Tree Speech, a cherished tradition of Henderson State, gives new students a history of the university's development. Significantly, the Black Lady is one of its most prominent characters. Emphasis on a negative, suicidal young woman at a rival institution builds school spirit and provides excitement. Freshmen who hear the story can enjoy the thrill of a colorful ghost, while feeling safe from any immediate danger.

Legendary Lovers

In contrast to jilted fiancées and scorned girlfriends, some female legend characters lose their lovers because of wars, duels, religious prohibitions, and other overwhelming circumstances that encapsulate American political and cultural history. The two wars that most often separate lovers in college legends are the Revolutionary War and the Civil War. Not surprisingly, Revolutionary War lovers usually appear in stories told at northern colleges, while Civil War lovers predominate in stories told at southern colleges. Battles of honor in which one man must die also tend to occur more often in legends from the South. Students at Roman Catholic colleges around the United States have enjoyed telling stories about forbidden trysts between priests or nuns and lay-persons of the opposite gender. Pregnant nuns and lovelorn priests are popular legend characters.[8] While these legendary lovers deal with disparate circumstances, they share a sense of the tumult and frustration of early romantic relationships.

One historically significant pair of star-crossed lovers from the 1700s belongs to the legendry of Tennessee Wesleyan College in Athens, Tennessee, founded in 1857. Students and faculty members at Tennessee Wesleyan cherish the legend of Nocatula and Connestoga, an Indian maiden and a British soldier who fell in love and died together in the late 1700s. Tellers of this legend often cite a historical fact: the Cherokee laid siege to Fort Loudon, held by the British, in 1760. After months of starvation, the British surrendered. On their way out of the fort they were attacked by Indians, and most of the British died. Oral tradition suggests that a desperate mother begged the Cherokee chief, Attakulla-Kulla, to spare her son. Mercifully, the chief accepted the woman and her son into his tribe. Later he married the woman, and they had a daughter named Nocatula Cooweena.

A plaque on the Tennessee Wesleyan College campus offers more details:

A wounded English officer from Fort Loudon was befriended by an Indian Chief and nursed back to health by Nocatula, daughter of the Chief. The soldier, given the name of Connestoga, "the Oak," was accepted into the tribe and married Nocatula. A jealous suitor attacked Connestoga with a knife. As he lay dying Nocatula confessed her eternal love and plunged a knife into her breast. Buried together. The Chief placed an acorn in Connestoga's hand and a hackberry in Nocatula's hand, symbolizing undying love. From these there developed two trees which stood on this spot for 150 years.

At Tennessee Wesleyan College, the site where the two trees once stood is treated with respect. The legend of the two trees is part of the college's founding; construction crews that built the college in 1857 took special care not to disturb the trees known by Nocatula's and Connestoga's names. In 1945, Nocatula's hackberry tree succumbed to disease and had to be taken down. Soon afterward, Connestoga's oak tree sickened and died. College personnel planted new trees where the original trees once stood.[9] Tennessee Wesleyan staff and students' reverence for the trees brings to mind the elves' devotion to the Two Trees of Valinor in Tolkien's middle-earth (Tolkien 1977: 33).

It has become traditional for orientation leaders to tell the story of Nocatula and Connestoga to each incoming group of freshmen at Tennessee Wesleyan. Plans are underway to build a Nocatula Garden, which will contain both an English formal garden representing Connestoga and a set of shrubs and plants native to east Tennessee representing Nocatula's Cherokee heritage. The class of 1953's reunion brochure states that this new garden "will not only help beautify the Tennessee Wesleyan College campus but bring the Cherokee maiden and her beloved together again." Local ghostlore suggests that Nocatula and Connestoga do not need to be brought together, as they already haunt the campus in each other's company. Ghostly figures, voices, and whispers have been reported in the vicinity of the two trees. Graduate student John Norris Brown's website notes that these ghosts "seem to be quite benevolent. Perhaps it's all that remains of an undying love between Connestoga and Nocatula" (Brown 2005a).

This touching story gives readers the comforting message that two people who truly love each other will always remain together. Like Baucis and Philemon of classical mythology, Nocatula and Connestoga take the form of trees of different types.[10] Alumni and administrators at Tennessee Wesleyan have planned a beautiful garden that represents the ethnicity of both the Indian maiden and her British lover, creating a sense of harmony between the area's original inhabitants and British/American settlers. The garden also reminds graduates of the college how important it is to stay loyal to their alma mater. Like many other campus ghosts, the spectral figures of Nocatula and Connestoga represent and support campus spirit.

Another pair of legendary lovers can be found at Northwestern State University, founded as Louisiana State Normal School in 1884 in Natchitoches, Louisiana. Like Nocatula, Isabella is said to have parted from her lover under grievous circumstances. Most versions of her story identify her lover as a passionate, belligerent man who died in a duel, but some versions identify him as a priest. Isabella's depression after her lover's death made her withdraw from the world. Choosing to become a nun, she isolated herself in Bullard Mansion, leaving bloody handprints on its walls.

Isabella's mark. Photograph by Geoffrey
Gould.

Madelyn Boudreaux, a student at Northwestern State University, e-mailed
Isabella's story to the Texas A & M folklore listserv in December 2000:

Creepy Oldness

The story has it that a young and of course very beautiful nun fell in
love with either a local man or a priest. Possibly she was not a nun but a
girl who lived in the convent, but there's no question that her name was
Isabella. Heartbreak, of course, followed, and she finally threw herself out
of the window of the convent. She then haunted the administrative building which burned in the early 80s. After it burned, she moved across the
street to take up residence in Varnado Hall, the dormitory.

In my year living in the dorm, I encountered many spirits, but as they
all came in bottles, if I saw anything supernatural, I didn't recognize it at
the time. Plenty of other girls in the dorm told of many spooky things,
99% of which could probably be attributed to confusion, adolescence,
liquor, and pranks.

At some point, there was a séance to move Isabella to the gym, although
it is rumored that she still moves around and can be seen in Varnado Hall. It
is considered no coincidence that this building also burned down, leaving

Isabella's postmortem arson at three out of four of her residences (the convent, the admin. building, and the gym). Perhaps, it is whispered, if the séance hadn't moved her, she would have taken Varnado with her as well. Or, perhaps, she wanted to spare the lives of all the girls who lived there.

Plenty of students claim to have seen Isabella in one form or another (in the shape of a huge white owl, for instance), and with as much creepy oldness as there is around Natchitoches (moving graves, gravestones inside of trees, the Tomb of the Unknown Confederate Soldier, and mid-18th century grave sites), there is plenty to fuel the folkloric fires. The town is the "first European settlement in the Louisiana Purchase," so it's got its own sense of history and antiquity.

This story's droll tone makes it a delight to read. Boudreaux vividly describes the "creepy oldness" of this college town, which adds depth to Isabella's story. Isabella's frequent moves from one building to another (in 1926, 1948, 1982, and finally 2001) show that Northwestern State University values her presence and wants to make her comfortable in each of her new dwelling places. According to campus tradition, Isabella must reside in the oldest building that is fit to hold her. She represents both campus spirit and the town's eighteenth-century heritage as the first settlement in the Louisiana Purchase. Like other ghosts that haunt old college buildings, Isabella proclaims the importance of local history and campus pride.[11]

Nonetheless, Isabella is no poster girl for proper behavior. As Boudreaux points out, she sets fires in campus buildings and only spares Varnado Hall because she likes the students and wants to protect them. Her passionate, histrionic personality makes her leave a bloody handprint in each building she inhabits. Why, one might ask, does Northwestern State University care so much about preserving this ghost that promotes pyromania and leaves bloody handprints? Besides portraying campus spirit in a wild and macabre way, Isabella embodies both individuality and suffering. Each handprint uniquely identifies an individual; no one can duplicate the imprint of Isabella's grief and painful death. As Jeannie B. Thomas points out in her essay on Indiana State University's "Barfing Ghost of Burford Hall," when bodily fluids go outside the body, pain is externalized and made clear (1991: 32–35). The administrators of Northwestern State University have given this unique, troubled, and loving soul the imprint of official indispensability. Representing her university's heritage and spirit, she shows students that she must never be forgotten.

Chapter Six

WAILING WOMEN

Some of the eeriest ghost stories on college campuses describe women who wail, weep, scream, or make other mournful sounds. The female figure who laments killing her own children—*"la llorona,"* the weeping woman—is well known in the southwestern United States.[1] Another important female legend character is the ghost who cries or screams because she has been sexually assaulted, brutally murdered, or both. Under the foundation of a building or in a basement, attic, elevator, or other liminal space, she makes so much noise that it is impossible for students to ignore her. Since the mid-1960s, probably earlier as well, American college students have told legends about weeping, wailing, and screaming female ghosts that demonstrate the danger of assault. As they listen to the ghost's story, students learn about the importance of staying safe. They may also learn about a female ghost with a close connection to rape and murder victims: a kind protector who watches over women living in the hall that she haunts.

Some campus administrators have hesitated to tell true stories about rapes and murders (Motifs T471, "Rape"; S110, "Murders"). Such stories worry prospective students, their parents, and donors to endowments. However, relatively recent legislation has made it impossible for colleges and universities to downplay sexual assaults and losses of life. The Student Right to Know and Campus Security Act of 1990 requires all institutions that receive federal funding to publish an annual report that includes crime statistics. The Campus Sexual Assault Victims Bill of Rights of 1992 stipulates that a college or university with federal student aid programs must tell victims how they can report what happened to them to law enforcement authorities. If no such notification occurs, a college or university may pay a $25,000 fine or lose its eligibility for federal aid.

Since the late 1980s, studies have shown that most sexual assaults on campuses involve people who know each other. Robin Warshaw, author of *I Never Called It Rape: The Ms. Report on Recognizing, Fighting, and Surviving Date and Acquaintance Rape*, concluded, after doing a survey on thirty-two campuses, that 84 percent of the rape victims knew their assailants and that 57 percent of the rapes happened on dates (1988). This influential study clarified the need to educate students about the dangers of date or acquaintance rape, which became even clearer when Ralph W. Hingson and others found that more than 70,000 students had been victims of an alcohol-related sexual assault or date rape (2002). During the 1990s and the first years of the twenty-first century, many college freshmen have watched videos about acquaintance rape as part of orientation or first-semester educational programs.

Legends about rapes reinforce this message, showing female students that boyfriends and other male friends may become assailants and showing male students that it is important to exercise self-control. In college legends of the 1960s and 1970s, most male attackers were (or seemed or be) strangers. Boyfriends risked becoming victims, as in the legend "The Boyfriend's Death" (Dégh 1968a). Many recently collected college assault legends from the 1990s and the early twenty-first century have followed a different pattern in which danger comes from the boyfriend himself: "Death by Boyfriend" rather than "The Boyfriend's Death." The increasing number of stories about dangerous boyfriends reflects young people's growing willingness to talk about dangers that can arise within close relationships.

Wailing women communicate with the living by crying, screaming, or making other mournful sounds. Their signature motif is E402.1.1.3, "Ghost cries and screams." In her illuminating book *Women Escaping Violence* (2001), Elaine J. Lawless explains that the narratives she collected from abused women are "muted screams of what cannot be spoken" (60). The horror of domestic violence can be too painful to put into words, and hesitation to name an attacker who is also a friend or loved one comes from beliefs deep within the structure of American culture. This horror and hesitation to speak come through in students' ghost stories about wailing women. Along with painful limitations, a sense of power emerges from these narratives. Even if the ghost cannot talk, she can scream—and she keeps on screaming until current students understand what happened to her. Her bold, relentless screams insist upon recognition and, if possible, justice.

Space and place are important in ghost stories about wailing women. Cathy Lynn Preston recently suggested that Max Lüthi's analytical terms apply to campus storytelling: the university's architecture resembles the folktale's castle; inner or hidden spaces of buildings and grounds resemble the legend's cave; students' stories about these spaces are legends; and a college's public self-presentation resembles the art form of the fairytale (2005).[2] Legends about wailing women who have been murdered and/or raped illustrate the symbolic importance of the college's or university's hidden spaces, where things happen that disturb the perfect surface of the fairytale for public consumption. From these hidden spaces comes evidence that women have died and, in some cases, evolved into guardian spirits that offer current students protection.

Ideology and Change

College students' legends record the ideas of their time and place; they also note changes in cultural patterns. As Linda Dégh says, the legend is "an ideology-sensitive genre par excellence" that "plays a leading role in the development and maintenance of a 'culture of fear'" (2001: 5). From the late 1960s to the early 1970s, legend-telling reflected changes in expectations for women living on college campuses. Through the mid-1960s, women commonly had to follow fairly strict rules about when men could visit their residence halls. However, once the upheaval of the late 1960s began, many institutions removed or loosened restrictions on visiting. In 1966, Richard Speck's murder of eight student nurses in Chicago made students and their parents feel anxious about safety. By the fall of 1968, rumors about the imminent arrival of a Hatchet Man were spreading from college to college. Changes in long-established visitation rules combined with fear of assault by murderous men to create a favorable climate for legend-telling.

The following legend was collected by Marcia Nadolny from a female friend at the University of Maine at Orono in the fall of 1966.

A Heavy Load of Laundry

It seems that there was a girl living in a single at a small midwestern college. Her room was at the very end of the hall on the first floor, right next to the staircase that led to the exit. This little room was separated from the other rooms on the floor by the bathroom and the maid's room. Anyway, this girl was studying late one night when she heard someone coming up the stairs. The steps were very heavy—as if someone was carrying a heavy load of laundry from the laundryroom to the basement. The steps got closer and closer to the hall door. Then they stopped. Slowly she heard the door open. As it opened, she felt a cold breeze coming under her door—as though someone had left the exit door open. She couldn't figure why it should be open, though, because it was after closing hours and it couldn't be opened without the alarm going off—unless someone had a key. At this thought she began to tremble. Her imagination went wild. "It must be a man sneaking in," she thought. The footsteps on the stairs were like those of an old man. She was really working herself into a panic by now. What should she do? She was too far from anyone to yell and besides it was very late to scream in case it was a false alarm. She decided to give the scream a try, so she sneaked over to her door and opened it very slowly. Suddenly she was overcome by someone who was terribly strong. She struggled to get away, to scream, to do anything, but she was helpless.

Three days later people began to notice that they hadn't seen her around lately. Her room was checked and they found everything just as she had left it—like she had gone to the bathroom and would be right back. No one had any ideas as to what had happened to her. Her home was called and she wasn't there—they thought she was at school. She had just disappeared. Her name was put on the missing persons list.

The following spring construction was started on a new dorm. And during the initial digging, the remains of her body were uncovered. Apparently, the man had kidnapped her that night while she was studying, taken her to the field in back of the dorm and raped her. Not wanting the body to be found, he had buried her on the spot.

Today, in the new dorm, the girls say that they can hear her screaming on the anniversary of her death. (Nadolny 1966)

Like "The Roommate's Death" and other legends about college women told in the mid-1960s, this text reflects tensions between women and men. In the 1960s, feminism's second wave reinforced American women's awareness of their strength and questioned the suitability of the proverb "Woman's place is in the home."[3] The central character in "A Heavy Load of Laundry" lives alone in a residence hall, with very few domestic duties. In the context of her era, she represents the danger of rejecting traditional expectations by becoming a victim of a terrifying and fatal assault.

The story's action begins with a strong sensory emphasis: first the sound of footsteps, then the chill of a sudden breeze. The footsteps sound ominously heavy, "as if someone was carrying a heavy load of laundry from the laundryroom to the basement." This sounds like a reproach to the student, who has been studying rather than taking care of a family's needs. She thinks the footsteps might be an old man's; he must have a key, as no alarm has gone off. Perhaps he is a relative who has grudgingly decided to do some laundry she has not done herself. The laundry's heaviness represents the weight of women's domestic duties. One proverb frequently quoted in New England is "Man's work is from sun to sun, but woman's work is never done."[4] This woman who spends little time doing "woman's work" dies at the hands of a male attacker.

Once the man comes into the woman's room, we hear nothing about him other than that he is "terribly strong," while she is "helpless": dominated, at his mercy. There is no physical description of the man, no indication that he is an identifiable person instead of a male monster. Here we can apply Elaine Lawless's observation that in some women's stories of domestic violence, men suddenly become monsters. Evidentiary motifs that emerge in women's life stories include T118.1, "Monster husband invisible," and D110, "Transformation: a man to wild beast" (Lawless 2002: 34). While this college student's situation differs from that of a woman who suddenly finds her husband or partner has become a monster, it has the same emphasis on unexpected discovery. The absence of physical description makes the man seem all the more frightening. He breaks into the woman's single room to take control of her body: to rape and kill her, then bury the evidence under a residence hall under construction nearby.

Three days after the girl's disappearance, her fellow students realize that she is gone. Like other characters in stories about missing students, she seems to have gone to the bathroom.[5] Communal residence hall bathrooms, often associated with ghosts, make people think about strange and unnerving possibilities. In this legend, the mention of the bathroom brings to mind exposure of the body at the time of a violent crime. Although the student has not actually gone to the bathroom, she has vanished, and no one knows how to find her.

The story ends with its central motif, "Ghost cries and screams." While living, the student hesitates to disturb others by screaming; she does not want to make noise "in case it [is] a false alarm." Her politeness reflects traditional feminine diffidence and concern for others, which keep her from summoning help. On the anniversary of her murder, the ghost of the dead student screams boldly and repeatedly. No longer bound by rules of proper behavior, she is free to demand recognition and justice. From the foundations of a new residence hall, she warns students to be careful. Her protective, strident presence gives female students the message that they should assert themselves and guard against assault.

Other screaming ghosts appear in residence hall elevators, which serve as liminal settings for representation of women's struggles and deaths. While going up or down in an elevator, suspended between one floor and another, a student may think about the danger of assault. A female ghost that makes its presence known in this small, confined space can have a powerful impact. As Alan Dundes explains in his study of the ballad "The Walled-Up Wife," the entrapment and murder of a woman can serve as a metaphor for oppressive male/female relationships (1996: 198). Ghosts of female students who have been raped and murdered may vocalize their distress in elevators, warning other women to watch out for dangerous men.

The following story came from Michael, a twenty-year-old Binghamton University student, in the spring of 2003.

Tie-Dye Shirt

A long time ago, I heard this story about some girl that is trapped in the elevator. Supposedly, when a person rides the elevator alone in a certain building, sometimes they start to hear this clanging noise. Just after that, they start to hear quiet screams that get louder and louder.

Eventually the person in the elevator begins to sense that someone is in the elevator with them. They sense that the person is a young girl wearing a tie-dye shirt. The person in the elevator typically is so freaked out that they bolt out the door as soon as it opens and run screaming to wherever they were going to go.

The story behind the girl is that sometime around the seventies or so, hence the tie-dye shirt, she was raped and murdered somewhere in the building. Now her spirit is trapped in the elevator, and she haunts people that ride in it.

As Jan Harold Brunvand has pointed out, horror legends such as "The Boyfriend's Death" show how Americans have expected young women to act during crises (1981: 14–15). In the above story, which combines horror with a supernatural element, a female student lets students know about her rape and murder by screaming in an elevator. Her first sounds—"quiet screams"—reflect the kind of reticence that contributed to the death of the central character in "A Heavy Load of Laundry." Soon, however, her screams grow "louder and louder," demanding attention from students who ride the elevator. As elevator riders hear the ghost scream, they start screaming themselves, showing that they understand what has happened.

This legend's time frame, "around the seventies or so," reflects the popular stereotype of the 1960s and 1970s as years of experimentation with hippie clothing, rock music, and drugs. Many campus legends designate the sixties and seventies as wild times when shocking things occurred. The victim in this story wears clothing that symbolizes both freedom and danger. Playing with words in an intriguing way, this story's narrator takes the female student from "dye" to "die." In countless horror legends and films, young women who experiment with sex, take drugs, or push other kinds of boundaries die violent deaths. Jokes about the "Final Girl," the one virtuous female character in a movie who does *not* die horribly, have pounded this point home.[6]

Told to scare, "Tie-Dye Shirt" resembles a campfire story in its focus on vulnerability to sudden attack. While the story reinforces conventional morality, suggesting the dangers of wildness and experimentation, it also demonstrates the power of the human or spectral voice. If students keep such voices in mind, they may stay safe in the future.

One Ghost or Two?

Sometimes a sad, scared ghost becomes a protector as legend cycles grow and change. Because this evolution takes place over time, researchers may not know at first that a building has housed more than one kind of ghost. For example, Benjamin Meiklejohn, a student at the University of Maine in 1992, decided to write a paper about the ghost of his own residence hall, Colvin Hall. He found not one ghost, but two: first a nameless woman who cried and then Caroline Colvin, the history professor and dean of women for whom the hall had been named.

In his folklore paper, Meiklejohn quoted from an earlier student's interview with Terri Gallant, who became Colvin Hall's resident director in 1979. Gallant said that during her first year, "The girls living upstairs said they heard a woman crying in the middle of the night, but when they looked for her they couldn't find anyone. There were only three rooms on the floor and they repeatedly heard the crying" (Brown 1987: 1). For Gallant, who was starting a new job in an unfamiliar building, stories about a crying woman served an initiatory purpose. Her residents' experiences provided evidence for a supernatural presence that made the hall both exciting and strange.

During Gallant's fifth year, a big change occurred: the hall went co-ed. As soon as the first men arrived, a female ghost became visible. Gallant said, "When men moved in, people began to see her. It was as if she didn't want them in the building." Women briefly saw the ghost while making sandwiches

Portrait of Caroline Colvin, the ghost of Colvin Hall at the University of Maine. Photograph by Christopher Tuthill.

in the kitchen late at night, but men heard her call their names and watched a female form materialize in front of them. She was, Gallant said, "slender with long hair that she always wore up. She was not very tall and was dressed in an old looking skirt and blouse" (1987: 1). Note the contrast between women's and men's experiences: women saw the ghost briefly while making sandwiches in the kitchen, traditionally associated with "women's work," but men saw her materialize abruptly, calling their names. Clearly, this ghost wanted to remind men to behave themselves. Rather than weeping wordlessly, she repeated their names, showing them that they had better take care.

Students in Colvin Hall called this ghost Caroline, identifying her as the dean of women in whose honor the hall had been named. Caroline Colvin's portrait, which has hung in Colvin Hall for many years, shows a serious-looking young woman wearing academic regalia, with her hair pinned up on top of her head. According to students' reports, the ghost of this helpful dean protected women and resisted change. While she worried about men's presence in her hall, she did not harm the men and generally caused no trouble.

Could this apparition of Caroline Colvin have been the same ghost that students had heard crying five years earlier? That crying ghost, who had appeared in three students' rooms, seemed more like a suffering student than the calm, solicitous dean after whom the hall had been named. The crying ghost differs so much from the dean that it seems necessary to recognize them as two separate spirits. There is, however, a connection between them. Besides serving as the University of Maine's dean of women, Caroline Colvin attended the university as an undergraduate student. A Colvin Hall resident with whom I spoke in the spring of 2006 knew about Colvin's undergraduate years; if earlier residents were also aware of the background of their hall's namesake, the crying ghost might represent Caroline as a young and uncertain student. During a time of transition, a miserable, crying ghost can encourage the appearance of another ghost that offers oversight and protection.

A comparable set of identities arises in Jeannie B. Thomas's "Pain, Pleasure, and the Spectral: The Barfing Ghost of Burford Hall" (1991). "Old Lady Burford," as the students called Burford Hall's ghost in the early 1990s, served as Indiana State University's dean of women in the 1940s. Students have said that her stern-looking portrait in the lobby can harm students who look at it too long: "Everybody claims that if you look at her picture for a period of time, something bad will happen to you" (29–30). Like a witch with an evil eye, she seems to have the power to ruin students' chances for happiness and success.

On the other hand, Burford Hall's ghost has a set of behaviors that identify her as a young, vulnerable person. Students of the early 1990s explain that she committed suicide in room 217 and has haunted that room ever since. Manifestations of her presence include sounds of vomiting and screaming, a toilet flushing, and a "hideous laugh" (Thomas 1991: 28). Like some of the spectral roommates discussed in chapter 4, she delights in scaring students who have recently moved into the residence hall. "Old Lady Burford" seems both old and young; she has an elderly, stern-looking face but acts like a confused, unhappy student. Such dual characterizations add depth and incongruity to campus ghost stories.

In May 2006, Nancy C. McEntire, a member of the folklore program at Indiana State University in Terre Haute, gave me a helpful update on the evolution of Old Lady Burford, now known as Barb. During the past several years, ISU students have identified Barb as the ghost of a student who died of alcohol poisoning. The sounds of her throwing up in women's bathrooms, late at night, make students feel worried. Believing that Barb is warning them about the dangers of alcohol consumption, students pay close attention to the mournful sounds of her late-night barfing. Currently, Burford Hall is closed for renovation. Students hope that when the hall reopens, their favorite ghost will still be there.[7]

Indiana State University's legends about Barb, also known as Old Lady Burford, strongly resemble the University of Maine's legends about Caroline Colvin. Some of this similarity may come from the fact that portraits of both women have hung in the buildings named after them for many years. A "founding mother" whose portrait students see every day can inspire legends.[8] While some of these legends describe an older woman, most of them focus on dangers to young female students: alcohol consumption, eating disorders, suicide, assault, and other threats to health and safety.

Most of the narratives in Benjamin Meiklejohn's 1992 collection identify Caroline (or Katherine) Colvin as a student who hanged herself in one of the rooms. Of course, if she had actually died while attending the University of Maine, she would not have gone on to become the university's dean of women, but that incongruity has not bothered legend-tellers. In some legends, an assailant stabs her to death in the attic, forcibly hangs her on the third floor, or violently kills her in a different way. In others, she hangs herself in the boiler room in the basement, then her boyfriend finds her body. Students feel her presence in bedrooms, where she taps on walls, opens doors, and drops things; in the basement, where she bangs on pipes; and in the north stairwell, where she trips people. Sometimes she appears as a "quick glimpse of something blue" in a mirror. Making fun of this ghost's ubiquity, students at the University of Maine have taken her portrait off the wall and placed it in such surprising locations as bathroom stalls, water fountains, dumbwaiters, freezers, and juice machines. Perhaps these choices of spots to stash the portrait should not surprise us. All but one of the locations listed here have to do with food service; the other—the bathroom stall—is, as Jeannie B. Thomas has shown, an exquisitely liminal space (1991: 33–34). In any case, it seems clear that Caroline's (or Katherine's) story formed an important part of new students' initiation into student life at the University of Maine in the early 1990s.

Since then, Colvin Hall's ghost seems to have faded into the background of student folklore. A staff member of Colvin Hall's Honors College told me that she knew ghost stories had circulated in the past but had not heard any specific details.[9] "Ghost Hunt," an article published in the *Maine Campus* on November 3, 2003, offers details about four skeptics' and four paranormal researchers' search for ghosts in Colvin, Coburn, Balentine, and Estabrooke Hall, as well as Hauck Auditorium and the Beta Theta Pi fraternity house. They find that a former housemother, "Ma Balentine," walks through

Balentine Hall, formerly an all-female hall, to make sure that no men are present. In Colvin Hall, however, the ghost-hunting team finds nothing more than "a general sense of creepiness." Although Caroline Colvin's portrait still hangs in the hall's main area and there have been a few "sightings," the team discovers no evidence of haunting. Their most dramatic findings come from the Beta Theta Pi House, where Evelyn, the brothers' former housemother, haunts "Evelyn's Room" in the attic and a girl named Jen, as well as a brother who overdosed on drugs, haunt a second-floor room called the "Birdhouse." The results of this ghost hunt show that in some halls, especially those that were once all-female, ghosts of older women continue to accompany ghosts of troubled students.

Ghostly deans and housemothers warn and comfort current students, reminding them of an era when staff members acting *in loco parentis* supervised the day-to-day lives of students in their halls. Today, most hall supervisors are professional resident directors, but at some universities, including the University of Maine, those who take these positions are graduate students. Many resident directors are in their early and mid-twenties. Resident directors and other staff members work hard to keep students safe and to enforce the college or university's rules. Nonetheless, certain ghost stories suggest that housemothers and old-fashioned deans can offer more comfort than young staff members. These spectral figures take students back to their institution's earlier days, reminding them about conservative rules for safe living. In particular, these ghosts remind women to watch out for men who may threaten their safety and well-being.

Sometimes a protective ghost predates the college or university's founding. Such a ghost haunts Mudge House at Carnegie Mellon University in Pittsburgh, founded in 1900 by the industrialist Andrew Carnegie. Jim, a recent graduate of Carnegie Mellon, told this story in March 2004.

Men and Only Men

At Carnegie Mellon University, there is a dorm called Mudge House. Mudge House used to be a mansion that belonged to a wealthy industrialist back in the nineteenth century. Now it is a converted dorm. Portions of the house have been renovated; however, the housing authorities have not been able to account for certain rooms in the house that are shown in the original blueprints. There is more to this house than just a philanthropic gift.

Back in the nineteenth century when the house was still owned by Sir Mudge, he had one daughter who was mentally challenged. Often times, she would run around the house screaming or doing random things. One day, one of the servants trapped her in her room and raped her. This drove the poor child even more insane, and after weeks of locking herself in her room, her father found her out in the courtyard. The poor child hung herself.

From that day, the master of the house boarded up the windows of where her room used to be and constructed a wall in place of her door-way and eventually donated the house to the University. Rumor has it that men and only men who live in the dorm, who walk around some nights, if they are walking around on the third floor looking for her room, hear sobbing behind the closed walls, and some men and only men who walk to the courtyard at night, may see her hanging from the balcony overlooking the courtyard.

Like the ghost of Caroline Colvin at the University of Maine, this ghost of an innocent child raped by a servant carries a gender-specific message. No female students can hear the poor child's sobbing and see her body hanging from the balcony above the building's courtyard; only men can hear and see her. Clearly, her purpose is to make men consider the tragic results of violence toward women. Her helplessness and desperation transform themselves, after her death, into a fierce determination to educate young men.

What makes this story both exciting and believable is its focus on precise architectural details. The description of hidden rooms and walled-up door-ways sounds like part of an intriguing mystery. Carnegie-Mellon's "Mudge House" website explains that this mansion, once owned by the Mudge family, underwent renovation when it became a residence hall (2005). In Jim's story, the building's renovation becomes a cover-up for a tragic rape and suicide. Students believe that rooms missing from the building's blueprints reveal the presence of an untold story. That story comes through eloquently in the sounds and sight of the ghost, which warn men to behave themselves with women.

In contrast to the Carnegie-Mellon story and others like it, some texts give students an almost mystical sense of surveillance by benevolent spirits. Such is the case at Cheney Hall at the State University of New York at Cortland, where a female ghost guards the building's central stairwell. This story came from Ted, a freshman at SUNY Cortland, in April 2003.

Fourth-floor railing of Cheney Hall at the State University of New York at Cortland, over which Elizabeth fell to her death after being pushed by her boyfriend. Photograph by Ashley Bleck.

Elizabeth

This is my first year in attending Cortland University. I have heard of several ghost stories that have happened around the campus from the upperclassmen. I will tell you the one that scares me the most.

There was this girl who lived on the fourth floor of this dorm building named "Cheney." I'm not sure what her name was, but I think it was Elizabeth. I could be wrong on that. Anyways, I did hear that she was murdered by her boyfriend on that floor. This happened, I think, in the 70s or maybe the early 80s.

So, after the girl's death, they put up a painting on the fourth floor to honor her, like some sort of tribute. Ever since, students have said that strange stuff happens on the fourth floor. For example, people say that they see an appearance of a female ghost with the arms stretching out. You get a weird vibe when you see it.

Oh, one last thing, some years later, another girl who was drunk as anything fell over the same stairs as Elizabeth, but she survived! Makes you wonder if Elizabeth was protecting her, doesn't it?

As told by a frightened male freshman, this legend of Cheney Hall describes an act of domestic violence that results in protection for other students (Motif E363.2, "Ghost returns to protect living"). The legend's central character is named Elizabeth—but is that truly her name? Ted does not know, but since I have collected other variants of the Cheney Hall legend, I can confirm that students have called the hall's ghost Elizabeth since the early 1990s. The popular commercial website "Haunted New York" also identifies Cheney's ghost as Elizabeth (2005). But this ghost's name is not especially important; what matters most is how she died and became a guardian of living students.

Ted does not specify exactly how Elizabeth died; he just says that her boyfriend murdered her on Cheney's fourth floor. Reflecting her most common mode of death in oral stories, the "Haunted New York" website explains that Elizabeth "was reportedly pushed from the fourth floor down the central staircase by her boyfriend in the early eighties" (2005). Here, as in the legend of Sara at Mansfield University, we see a prominent, centrally located staircase as a setting for tragedy. Sara throws herself downstairs because her boyfriend has rejected her, but Elizabeth's boyfriend pushes her downstairs himself; he literally, not figuratively, "dumps" her. While Sara and Elizabeth both die and become ghosts, only Elizabeth turns into a protector of other women. As a victim of relationship violence, Elizabeth makes it her mission to protect other women from similar tragedies.

Note that the female student in the second part of the story is *not* a domestic violence victim; instead, she drinks too much and "falls over the same stairs as Elizabeth." Drinking constitutes a familiar peril in the early twenty-first century, as some of the warning legends in chapter 4 and the most recent legends about the ghost of Burford Hall demonstrate. It seems right for Elizabeth, who suffered and died, to protect female students from dangers that threaten their lives. The visual image of "a female ghost with the arms stretching out" confirms that Elizabeth is a protective spirit whose arms will catch women who take too many risks. Her outstretched arms, like the arms of Renaissance angels, have the power to comfort young people.

Both angels and saints come to mind when we listen to Cheney Hall's ghost story. Legends of Christian saints' lives have offered inspiration and solace to believers since the early days of Christianity. Some legends about young female saints have a close connection to college buildings. The patron saint of Balliol College at Oxford University is the virgin martyr Saint Catherine of Alexandria, who did not die upon her spiked "Catherine wheel" because the wheel mysteriously broke into pieces. Her legend gives her credit for many conversions and subsequent martyrdoms after her death at the beginning of the fourth century. Balliol College holds a Saint Catherine's Day Dinner each November 2 and preserves documents related to her life and death. Similarly, Oxford's Christ Church College honors the memory of its patroness Saint Frideswida (c. 650–735), who refused to marry King Alger and escaped from him after he suffered mysterious blindness.

Legends about holy young women and their shrines help us to see Cheney Hall's Elizabeth in perspective. Elizabeth, who died at the hands of her boyfriend, remains on the hall's staircase, protecting other young women from a similar fate. Ted's story shows that Cortland students marvel at the survival of the drunk young woman who fell downstairs. Their amazement at Elizabeth's protective power comes close to religious veneration. In contemporary college culture, Elizabeth functions as a secular saint.

According to Ted's story and others told by Cortland students, a painting or mural on the fourth floor of Cheney Hall honors Elizabeth. The "Haunted New York" website supports this contention: "After the tragic death of the young woman, a mural was designed in her honor. Students living on the fourth floor of Cheney reported a feeling of unease when viewing the mural— as if they were being scrutinized by Elizabeth's representation in the massive painting" (2005). When I interviewed the current resident director of Cheney Hall in November 2005, I was surprised to discover that the hall had no mural and had probably never had one. Although Cortland students enjoyed scaring one another with ghost stories about two female students falling downstairs, they had no access to a mural. "Since Cheney is the oldest building," the resident director told me, "it is fitting that it has a ghost story." The two of us laughed about a building constructed in 1950 seeming very old; however, we knew it was not unusual for such an "old" campus building to house a ghost.[10]

Elizabeth's story lets students take comfort in the protective presence of a female figure who wants, above all, to save other women from an early death. Some versions of Elizabeth's story say that her boyfriend killed her, while others say that she killed herself after fighting with him. Whether the cause of death is murder or suicide, her life's abrupt end shows that relationships may end tragically. Ghosts like Elizabeth deliver a crucial message: "Never forget."

Danger, Safety, and Belief

Legends about residence hall murals and portraits demonstrate the importance of objects that commemorate notable individuals or events. Some objects have tangible form, while others exist only within campus legends. When the resident director of Cheney Hall told me that there was no mural on Cheney Hall's fourth floor, I felt disappointed. However, as I thought about this apparent incongruity, I realized that a memorial sketched by a legend could be just as meaningful as an actual mural. Perhaps it had even more meaning than a real mural would have, as each storyteller and listener could fill in the image's details.

A mural that exists only within the imagination may mean more to students than an actual mural because of their belief in a miraculous event that took place not long ago. In her work with Pentecostal women who told stories about miracles, Linda Dégh learned that belief in the possibility of miracles can make believers "radiant and sane" (2001: 318). Similarly, belief in Cheney Hall's miracle makes students feel safer and happier. If the mural had an undisputed existence, there would be no need for belief and less impact on individuals who welcome the presence of the extraordinary in their lives.

In some college ghost stories, malfunctioning lights and other appliances reinforce belief in a supernatural presence. Catherine, a nineteen-year-old freshman at Marist College in Poughkeepsie, New York, told the following story in April 2005.

Jealous Ex-Boyfriend

In the 70's a female freshman was shot and killed by her jealous ex-boyfriend in the cafeteria. Students now report lights and TVs turning on and off by themselves. This happens in Sheahan Hall, one of the freshman dorms. This is the dorm where the murdered student used to live. Luckily I lived in Leo when I was a freshman.

Does Catherine's story deviate from the pattern of wailing women that I have explored in this chapter? Certainly the text includes no specific cries or screams; however, televisions that inexplicably turn themselves on and off give voice to the ghost in their own way. Along with these self-activating TVs, lights with wills of their own seize current students' attention. This legend's most important feature is its proof that the anguished ghost makes contact with women who need to know what happened to her. That is the crux of "Wailing Women" stories: prevention of further tragedies through a ghost's urgent messages.

This young woman's boyfriend kills her in the college's cafeteria: a space for food preparation and service. It does not seem accidental that many female ghosts haunt domestic spaces. Even now, forty years after the beginning of feminism's second wave in the United States, old stereotypes haunt us. Although Sheahan Hall's ghost story is based on an actual murder that took place in a cafeteria, emphasis on the murder's location foregrounds the area's significance, reminding readers that gender-related expectations can have tragic consequences.

The most thorough record of the Sheahan Hall murder can be found on the website of Christina Hope, a Marist College student who was a resident assistant at Sheahan Hall during the academic year 2001–2002. Her website, "The Hauntings of Sheahan Hall" (2004), includes relevant newspaper articles, five interviews, a bulletin board for postings of recent ghost stories, and a theory about the meaning of the Sheahan Hall hauntings. A brief summary of the crime explains that Shelley Sperling, a seventeen-year-old freshman, was walking into Marist College's cafeteria on February 18, 1975, when her high school boyfriend ran after her and shot her several times. Because he was "jealous of Shelley's new life at college," her boyfriend had previously attacked her with a brick, fracturing her skull and one hand. This time, she did not survive (Hope 2004).

Shortly after Shelley Sperling's death, Father Leo Gallant wrote an article for the school paper, *The Circle*, in which he noted that the beauty of Shelley's memorial service brought members of the campus close together. "Once having tasted real community," Father Gallant observed, "maybe more will seek to build it on campus, in the dorms. Shelley isn't through with Marist" (Hope 2004). Like many tellers of campus ghost stories, Father Gallant emphasized the helpfulness of the dead (Motif E363, "Ghost returns to aid living").

Like Father Gallant, Christina Hope thinks that Shelley has a mission to accomplish. In the section of her website titled "My Theory," she explains that Shelley "is haunting Sheahan for a reason . . . she wants people to know about her story and what happened to her." Shelley's education of current students fits the pattern formed by other wailing female ghosts in college residence halls. However, Christina adds another dimension to this pattern. Explaining that fate brought her to Sheahan Hall, she says that she needs "to let the college population know the truth about what happened to [Shelley] and to give them the actual facts concerning her death." Then, Shelley will finally have the chance to move from limbo to heaven, free from the tragic history of her murder at Marist College (2004).[11]

As the above statements show, belief motivates interpretations of the ghost's meaning, which vary according to the believer's age and position in the campus community. Father Gallant, a chaplain of the Marist Brothers at the college, saw the dead student's purpose as bringing students and faculty members together, while Christina and other students thought about what they could learn from the ghost's tragic history. Students who posted messages on the "Hauntings of Sheahan Hall" bulletin boards expressed excitement about reports of radios turning themselves on and water starting to flow in certain sinks of Sheahan Hall's bathrooms. Reports of these unusual events sustained belief in Shelley's presence.

In the spring of 2006, I corresponded on e-mail with Christina Hope, who kindly filled me in on some of the unusual things that had happened in Sheahan: doors slamming, computers and fans turning themselves on and off, and a female ghost materializing twice. On one occasion, Christina herself saw Shelley's ghost. After leaving photocopies of Shelley's and her boyfriend's yearbook pictures on her bed, she left to do her RA rounds, then returned to see "a girl in there with long brown hair and a crocheted type sweater on that was tan, cream colored and brown (stripes) looking at the pictures." As Christina watched, the ghost "disappeared into the wall." Later, when Christina tried to put Shelley's picture into her website, the picture disappeared: "I 'prayed' to her to tell her to give me a sign if she didn't want me doing something with this site, but asked her not to freak me out, so I ended up taking her out of the picture."[12] Like a saint or a guardian angel, Shelley stayed near the preserver of her history and responded to her prayers (Motif E341.3, "Dead grateful for prayers").

As in the stories about Shelley Sperling, another legend about a haunted cafeteria offers audible and visual proof of a ghost's power. At the State University of New York at Stony Brook, the ghost of a female student both screams and darkens the building where she died. Conrad, a twenty-one-year-old transfer student at Stony Brook, told the following story in March 2004.

Dark All Day Long

When I was a transfer student coming into Stony Brook, I heard a lot of rumors about my new residence hall. I lived in Tabler Quad at the time and supposedly it was haunted. There were so many rumors and stories floating around about it. The first I heard was about the dining hall. Tabler used to have a dining hall until somebody got raped and killed in it.

The dining hall is now deserted and it's just a glass building that remains dark all day long. People say that at certain times during the night, you can hear a girl screaming and you see a reflection in the window.

After telling this story, Conrad insisted that he believed in the ghost of Tabler Quad. He had first heard the story after arriving on campus as a transfer student, when worry about the area's crime rate had set his nerves on edge.[13] In the midst of an ambitious renovation project, Tabler Quad stood empty. With large glass panels and no light from within, the dining hall provided an ideal setting for rumors and legends about threats to women's safety. Dark, deserted, and dangerous, it epitomized students' fears.

Conrad says that Tabler Dining Hall is "just a glass building," but it is much more than that: a memorial to victims of rape and assault. As Martha Norkunas points out in *Monuments and Memory*, monuments to women mark their presence on the landscape (2002: 11). While Tabler Dining Hall functions as a monument only within the boundaries of a legend, it serves as a powerful reminder of women's suffering. At night, the building reverberates with screams that draw people's attention. This female victim refuses to be silenced and insists on remaining visible. Her screams remind both women and men to avoid the consequences of rape by an acquaintance or a stranger.

Like such fantasy classics as *The Lord of the Rings*, campus ghost stories highlight the perils of making one's way through an unfamiliar environment to achieve hoped-for success. Wailing women, whose own lives end tragically, become guides for a longer and more fulfilling life than they had themselves. As J. R. R. Tolkien reminds us, one of the most important benefits that we can gain from good fantasy is the consolation of a happy ending, which offers "a sudden and miraculous grace" (1965: 68).[14] While wailing women's own stories do not end happily, many of these stories culminate in scenes where ghosts functioning as protectors, even as secular saints, keep women safe. These moments of comfort and safety soothe our spirits: a triumph of the student-generated legend over the administrative fairytale.

Chapter Seven

SPECTRAL INDIANS

On some American college campuses, students have perceived the presence of Indian ghosts, whose behavior is related to their ethnic identity (Motif E425.2.4, "Revenant as American Indian"). Some of these ghosts stand silently, affirming their connection to ancestral lands and burial grounds. Others run away, evading the people who have suddenly spotted them. Whether they stay for a short time or a longer one, ghosts of the United States' original inhabitants make people reassess historical and cultural issues.

When Indian ghosts come to a campus, they engage in what Kathleen Brogan identifies as "cultural haunting": representation of a communal, ethnically based tragedy through one spectral figure (1998: 4–5). Cultural haunting unsettles and troubles its perceivers; it involves obscure and difficult issues, as well as little-known history and a strong sense of guilt. Avery Gordon, the author of *Ghostly Matters: Haunting and the Sociological Imagination*, has written about "that which makes its mark by being there and not there at the same time" (1996: 6). On many college campuses, the presence of Indian ghosts signals their people's absence. Students who come into contact with these ghosts may experience what Gordon calls a "transformative recognition": a growing awareness that reality is more complex, disturbing, and surprising than most people realize (8). While such a recognition does not come easily, it profoundly influences people's view of the world.

Breaking into current space and time, Indian ghosts deliver compelling messages. Some stories of spectral Indians intertwine with rumors of college campuses having been built above Indian burial grounds. Standing on the burial grounds of their ancestors, ghosts show students a sacred dimension that demands to be acknowledged, while revealing the callousness of the entrepreneurs who built the campus. Stories of this kind differ from the romanticized literary legends about Indians that Simon J. Bronner describes in his study of campus folklore, *Piled Higher and Deeper*; justice and reverence are what matter here, not romantic love or sudden death (1995: 144). However, some legends about romantic love, death, and revenge continue to be popular on college campuses.

Most of the students from whom I have collected legends about Indian ghosts have been college freshmen: travelers from their homes to a new place where legends and rumors offer an important kind of learning. With a heightened sensitivity to both oral and visual stimuli, freshmen pay careful attention to their new environment. Ernest Boyer, author of *College: The Undergraduate Experience in America* (1987), calls the transition to college life a "major rite of passage" where the first few weeks' impressions have a strong impact (288). Gazing at their new surroundings, acutely aware that they are no longer at home, many college freshmen listen closely to legends and rumors, interpreters of both the past and the present.

Outsiders and Insiders

Most of the Indian ghost stories that I have collected have come from non-Indian students, who see Indians as different from themselves. Many Anglo-American ghost stories focus on otherness: being dead, not alive; paranormal, not normal; disruptive, not orderly. Ethnicity is one dimension of otherness that can shock or frighten the observer. For non-Indians, Indian ghosts represent danger from a source that is difficult to understand.

Although non-Indian students perceive Indians as being different from themselves, some of them have learned, during summers at camp, to identify themselves as members of a group with "Indian" customs. As Philip J. Deloria explains in *Playing Indian*, American children have been encouraged to imitate Indians' dress and rituals since Ernest Thompson Seton's "Woodcraft Indian" experiment began in 1901 (1998: 95–115). Camp Fire Girl, Boy Scout, and Girl Scout groups have encouraged children to develop skills valued by Indians. Organizers of the Camp Fire Girls in the early twentieth century encouraged young women to choose Indian names and to make deerskin dresses that expressed their abilities and aspirations. Boy Scout and Girl Scout camps have also made Indian names part of their identities. Three units at the Girl Scout Camp May Flather in Mount Solon, Virginia, for example, bear the Indian names Shawnee, Sinewa, and Sherando; many other camps have chosen similar names for their units and bunks. Through such influence, children briefly identify themselves as belonging to a quasi-Indian group. As Deloria suggests, such playful experimentation with Indianness reflects Americans' awareness of "an authentic Other," as well as their desire to find more satisfaction in everyday life (1998: 101).

Another interesting aspect of children's and adolescents' tradition has been their circulation of legends about hostile Indians who threaten young people's safety. At Lake Ronkonkoma near Sayville, New York, for example, teenagers tell stories about a young Indian woman who fell in love with an Indian prince living on the opposite side of the lake. When she sneaked out in a canoe to meet her lover, the spirits of the lake made the canoe sink, expressing disapproval of young people from different backgrounds coming together. Now, one narrator says, "Every year the angry Indian princess kills two lovers and pulls their souls down to the bottom of the lake. And every year at least one young couple dies" ("Scary Urban Legends" 2006). Legends like this one give young people cautionary messages about how to behave and stay safe, but they do not show much familiarity with Indians' history. Although Lake Ronkonkoma was sacred to Indians living near Sayville when whites came to the area, no Indian settlements were located on the lake itself, and the terms "Indian prince" and "Indian princess" came from white settlers' romanticism.

Since many stories of spectral Indians come from narrators who do not know Indians well, it is important to consider Indians' own viewpoints. In his short story "Bone Girl," the Abenaki author Joseph Bruchac offers some thoughts about ghosts through the persona of an alcoholic in his sixties, Russell Painter:

> *Are ghosts outsiders? That is the way most white people seem to view them. Spirits who are condemned to wander for eternity. Ectoplasmic remnants of people whose violent deaths left their spirits trapped between the worlds. You know what I mean. I'm sure. I bet we've seen the same movies and TV shows. Vengeful apparitions. Those are real popular. And then there is this one: scary noises in the background, the lights get dim, and a hushed voice saying "But what they didn't know was that the house had been built on an Indian graveyard!" And the soundtrack fills with muted tomtoms. Bum-bum-bum-bum, bum-bum-bum-bum. (Bruchac 1993, 237)*

With devastating irony, Bruchac targets two of the prime features of stories about spectral Indians: the revelation of a little-known burial ground and the sound of drumbeats. Scary though both of these might seem to the uninformed, to Russell Painter—and, we assume, to Bruchac—these two story elements are annoying clichés from the mass media. "Muted tomtoms" do not signal ghosts' presence; they just show that the listeners have been watching too much TV and seeing too many movies.

What, then, do ghosts mean to Painter? He suggests that ghosts are *not* outsiders, as they are "still with us and part of us. No farther away from us than the other side of a leaf that has fallen" (1993: 238). In effect, ghosts are family members. Indians, Painter explains, tend to live in the same place, while whites move around. Belonging to their homes just as much as living people do, ghosts are "familiar spirits" who deserve respect and attention (244). When Painter leaves his wife, he wanders around town in an alcoholic daze. After a while he finds Bone Girl, who died two hundred years ago; he recognizes her when he sees her old-fashioned dress and high-button shoes. Eager to avoid another meeting with this reservation ghost, he sobers up, goes back to his wife, and invites his nephew Tommy to live with him. Bone Girl is a ghost who warns, a grim but helpful spirit who wants to set Painter straight. He changes his lifestyle, appeases the ghost, and continues to coexist with her on the reservation.

Traditional stories about Indian ghosts represent the varying beliefs and practices of North America's original inhabitants. In the "Ghosts" section of their collection *American Indian Myths and Legends*, Richard Erdoes and Anfonso Ortiz present a wide range of supernatural figures: Zuñi and Sioux spirit wives, a ghostly Pima-Papago grandmother, a Pequod ghost-witch, and a tall, love-struck Cheyenne spirit called the "Double-Faced Ghost" (1992: 427–64). In the Hopi legend "A Journey to the Skeleton House," skeleton spirits offer to help living people if the people help them in return (442–45). Not all Indian ghosts offer help, but all of them, as Bruchac's Russell Painter says, deserve attention and respect. They are familiar spirits who significantly influence community members' view of their world.

Desecration and Punishment

Non-Indians' stories about Indian ghosts tend to focus on strangeness and suffering. For example, Ray B. Browne's collection of Alabama tales, *"A Night with the Hants"* (1976), includes several intriguing stories about Indian burial grounds. One story, "Digging in the Indian Grave," describes what happens when a mother and son start digging up an old grave in a grove of trees. Three times they hear groans, each one louder than the one before. The son asks, "What was that, Mother?" and she replies, "I don't know, but I'm not going to stop to find out" (55). Curiosity blends with fear; will the Indians' suffering, demonstrated by the three groans, bring negative consequences to the mother and son? Not wanting to find out, the two of them run away from the grave. Their careless disturbance of a sacred burial site has brought them close to the pain of the past, reminding them that actions have consequences.

The motif Q212.2, "Grave-robbing punished," conveys traditional wisdom about what happens to those who do not show proper respect for the dead. So does Aarne-Thompson type 366, *The Man from the Gallows*, in which a ghost comes back for its stolen body part. Traditionally, people who disturb the dead can expect punishment. Unfortunately, this taboo has not prevented people from desecrating Indian gravesites. Curiosity, research interests, and a desire to make money have all contributed to the disturbance of Indian graves. In 1990, the Native American Graves Protection and Repatriation Act (NAGPRA) mandated the return of Indian remains to the appropriate tribal organization. Gradually, museum directors, anthropologists, and others have been complying with that law. However, stories about disrespect for Indian remains, including disturbing accounts of recent excavations of a large shell mound near San Francisco, continue to circulate.[1]

One remarkable story about appropriation of Indian bones can be found on the website "Ghost Stories Told by Students" (1998), created by librarians at Wells College in Aurora, New York. This story, "Delaware John," describes the execution of one of the last Indians who stayed on the north shore of Lake Cayuga after George Washington sent two generals to break the power of the Iroquois. During the fall hunting season in 1803, Delaware John became jealous of his hunting partner, George Phodoc, and decided to shoot him. Thinking that he was shooting Phodoc, Delaware John accidentally murdered Ezekiel Crane, who had recently settled in Seneca County. At his trial in Aurora, Delaware John asked to be shot like a warrior, but the judge sentenced him to death by hanging. Before his death, Delaware John agreed to give his body to Dr. Frederick Delano, the local physician, in exchange for a jug of whisky. Dr. Delano wired together Delaware John's skeleton and hung it up in a prominent place in his office. For sixty-seven years, several physicians displayed the skeleton in their offices. Finally, in the spring of 1879, Dr. Elijah Baker had the skeleton buried in Oak Park Cemetery. The only mourner at Delaware John's burial was Fred Baker, the doctor's son, who sent an account of what happened to Wells College professor Temple R. Hollcroft in 1952. Baker mentioned that the jury foreman at Delaware John's trial had been Elijah Price, his grandfather, after whom Dr. Elijah Baker had been named.

This story differs from other narratives on Wells College's website because it comes from Professor Hollcroft's papers and book excerpts, not from students' oral tradition. The other stories on the website, including "The Red Door," "The Frightened Roommate," and "The Melting Bicycles," unequivocally qualify as ghost stories. No ghost comes up in the historical accounts of Delaware John's death and burial, but the inclusion of his story on the website shows that Wells College's librarians view Delaware John as part of their institution's spectral heritage. The bargain before his death and the desecration of his skeleton epitomize disrespect for Indian remains.

Delaware John's name identifies him by his ethnicity. Like Mark Twain's character "Injun Joe" in *The Adventures of Tom Sawyer* (1899), Delaware John seems to dislike all whites. Joe is a half-breed, but John is a full-blood who stubbornly refuses to leave the land from which most of his people have fled. After mistakenly shooting Ezekiel Crane, he begs for an honorable death, but the authorities deny his request. The best he can do is to exchange the bones of the corpse he will soon become for a jug of whisky. Soon, his skeleton becomes a piece of office decoration for a series of white doctors in the town of Aurora.[2] For all of these reasons—the whites' refusal to respect his wish to die a warrior's death, their purchase of his body with whisky, and their placement of his bones on public display—Delaware John serves as an agent of cultural haunting, making others aware of his ethnic group's suffering. His hanging and the exchange of his bones for whisky symbolize white settlers' removal of eastern Indians through a combination of persuasion, purchase, and punishment.

Delaware John's story ends peacefully. Dr. Elijah Baker, whose father served as the foreman at John's trial, decides to give the bones an honorable burial and asks his son, Fred, to serve as mourner at the cemetery. Fred shares the story of what happened with Professor Hollcroft, who serves as Wells College's historian. Students who read this part of Wells College's ghost story website learn that some people have tried to allay historical injustices by doing the right thing, albeit almost a century too late. Although Delaware John does not haunt a college building as some ghosts do, his presence on Wells College's ghost story website educates students and other wanderers through the realm of cyberspace.

Early Educational Experiments

Indian ghosts reflect the process of spectralization described by Renée Bergland in *The National Uncanny* (2000). Looking at a wide range of speeches and literary works, Bergland shows that the dominance of mainstream American culture made it necessary for whites to envision Indians as ghosts. As the "ghosting" process continued, Indians seemed to disappear from American society; indeed, many of them had died because of forced removal and diseases to which they had not been exposed before. Early experiments in Indian education at American universities reflected that sad process. In some cases, legends have offered dramatic accounts of what happened.

Some of North America's most prestigious colleges and universities began with European settlers' desire to educate young Indians and convert them to the Christian faith. The founders of Harvard, Yale, Princeton, Dartmouth, and William and Mary wanted to convert Indians to Christianity and to give them a good education. As might be expected, very few Indians wanted to be converted and changed by European-style education. Most of the students who enrolled dropped out soon afterward, preferring to go back to their people's traditional way of life. Because some records of early Indian students' enrollment are more detailed than others, I will describe what happened on the campuses of Harvard, Dartmouth, and William and Mary.

Harvard, the oldest university in the United States, was founded in Cambridge, Massachusetts, in 1636 and received its charter in 1650. Samuel Eliot Morison's *The Founding of Harvard College* quotes from the charter's request for "necessary provisions that may conduce to the education of the English and Indian youth of this Country in knowledge and godliness" (1935: 248). One of Harvard's first buildings, the Indian College, went up in 1654. Eleven years after the building's construction, no Indian students remained at Harvard. Although the Indian College ceased to exist in 1693, the legacy of interest in Indian students revived almost three centuries later. In 1970, Harvard's Graduate School of Education founded its American Indian Program, which became known as the Harvard Native American Program in 1991. The university recently celebrated the 350th anniversary of the Indian College's founding.

Like Harvard, Dartmouth College began with a firm commitment to educate and evangelize Indian youths. In 1769 Eleazar Wheelock, a congregational minister, received a charter "for the education and instruction of Youth of the Indian Tribes in this Land . . . and also of English Youth and any others."[3] Wheelock financed the college's first buildings with money that Samson Occam, a Mohegan student, had raised in England. Indian enrollment remained very low until 1969, when the new president, John Kemeny, established a goal of 3 percent Indian enrollment at the undergraduate level.

The college achieved this goal in 1991. Dartmouth's Native American Studies Program has thrived, and the college's athletic teams now call themselves "Big Green" instead of "Dartmouth Indians," so it is clear that the administration wants to show respect for former and current Indian students.[4] At their fall orientation, new Dartmouth freshmen do not learn about Indian ghosts; instead, they hear about the ghost of murderous Doc Benton, whose story is included in chapter 1.

In contrast to students at Dartmouth, students at the College of William and Mary tell stories about unhappy Indian ghosts. William and Mary, the second-oldest institution of higher education in the United States, received its royal charter for the education of Indian and English young people in 1693. Admission of Indians began in 1700, but few tribal leaders allowed their children to attend; instead, they sent young prisoners of war to the college. During the Tuscarora War (1711–13), the presence of Indian students at the college kept Williamsburg safe from attack. Virginians tried to increase Iroquois and Cherokee enrollment at the college in the mid-eighteenth century so that members of those two powerful groups would not form an alliance with the French. A few Cherokee students came to the college between 1753 and 1756, but they disliked staying indoors, reading books. Most students at the college in the 1760s had been hostages or prisoners of war. In 1777, the Indian school came to an end (Brudvig 1996).

Although William and Mary's mission to educate Indians ended more than two hundred years ago, twenty-first-century student tour guides have made sure that prospective students know about this part of the college's history. Sally, a twenty-year-old student who visited the College of William and Mary in April 2000, learned this story from a tour guide and told it in April 2003.

Against His Will

At William and Mary University, during the 1800s there was an Indian tribe near the University. And for some reason they wanted to educate one Indian boy and it was against his will, so they took him and put him in the school. I think at the time it was an all boys' school, but they weren't allowed to go out at night or leave the dorms.

One night the boy escaped and went to find his Indian tribe. He was missing the next day and when they went to find him, they found him dead in the forest. It was rumored that it was a set up, that some Indian hater killed him. In the attic of the dorm where the boy lived, you can hear drum beats and feet dancing, like tribal Indian drum beats.

In Sally's story, time slips out of joint; Indians came to the College of William and Mary in the 1700s, not the 1800s. That inaccuracy does not matter much, as the story succeeds in conveying a sense of injustice. Sally says that the Indian boy was taken "against his will" and was not "allowed to go out at night or leave the dorms." When he finally escapes, "some Indian hater" kills him, and rumors say that the death was a "set up." We do not know who this Indian hater was, but it is not difficult to understand that the Indian boy has suffered a wrongful death. College officials gave him what they thought he needed, but he preferred to risk his life to return home. After his death, drumbeats and the sound of feet tapping on the floor of the boys' dormitory remind students how important it was for the Indian boy to go back to his people's traditional culture.

Sally's story not only recalls racism but also creates a lively portrait of a rebellious young man. Her dramatic description of his restless ghost gives the college's history a new dimension of meaning for pre-freshmen. Like the young Indian, they may chafe against academic restraints; being free to wander may have more appeal than spending long hours in lecture halls and laboratories. Much campus folklore focuses on subversion of established rules and regulations. While sympathizing with the young Indian's plight, students learn some significant aspects of early education in the United States.

Indian Boarding Schools

More extensive and damaging than elite universities' experiments with Indian education was the United States government's Indian boarding-school movement, which began in the late 1870s with the founding of Carlisle Indian School in Pennsylvania. According to the anthropologist Carolyn Marr, post–Civil War reformers wanted to transform young Indians into "patriotic and productive members of society" through strict boarding-school regimens. "Before" and "after" photographs of children who entered the schools show that their hairstyles and dress changed dramatically (2006). Away from their families, under the control of school officials who were trying to take away their cultural heritage, Indian children forgot how to speak their original languages and learned what the government thought would be good for them.

Some learned industrial skills, while others followed different vocations that the government deemed appropriate for members of a vanquished race.

The results of this repressive indoctrination have drawn the attention of social scientists and creative writers. David Wallace Adams's *Education for Extinction* (1997) emphasizes the genocidal quality of American Indian boarding schools, as does Ward Churchill's *Kill the Indian, Save the Man* (2004). Many children died while attending Indian boarding schools, but it is difficult to ascertain the exact number of deaths.[5] Because of this tragic loss of young Indians, as well as the removal of the children's cultural heritage, creative writers have written poetry and fiction about boarding-school students. John E. Smelcer's novel *Stealing Indians* (2006) includes several poignant ghost stories based on folk narratives about deaths at Indian boarding schools. Another creative writer who evokes the sadness of boarding schools' repression of culture is Louise Erdrich, whose poem "Indian Boarding Schools: The Runaways" appears in many anthologies (1984: 11).

Students at Haskell Indian Nations University in Lawrence, Kansas, know about the ghosts of boarding-school students, since their institution began as the United States Indian Industrial Training School in 1884. Gradually, this vocationally oriented boarding school evolved into a high school. After the last high school class graduated in 1965, Haskell became a junior college (1970) and then a university (1993). Since the turn of the twenty-first century, journalists have recognized Haskell as a university haunted by many ghosts (Eakins 2001; Pierpoint 2001). Complex cultural, political, and ecological issues have made Haskell's ghosts noteworthy for Indians and non-Indians across the United States.

Like a number of other colleges and universities, Haskell has an on-campus cemetery that provokes speculation, but Haskell's cemetery is unusual. The children who were buried there died between 1885 and 1913, when the Indian boarding-school movement was at its height. According to Stephen A. Colmant, a doctoral student at Oklahoma State University, most of the children in the cemetery died when they were about ten years old. The youngest, Harry White Wolf, was only six months old at the time of his death. Why these children died so young is not clear, but stories circulating at Haskell explain that children died because of smallpox and other diseases introduced by whites, as well as deplorable living conditions at the boarding school. Colmant suggests that Haskell's cemetery symbolizes "hardships endured and overcome." Because it reminds Indians how ruthlessly the United States Government tried to eradicate their culture, the cemetery encourages loyalty to traditional culture within families and communities (Colmant 2006).

Similarly, ghost stories told on the Haskell campus have emphasized positive effects. Students and staff members at Haskell Indian Nations University have told stories about child ghosts wearing turn-of-the-century clothes that have appeared on campus lawns and pathways. Many members of the campus community believe that these are the spirits of the Haskell Babies, who died because of harsh living conditions at the boarding school and were buried on the school grounds (Eakins 2001). These child ghosts have become protectors of students on the college campus. Like Elizabeth at the State University of New York at Cortland and other ghosts of murdered women, they have protective power. Ever since the Kansas Department of Transportation proposed a new highway bypass through the southern end of the Haskell campus, protesters have opposed desecration of the ground in which the Haskell Babies were buried (Pierpoint 2001). So far, there has been no resolution of this conflict.

In April 2006, I interviewed several of the Residential Life staff members at Haskell Indian Nations University by telephone. Haskell's director of Residential Life told me that ghost stories circulated most actively in the residence halls. After speaking with hall staff members, I discovered that there were at least two kinds of ghost stories: those that described the Haskell Babies' activities and those that chronicled startling visits from older ghosts. Kindly and patiently, several Residential Life employees told me about visits from ghosts that had enlivened their evenings.

It was exciting to learn that a ghost had recently appeared on the Haskell campus. People had not only seen this ghost but also had taken its picture with a camera phone. John Sithins, a member of Haskell's Residential Life staff, told me this story in April 2006.[6]

The Face on the Door

This was last—I think it was in March. I've been working in the building two years this May. Before I saw the face, I had noticed that when there was a powwow on campus, our handicapped door would pop open and closed with nobody coming in. We would make a joke that somebody was coming to the powwow.

This one week I was there by myself. This happened when we had a snowfall around 3:00 in the morning. I heard the handicapped door pop open. When I heard the door pop open, I felt a chill come down my spine. That never happened before. I walked up to the door and looked outside.

When I stepped back, I saw that on the upper righthand corner of the door there was a face: the right side of a human face. You could see the crow's feet, the pock marks on the face. You could see the chapped lips of this face on the door. A minute before I saw this face, the staff at Pocahontas had radioed security. They had seen an old woman with white hair going up and down the stairs of their building.

When I saw the face, I called Security too and they came on over. Someone took a picture of the face with a camera phone. I've got several copies of it.

ET: Who do you think the face was?

It was a male face. If you saw photos from the early 1800s, that's what it looked like. When a security guard checked, the face was on the *inside* of the building. There was a total of eight to ten people who saw that face. You know, I don't think that door has popped open again since then.

With a few vivid details, Sithins helped me visualize the face of an old Indian man who had suffered severely. This face had pock marks—scars from the smallpox epidemic caused by European colonization—as well as chapped lips, probably from exposure to wind and rain. The crow's feet or wrinkles on the old man's face showed that he was an elder with significant life experience. As an elder, he could teach Indian staff members and students about troubles that they had not directly experienced.

Sithins's reaction to the old man's ghost showed that the ghost had made him feel both comfortable and uncomfortable. At first, when the handicapped access door popped open and shut, he joked with co-workers that "somebody was coming to the powwow." It seemed all right that an invisible person—a member of the extended family—was joining in the celebration. But later, when Sithins was alone, he felt a chill down his spine and called Security. A minute before, staff members at Pocahontas Hall had reported a white-haired female ghost to Security. A member of the Security staff took pictures: persuasive visual evidence that a spectral visitation had actually taken place. The strength of this visual evidence explains why Sithins and the others felt scared. While it is easy to joke about the ghostliness of a door opening and closing, a photograph of a sober-faced apparition leaves no room for doubt.

Like Sithins, I find the apparition of the old man's face to be both impressive and troubling. This face represents the tragic consequences of early

European influence: smallpox and other serious diseases, as well as loss of land and stature. In *Cultural Haunting*, Kathleen Brogan explains that a baby's ghost symbolizes the tragedy of slavery in Toni Morrison's *Beloved* (1998: 61–92). Similarly, the face of this old Indian man conveys the sad history of Europeans' domination of Indians. Viewing the face and confirming its reality by taking pictures with a camera phone, members of the Haskell community remember the pain of the past.

Love and Revenge

Some campus legends about Indian burial grounds follow plot patterns of the nineteenth century, focusing on love, war, self-sacrifice, tragic death, and forgiveness. Others from more recent times recognize the potential for Indians' revenge. Some important texts come from southern states, where the Indian Removal Act of 1830 caused severe hardship, dislocation, and suffering. Narratives about three statues in Tennessee, Michigan, and upstate New York help us understand how some stories about past tragedies have evolved.

Chapter 5 includes an overview of the legend of Nocatula and Connestoga at Tennessee Wesleyan College in Athens, Tennessee. Nocatula, the daughter of a Cherokee chief and a white woman, falls in love with Connestoga, a wounded English soldier. She nurses her lover back to health, then loses him when a jealous suitor stabs the soldier with a knife. Proclaiming her love, Nocatula stabs herself (Motif N343.4, "Lover commits suicide on finding beloved dead"). Her father places a hackberry in his daughter's hand and an acorn in Connestoga's hand; two trees grow from their graves, symbolizing eternal love.

This legend encodes cultural values of the nineteenth century. Its central figures are warlike Indians, including a merciful chief and a jealous suitor. Attakulla-Kulla, a Cherokee chief born around 1712, was well known for his fairness and willingness to help the British. In this legend, he becomes a figure of almost mythic kindness. With his white spouse, Chief Atta-Kulla-Kulla has a daughter who shows that she is faithful and loving as well as beautiful. The chief's mercy and the young lovers' everlasting devotion make their story memorable and inspiring. Students and administrators at Tennessee Wesleyan University have become very fond of the legend of Nocatula and Connestoga, which represents both romantic devotion and school spirit.

The central feature of the Nocatula Garden at Tennessee Wesleyan is a statue of the beautiful young Cherokee woman who committed suicide

Statue of Nocatula at Tennessee Wesleyan University. Photograph by Tennessee Wesleyan staff.

because of her love for her British soldier. With feathers on her head and attractive clothing appropriate to her era and ethnicity, the statue of Nocatula welcomes visitors to her garden. Soon a statue of Connestoga will join her there, completing the representation of happily united lovers.

Besides representing love and loyalty, the legend of Nocatula and Connestoga suggests that an Indian's tragic death may bring blessings to the area where the death took place. In his study *Beyond Ethnicity*, Werner Sollors explains that nineteenth-century white Americans expected blessings to come from dying, melancholy Indians; sometimes they viewed dead Indians as ancestor figures (1986: 114–30).[7] This view of Indians as adopted ancestors was easier to accept than images of men, women, and children who had lost their land and moved to reservations. Sollors's argument applies fairly well to the story of Nocatula and Connestoga, which emphasizes love between a mixed-blood Indian woman and a white man rather than battle, victory, and defeat. Seeds given to the young lovers by Nocatula's father symbolize his blessing. As the oak and hackberry trees grow and endure, they suggest that love can transcend conflict between ethnic groups.

In sharp contrast to nineteenth-century legends of loving, altruistic Indians, some twentieth-and twenty-first-century legends describe angry Indian women who threaten others' safety. In 1978, Thomas Pappas, a student at Wayne State University in Detroit, collected the following story from his friend Doug.

Minnehaha's Ghost

Somewhere in Ionia there is a graveyard with a mausoleum, and this mausoleum is supposed to contain the remains of the Indian woman, Minnehaha. She was, as I have heard, very hostile by nature. And there is a small statue of her on top of the building, holding a knife over her head.

As the story goes, if you stand in front of the mausoleum and call out her name at the stroke of midnight, her ghost will appear from the mausoleum holding the deadly knife in her hand: as if to strike down those who disturbed her rest. As I was told, no one ever stayed around long enough to find out her intentions. (Pappas 1978)

Doug's description of Minnehaha's grave sounds dreamlike. Does such a mausoleum actually exist? I have found no evidence that it does. Lacking an actual site to explore, I will consider Minnehaha's characterization in Henry Wadsworth Longfellow's long narrative poem "The Song of Hiawatha" (1992 [1855]). Longfellow describes her as "Minnehaha, Laughing Water, Handsomest of all the women": a radiantly positive character (1992: 75). However, Hiawatha's wise grandmother, Nokomis, warns her grandson about the danger of an alliance with a woman from another group of people: "Very fierce are the Dacotahs, / Often is there war between us. / There are feuds yet unforgotten, / Wounds that ache and may still open!" (69). Later, after Minnehaha's death, Hiawatha sees a vision of white men's "great canoes of thunder" arriving, making his people fight with one another and scatter like autumn leaves (153). This heritage of strife, both among Indian peoples and between Indians and whites, provides ballast for the legend of Minnehaha's vengeful ghost.

"Minnehaha's Ghost" presents a darker view of white/Indian conflict than Longfellow envisioned. Like the many campus statues that supposedly come to life on special occasions, Minnehaha, frozen in stone, waits for a victim, holding a knife over her head. If a young person dares to call her name at the stroke of midnight, she will come forward, clutching her "deadly knife"

Seventeen-foot-tall monument in memory of Sa Sa Na Loft, who died in a train wreck in 1852. Photograph by Geoffrey Gould.

in one hand. This scenario fits the pattern of young people's visits to forbidden, dangerous places (Ellis 2004: 112–41). There is also a connection to the "Bloody Mary" ritual discussed in chapter 3, in which saying a ghost's name makes the speaker vulnerable to attack. If young intruders call Minnehaha's name, she may hurt or even kill them. While such consequences are well established in children's and adolescents' folklore, Minnehaha's ethnicity makes her stand out in the crowd of hostile female spirits. In the context of whites' oppression of Indians, she has good reasons to go after careless intruders.

The ghost of another Indian woman haunts an obelisk in Evergreen Cemetery in Owego, New York, near the campuses of Cornell University and Binghamton University. In January 2005, two freshmen at Binghamton University, Cal and Frank, told me that they had recently visited the monument with a group of friends. Cal explained, "There's an Indian statue at Evergreen Cemetery. Kids drive to the cemetery late at night and flash their lights on and off. In daylight, if you stand by the statue and look down at the town, following two points, you'll see a store that recently burned down." Frank reminded me that a store in Owego had burned down not long ago under mysterious circumstances. According to these two students and their friends, the culprit was an angry Indian ghost (Motif E578, "Dead persons build fires").

Focus on this ghost's destructive power seems ironic, as the young Indian woman buried beneath the monument was a local heroine at the time of her death. Sa Sa Na Loft, a twenty-one-year-old Christian from the Mohawk Woods reservation in Canada, perished in a train wreck in Deposit, New York, on February 18, 1852. Feeling admiration for this young woman, who had come to raise money for the religious education of her people, townspeople paid for the construction of an obelisk seventeen feet high on a hillside above the town of Owego (Moyer 2004). Since then, many visitors have made a pilgrimage to Sa Sa Na's grave. When I visited her grave myself in July 2006, I noticed that coins covered the metal plaque beneath the obelisk. These coins marked her status as an important person, loved and missed, who could bring good luck to passers-by.[8]

In Cal's description, the straight line from Sa Sa Na's monument to a store in Owego that recently burned down becomes a trajectory of fiery destruction. Sa Sa Na's ghost seems to have the power to incinerate places owned by people that she wants to harm.[9] But why would she want to destroy this store? Could it be because the owners of the store are white? Although Sa Sa Na enjoyed good relationships with whites during her education and travels, she might have preferred to stay with her own people instead of being interred by strangers on a hillside in Owego. An inscription on her monument states that she was "by birth a daughter of the forest, by adoption a child of God." Citizens of Owego wanted to honor this young woman, but Sa Sa Na's brother, Rok Wa Ha, did not want to leave his sister's body in the state of New York. Prominent Owego citizens ultimately persuaded him to comply with their wishes, and Sa Sa Na became an honorary daughter of the town of Owego (Douglas 2001). Perhaps, as a ghost, she would want to punish the proprietary whites and return home (Motif E545.18, "Ghost asks to be taken to former home").

Although a desire for punishment or revenge often motivates ghosts' behavior, it does not fully explain college students' view of Sa Sa Na as a fire-starting ghost. The most likely explanation comes from the influence of popular films. In Stephen King's *Firestarter* (1984), a young woman has the power to incinerate people; King's later film *Creepshow 2* (1987) features a statue of a wooden Indian that comes to life, then goes on a murderous rampage to avenge the killing of owners of a store (Motif D435.1.1).[9] Many "Cowboy and Indian" movies have depicted Indians as burners and destroyers of whites' property.[10]

These negative stereotypes still have enough strength to shape some young people's ideas, motivating them to draw a line in the air from a seventeen-foot monument to a store that mysteriously burned down.

In legends, images of avenging Indians have historical meaning. One Indian woman with a deadly knife and another who can burn down buildings remind us of past discord between Indians and whites. These two women's expressions of revenge contrast sharply with the serenity of Nocatula, who rests peacefully with her British soldier in the garden framed by their trees at Tennessee Wesleyan College. However, even Nocatula and Connestoga have ghosts that some observers have seen wandering restlessly. Ghost stories remind us of past tensions, making us reassess the impact of the past upon the present.

Landscape

On some college campuses, landscape features evoke memories of people who lived there before settlement by Europeans. Three examples of campuses of this kind are the University of Wisconsin at Madison, Louisiana State University at Baton Rouge, and Binghamton University in New York. All three of these universities have a relatively small number of Indian students; the University of Wisconsin at Madison has 1 percent, and the other two have fewer than 1 percent.

Each of these three campuses has landscape features that bring an Indian presence to mind. Most dramatically, at the University of Wisconsin at Madison, effigy mounds, cemeteries, and ancient campsites fill at least twenty-two archeological sites. No other university in the world has as many varied effigy mounds and earthworks as this campus has. Mounds shaped like birds, panthers, and turtles are common in this part of Wisconsin. The archeologist Robert Hall has made the important point that these effigy mounds closely resemble depictions of powerful spirits of the upper and lower worlds in many midwestern Indian tribes' cosmology (1993). It is not surprising that University of Wisconsin students feel the impact of these mounds' presence and tell stories about university officials taking some of the mounds away. Students have told stories about one mound being removed for the construction of Bascom Hall; they have also talked about dust from another mound being used to fill in the hollows of State Street. Besides the remarkable effigy mounds, Indian springs at or near the University of Wisconsin enhance the campus landscape. Stories have been told about an Indian "wishing spring" on the shore of Lake Mendota, where students go to seek blessings. A "spirit spring" at the University of Wisconsin Arboretum is famous for its medicinal virtues (Brown 1938; Krouth 1997).

At Louisiana State University, ancient Indian mounds on the northwest corner of the campus once served as the focal point of rituals. Although archeologists do not think these mounds were burial sites, Brian Bordelon, writing in the magazine *Gumbo* in 1991, suggests that the mounds comprise "the most mystical site on L.S.U.'s campus; the ominous-looking trees on the mounds are haunted by the ghosts of the Indians from ages past." Frank de Caro, who kindly helped me to locate that article, has said he doesn't think that "belief in the mounds' being haunted is very widespread" (2003). Nonetheless, these mounds serve as markers of an Indian culture that students have recognized as an important part of their campus landscape.

At Binghamton University, whose campus I know best, there are no mounds or springs, just an encircling ring of hills near the confluence of two rivers. Ever since I arrived there in 1977, I have heard rumors that Binghamton is one of our country's "most haunted" places, because of the joining of two rivers where Indian settlements flourished for many years. Rod Serling, creator of the popular television series *The Twilight Zone*, grew up in Binghamton; students say this is one more piece of proof that the area is strange and spooky.

Binghamton University has many buildings with Indian names that create an onomastic landscape. Impressionable new students whose residential area is College-in-the-Woods drive, with their families, up to the doors of Mohawk, Onondaga, Oneida, Cayuga, or Seneca Hall; they eat their first dinner in the Iroquois Commons. These names are relics of spectralization, reminding students of a presence that has become minimal. Other State University of New York campuses have residential complexes with similar names and similarly low Indian enrollments. At the State University College at Morrisville, for example, Cayuga, Mohawk, Oneida, and Onondaga halls comprise the residential area called Indian Quad, and students eat at Seneca Dining Hall.

Rumors

In the spring of 2003, one of my students told me that Binghamton University used to be an Indian burial ground; several others collected narratives about Indian ghosts. Trying to figure out where the burial ground rumor had originated, I discovered that several teaching assistants in a large anthropology class had been telling students their residence halls stood above Indian graves. Since professors and teaching assistants are supposed to be bearers of truthful reports, the students believed what they heard and shared the news with their friends. In much the same way that stories told by camp counselors circulate among campers, this rumor spread rapidly.

One of my colleagues at Binghamton University expressed concern about the rumor, saying that students should not be allowed to spread such false-hoods. Our campus's reputation could suffer, he said, if students kept telling each other their residence halls stood above Indian graves. If this colleague had been a folklorist, he would have known that rumors cannot be stopped so easily.

What the teaching assistants had been telling their classes turned out to be technically untrue but intriguingly reminiscent of a local grave desecration that had occurred near the campus. Binghamton University's public arche-ologist, Nina Versaggi, told me that gravel miners had dug up Indian bones and artifacts at Willow Point, on the banks of the Susquehanna River, during the 1930s. William A. Ritchie, author of *The Archaeology of New York State*, documented some Indian burials on the Clark/Palmer site where the gravel miners were working (1980: 304, 311–12). Gravel mining continued, in spite of the discovery of Indian remains (Versaggi 2004).

This disturbance took place, of course, long before the National Graves Protection and Repatriation Act (NAGPRA) of 1990. As Versaggi explained in an interview in 2003, this act was passed "to right some . . . historical wrongs" (PAF). During the spring of 2003, the same time period when rumors about the Indian burial ground were spreading, Binghamton's Public Archeology Facility was working on returning human remains from an Indian burial ground in Nichols, New York, dislodged during highway construction, to the Haudenosaunee Committee of the Iroquois Confederacy. Did students know about the bones or about the grave desecration that had happened half a mile away? It seems likely that they did not; nonetheless, they energetically spread the rumor of an Indian burial ground on campus, heightening others' awareness of injustices that had occurred in the past.

On other college and university campuses, rumors about Indian burial grounds have become part of student folklore. Some of these rumors refer to the era before white settlement. Troy Taylor, author of *Ghosts of Millikin: The Haunted History of Millikin University* (1996), explains that the first set-tlers of Decatur, Illinois, decided to occupy an area where Indians had buried their dead. Because this site was "somehow more closely connected to the next world," Indians had kept it for burials only, preferring not to live there (1996: 17). When white settlers built the town, "vengeful Indian spirits" rose from their burial ground to torment the living (48). Taylor views the early disturbance of Indian graves and later construction at Millikin University (which received its charter in 1901) as the reason for Indian spirits' continuing to haunt the campus (18). As in many other legends told by whites about Indians, disturbance and disrespect keep ghosts moving.

At the University of Tennessee in Knoxville, students have associated three parts of their campus with Indian burial grounds. The first is Reese Hall, which Alan Brown identifies as a haunted dormitory in his *Stories from the Haunted South* (2004: 247). According to John Norris Brown, author of the website "Ghosts and Spirits of Tennessee," maps of Knoxville from the early 1800s reveal that Reese Hall stands upon two cemeteries: one for Indians, another for white settlers. "Disturbingly," Brown says, "there is no record of any of the graves being moved. The graves are probably still there, located under the foundation of the building and the parking lot!" Because the ghosts are unhappy, they scare students in Reese Hall, especially around Halloween. The two other parts of the University of Tennessee haunted by restless Indian spirits are McClung Museum, which stands above a burial mound, and the agricultural campus (Brown 2005b).

Still another rumor has circulated at Ohio University in Athens, notorious for being one of the "most haunted" universities in the country. The website "Forgotten Ohio" claims that this university's West Green stands upon an Indian burial ground where students occasionally hear chanting, as well as the sound of a spectral river running nearby. Even more colorful is the rumor that a headless buffalo named Stroud haunts West Green. According to "Forgotten Ohio," Confederate soldiers killed the buffalo and hid loot from nearby farms in the buffalo's head. The buffalo head hanging on the wall of Buffalo Wings and Rings in Athens might be Stroud's head—or it might not (2006). As this set of rumors and legends shows, campus spirit has a close connection to its human and animal ghosts.

Presences

Some campus ghost stories told by non-Indians describe a generalized presence rather than a specific Indian ghost. Stories of this kind combine sights, sounds, and feelings that make the narrator feel uneasy. Sometimes the presence belongs to an Indian burial ground; in other cases, the presence makes less sense. Because it can be difficult to put a feeling of uneasiness into words, stories about spectral presences tend to sound vague and mysterious.

Such is the case in this text narrated by Paula, a twenty-three-year-old student at the College of New Jersey in Ewing, in November 2004.[11]

Holman Hall

> There's a building on campus . . . Holman Hall, yeah, that's the name. It's a weird building because the floors aren't lined up together. Like there's a basement part, but you can walk into that floor from outside on one side and the rest of that floor is underground.
>
> Then too if you go upstairs to the first floor, that floor exits outside as well. So the part where the entrance is to the basement, the first and second floors kinda overhang there, like a portico or something. So supposedly that section is built on an Indian burial ground. So when people are working late at night on art projects they hear Indian chanting and feel a presence.
>
> Chris said he's heard the chanting and felt something around him. I think sometimes the ghosts can get violent. But I know the student paper had the story in it. But usually the students just get really freaked out and leave.
>
> Whether someone's actually seen a ghost, I'm not sure about that.

Paula's story about Holman Hall emphasizes the building's architectural peculiarity. Art students think Holman is a "weird building" because of the unevenness of its floors. Since the floors are not aligned with each other in the expected way, they set the stage for something unusual to happen. While students work on their art projects late at night, they hear chanting and feel a presence. As Joseph Bruchac's story "Bone Girl" indicates, these story elements seem clichéd to Indians who wryly observe white culture. For non-Indian students, though, hearing chanting, perceiving a presence, and wondering whether the building stands above a burial ground can have an unsettling impact. Suddenly, the familiar art building seems to have been repossessed by spirits of the area's original inhabitants, whose descendants no longer live there. The spirits do not seem harmful, just insistent. Chanting, making their presence felt, they remind students of their people's absence.

In a different context, folklorist Kimberly J. Lau has shown how an unusual floor plan can become part of subversive campus folklore. Her article

"On the Rhetorical Use of Legend: U.C. Berkeley Campus Lore as a Strategy for Coded Protest" (1998) includes a detailed description of Dwinelle Hall, whose uneven floors and hidden staircases make it difficult for students to find their way around. Tour guides tell prospective students that Dwinelle's architects were two brothers, each of whom insisted upon doing things his own way. Lau explains that Dwinelle's architecture serves as a "metaphor for the university's administration and bureaucracy" (7). Tour guides delight in telling students that the campus is not as well organized as officials say it is. Similarly, students who are studying art late at night may take pleasure in repeating the College of New Jersey's legend of an Indian presence and burial ground, which suggests that the college has not shown proper respect for the dead.

Another text about an Indian presence comes from Aiko, a Montclair State University student who shared her experiences with the publishers of the "Weird New Jersey" website (2005). The website's publishers, Mark Sceurman and Mark Moran, kindly agreed to share this eerie campus ghost story with me.

Strange Happenings at Montclair State

Apparently, as the story goes, the site where the Clove Road Apartments sits used to be an ancient Native American burial ground. I do know that part of the history of Montclair includes several Native American groups which used to inhabit the area before it was officially settled. It could be that the story was created as a way to scare anyone new to the campus and the Clove Road Apartments.

I lived in one of these apartments in 1996 with three other roommates. We experienced several random, unexplained phenomena that to this day I often question and refrain from speaking about openly. Some of the things that occurred which are of interest include: hairdryers and other electrical appliances turning on on their own, second floor lights flashing on and off when no one was upstairs, someone knocking on bedroom and bathroom doors when only one person was known to have been in the apartment, weird "unearthly" noises being heard coming from the woods directly behind the apartments, and shadows of what we originally thought were animals (deer) lurking around in the woods.

Also, an unsettling feeling of nausea would overcome any one of us that discussed these weird events at length. There were times when the apartment would get unreasonably chilly even though the thermostat was cranked up to 80 degrees. Several guests witnessed the events that plagued us if they spent long enough periods of time in the apartment. Originally people thought that we were just making up stories to spook one another, or that we had overindulged in drinking and "hallucinated" these events. We (my roommates and I) began to accept that perhaps we were imagining things, until we began to hear of similar stories about other apartments in the Clove Road complex. One story went so far as to claim that a girl awoke one night to see the ghost of a young man in late 18th century clothing standing over her bed and looking at her lovingly. This girl thought perhaps her roommate's boyfriend had mistaken her for her roommate and was standing at the wrong bed, until she called out to the "man" to tell him that he was in fact at the wrong bed, when the image suddenly vanished like mist.

We all got a little freaked out after hearing that one. I did not live at Clove Road long. I moved home with my parents the following spring because of the discord that I was experiencing at the apartment with my roommates. We were all best friends and suddenly were fighting and not getting along, which may not sound like a big deal, but I attribute it to something "unnatural" that was affecting us.

This unusually long ghost story describes a complex set of sensory experiences: sight (machines going on and off, shadows, the apparition of a young man), sound (knocking and unearthly noises), and, creepiest of all, an "unsettling feeling of nausea" that affects any of the students at the Clove Road Apartments who dare to talk about what happened. The multi-sensory nature of this spectral assault leaves the students feeling overwhelmed. As in many other ghost stories, the nature of the ghost(s) seems hard to understand. However, the emphatic mention of "an ancient Native American burial ground" at the beginning of the story suggests that angry Indian spirits are to blame for the peculiar things that happen.

While the story's narrator takes the strange events seriously, she considers the possibility that the rumor about the Indian burial ground was created to scare newcomers to the campus or to Clove Road Apartments. Apparently, she has learned enough about freshman initiation to know that such rumor-mongering happens fairly often. However, after presenting this disclaimer, she recounts a set of personal experiences that makes a convincing case for the rumor's authenticity. She and her three roommates go through such an alarming sequence of odd perceptions that a spectral presence seems to be the only viable explanation.

Throughout her story, Aiko emphasizes the strangeness of sights, sounds, and feelings. The words "unearthly," "unreasonably," and "unnaturally" convey the message that nothing rational can account for the occurrences. Toward the end of the story, she mentions that others thought she and her friends were just drinking and hallucinating but changed their minds after hearing what happened. By the time the spectral young man— apparently a ghostly lover—leans over one of the female roommates, the story seems quite persuasive. Is the young man in eighteenth-century clothing an Indian or white? It is impossible to know. Very quickly, the young man's image vanishes "like mist."

At the story's end, we hear that the ghostly assaults have made the roommates angry at each other. There seems to be no reasonable explanation for the fact that these roommates, who have been best friends for a long time, are suddenly at each other's throats. Aiko explains this state of affairs by the presence of something "unnatural." Hostility between white settlers and Indians, epitomized in the disturbance of a sacred burial ground, casts a long shadow. Although roommates' bickering reflects this hostility on a small scale, it is, nonetheless, a serious reflection of past tensions that continue into the present.

Apparitions

Like stories about ghostly presences, stories about apparitions stress eerie, inexplicable feelings. Sometimes, as in the above text from Montclair State, a ghost briefly appears while students struggle to understand what is going on. More often, however, the apparition provides the story's main focus. Seeing an Indian materialize shocks the non-Indian viewer, showing that the past can break into the present.

Many legends about apparitions are very brief, almost telegraphic in their terse communication of details. Such is the case in this story sent by Matthew, resident director of Presidents Park at George Mason University in Fairfax, Virginia, to Professor Peggy Yocom in November 2000.

Presidents Park

Basically it is rumored in the Park that from Sub2 back is an Indian burial ground. It is said that some students have experienced the ghosts of the children buried here. One woman in Jefferson last year said she saw a vision of a little Indian boy in her closet. It is also said that the showers in Jefferson sometimes turn on for no reason.

Because Matthew serves as Presidents Park's resident director, his story sounds persuasive. Resident directors usually stay in close touch with their students; if ghosts appear, RDs will probably hear about them. The fact that Matthew wanted to share this legend with his professor shows that he thought it was important. While the story has few details, its linkage to a rumor about an Indian burial ground gives it depth and meaning.

Some background information on Presidents Park helps us to place this legend in context. Presidents Park is a large housing complex for freshmen only. Its thirteen buildings bear the names of some of the most famous presidents of the United States, including Washington, Jefferson, Lincoln, Monroe, Jackson, Roosevelt, and Kennedy. These presidents' names bring to mind a wide range of decisions and programs, some of which were disastrous for American Indians. For example, Thomas Jefferson encouraged Indian nations to buy goods on credit, then get out of debt by selling their lands to the United States Government. James Monroe encouraged General Andrew Jackson to pursue and kill Seminole Indians in Florida; later, when Jackson became president himself, he signed the Indian Removal Act of 1830.

The ghost of the little Indian boy appeared in Jefferson Hall, adjacent to Monroe Hall. Those two presidents' names may or may not have seemed significant to students who repeated the story. However, the fact that the vision occurred in a closet is difficult to overlook. As in the story of the ghostly lover in chapter 3, a closet represents keeping something hidden. Curious about what happened to American Indians in the area where they are going to college, students can bring some details "out of the closet" by telling ghost stories.

Other stories of Indian ghosts emphasize both Indians' deaths and the deaths of white settlers. The following story came from Nathaniel, a thirty-year-old graduate of the University of Connecticut at Storrs, in April 2003.

Looking for his Head

When I was in college we used to tell these stories about the woods around here, near the University of Connecticut. Supposedly there was this settler that was killed by Indians and his head was cut off. People said you can see him at night wandering around with a lantern looking for his head.

In the same area there is an Indian that was killed. He was a hunter, so he still walks the same hunting trails he always has. Things get moved around all the time in the houses along the trail. There was an old lady who insisted it was true. She lived alone, so she said no one else could have moved her stuff. She was old, so no one believed her.

Headless ghosts have held students' attention for many years (Motif E422.1.1, "Headless revenant"). At Cambridge University in England, the headless ghost of Archbishop Laud haunts his former college (Yeates 1994); at colleges in southern New York State, Washington Irving's Headless Horseman still enjoys some notoriety; and in the fictive world of J. K. Rowling's *Harry Potter* books, Nearly Headless Nick delights Hogwarts students. Nathaniel's text, however, offers more than the macabre fascination exerted by a ghost with no head. This settler died at the hands of Indians, so he represents the long and bloody conflict that marked the settlement of the American colonies.

The second half of the story introduces a dead Indian who "still walks the same trails he always has." In a way he resembles the headless settler, because he keeps doing one thing over and over, but there is more to his story than that. Along the trail where the Indian walks (and presumably is seen by local inhabitants), things inexplicably move around inside people's houses. Expecting to find order, the residents find disorder, and they wonder what is wrong. One old woman insists that the Indian ghost has entered her house, but nobody believes her. Cassandra-like, she tries to tell others about the Indian ghost. What message is he trying to convey? Perhaps he needs to help others understand the struggle that resulted in his death. This Indian ghost wants to make people think, and in at least one case, he succeeds. Hearing his story at the University of Connecticut, students learn to ask questions about what happened to Indians in early New England.

A few students at Binghamton University have told stories about seeing Indian ghosts. One, narrated by a nineteen-year-old white female student in April 2003, takes the form of a memorate:

Mist and Fog

One time I was walking from Johnson Hall from a friend's place back to my place in Digman. And it was really late, almost 3 AM, and my friend

Volleyball court at Binghamton University, where two spectral Indians appeared one misty morning. Photograph by Geoffrey Gould.

said that he would walk me back to my hall, so while we were walking there was a lot of mist and fog in the air. It was my freshman year and my first two weeks at Bing, and the fog was really thick, unusually thick.

While me and my friend were walking, I look to my left towards the volleyball court and I see two Native Americans, dressed in their traditional clothes standing there for a minute and then suddenly they ran into the thick fog. I got so scared I clung onto my friend's arm and told him what I saw and he didn't believe a word I said.

But the scary part is, the next semester in my anthropology class, my professor told me that the campus was built over Iroquois land and many Natives were buried under Dickinson and Newing. I mean it could've been people messing around, but why would they do something like that?

Several parts of this story immediately get my attention: the mist and fog, which, as in Marion Zimmer Bradley's *Mists of Avalon*, signal a shift to another mode of life in the same location; the late hour, when unusual things are more likely to happen, and the "traditional dress," which shows respect for the old ways. Like many other legend-tellers, this narrator authenticates her experience by explaining about the information from her teacher after describing her surprising experience. Her friend, interestingly enough, sees nothing. But the most important aspect of this story seems to be its function as an initiatory experience. This nineteen-year-old student sees Indian ghosts during her "first two weeks in Bing," while she is making the first adjustment to living away from home. Looking at a small part of the campus landscape—a volleyball court on a patch of sand—she sees evidence of a vanished way of life. The two Indians who appear in front of her and her friend seem like counterparts of themselves in an earlier time period. Not only is she sensitive to her new environment; she also shows an eagerness to learn about the past—more specifically, to figure out why two Indians so quickly move from presence to absence.

When legends about Indians are told in tandem with rumors, they give students a view of troubling injustices. For freshmen in particular, rumors about desecrated burial grounds raise questions about how the buildings and roadways of their campus landscape were constructed. If these buildings and roads were built "over the dead bodies" of the original inhabitants, then something seriously wrong has taken place. Images of ghosts running, then fading away, help the listener understand how an earlier way of life has vanished.

Standing on the land of their ancestors, Indian ghosts remind the living to remember past struggles and to honor the dead. Having long memories and a strong sense of justice, these spectral Indians communicate without speaking; their presence says more than words can say. Through spectral Indians' stories, students learn to question mainstream history and to try to prevent new acts of injustice from harming ethnic groups in the future.

Chapter Eight

LEGEND QUESTS

A
s college students listen to each other's ghost stories, they learn about long-ago tragedies and recent encounters with the supernatural. Imagining what happens in stories sends shivers down the spine, but feeling the presence of the supernatural oneself goes beyond momentary thrills. In his essay on the world of magic that he calls Faërie, J. R. R. Tolkien notes that Faërie cannot be "caught in a net of words"; it is "indescribable but not imperceptible" (1965: 10). Difficult though it is to describe such a place, people have tried to put their extraordinary experiences into words. College students have eloquently conveyed the excitement of their collisions with supernatural forces, explaining why they want to take the risk of undergoing such an experience. During visits to on- or off-campus locations where supernatural events have taken place, students hope—but also fear—that something amazing will happen to them. When they begin a visit of this kind, they enter a mysterious realm filled with sensory stimulation and ambiguity.

Since the early 1970s, many folklorists have called such visits "legend trips." While this term accurately indicates a journey, it makes no reference to the journey's purpose. I suggest that another term, "legend quest," does more justice to older adolescents' reasons for visiting legend sites. Among these reasons are desires to understand death, probe the horror of domestic violence, confront racism, and express the uneasy relationship between humans and technology. There is also a strong emotional component: an attempt to feel both thrilled and afraid under relatively safe circumstances.

Student development theorists have offered insight into late adolescents' search for meaning. In contrast to Jungians' interpretation of adolescents' search for a more complex sense of self, discussed in chapter 4, some developmental psychologists have focused on achievement of a purposeful life through self-definition. Erik Erikson's studies of adolescent identity formation emphasize self-definition through interaction with others. Erikson suggests that adolescents want to discover "who and what they are in the eyes of a wider circle of significant people as compared with what they themselves have come to feel they are; and how to connect the dreams, idiosyncrasies, roles, and skills cultivated earlier with the occupational and sexual prototypes of the day" (1965: 299). Adolescents' focus on roles, skills, and general identity development takes them through certain stages of development as they approach adulthood.

According to James E. Marcia, most adolescents go through several stages of identity development (1966: 551–58). These stages include diffusion (lack of exploration of roles or reference groups), moratorium (active exploration of roles and reference groups), foreclosure (choice of roles without exploring alternatives), and achievement (commitment to roles and reference groups after some exploration). Legend quests fit the moratorium stage, giving college students important kinds of self-knowledge. By visiting sites associated with legends, students discover how to take risks and handle fear (Motif H1440, "The learning of fear"). As they look toward the future, they enact roles from past tragedies, proving their own resilience and readiness for further challenges.

Alan S. Waterman's study of adolescents' identity formation (1985) has shown that going to college stimulates the discovery of a strong sense of self. College campuses offer a wide range of experiences that both evoke and answer questions about personal capabilities. Studies by Waterman and others during the 1970s signal a connection between college students' poetry writing and identity achievement (Waterman, Kohutis, and Pulone 1977; Waterman and Archer 1979); other studies have indicated a relationship between cultural interests and resolution of identity (Waterman and Waterman 1971). Waterman wisely observes, "Rather than there being a direct, facilitative connection among cultural interests, poetry writing, and identity formation, all three may derive from some common underlying psychological quality related to curiosity and exploration" (1993: 67). Like poetry and other cultural pursuits, legend quests give intellectually curious college students an important way to explore roles that clarify their emerging identities as adults. Unlike other forms of culture, however, legend quests follow a distinctive pattern of fear-seeking in relation to specific legend scenarios.

Linda Dégh was the first folklorist to write articles on adolescents' nocturnal journeys to haunted locations, including two bridges in southern Indiana, in 1969 and 1971. In *Legend and Belief*, she argues that most adolescents' legends are quest stories: young storytellers travel to haunted places, telling stories as they "prepare for the anticipated legend in action" (2001: 253). Kenneth A. Thigpen, author of "Adolescent Legends in Brown County: A Survey" (1971), suggests that putting oneself under the power of the supernatural is central to the success of such visits. Certain ritual actions, such as blinking car lights, sitting on accursed seats, and approaching forbidden tombstones, can result in extraordinary occurrences. Thigpen identifies a three-part structure. Part one is an "introduction to the plausibility of the phenomenon" by someone who has already visited the site. Part two happens at the site itself, when people "act out the specified requirements to cause the fulfillment of the legend." Here the supernatural collides with reality, shocking and frightening participants. In part three, people discuss what happened, composing a story suitable for narration at the beginning of a later visit to the same place (1971; 204–5).

The main advocate of such visits' importance has been Bill Ellis, whose books and articles have delineated the legend trip's meaning. Ellis has urged folklorists to accept the importance of legend trips themselves, not just the legends that get them started. Like Thigpen, Ellis sees the legend trip as a three-part process: storytelling, rituals to invoke a supernatural presence, and finally discussion of what happened (2004: 114–15). His analyses of legend trips have yielded intriguing and thought-provoking conclusions. Ellis notes that outrageous pranks and sexual experiments are important parts of the American legend-trip tradition, with antecedents in folklore of the British Isles. For example, written records of visits to British holy wells and graves of saints in the seventeenth and eighteenth centuries show that young people enjoyed drinking and partying at such locations late at night (2004: 116–17).

Ellis, who has surveyed more than two hundred descriptions of journeys to legend sites, defines the legend trip as a "ritual of rebellion." This ritual, he says, "serves mainly as an excuse to escape adult supervision, commit anti-social acts, and experiment illicitly with drugs and sex. Both legend and trip are ways of saying 'screw you' to adult law and order" (2003: 188). Cursing and stamping on a grave, drinking, smoking marijuana, and stealing tombstones all defy adults' moral standards while proving how brave and rebellious the trip's participants are. Feeling frightened by the site's spooky atmosphere, young couples may snuggle up to each other, enjoying some forbidden sex (2004: 116).

I agree that rebellious behavior is one notable ingredient of such journeys, but I do not find it to be the main motivator among older adolescents. What seems to intrigue college students most is the opportunity to play a role in a strange, perhaps supernatural drama linked to past tragedies. By visiting legend sites, students try to discover whether supernatural forces are real and to answer other important questions. They also experience intense feelings that range from excitement to horror and fear. Like the central character of

"The Youth Who Wanted to Learn What Fear Is," they go on a quest to discover what stimuli will make them feel "scared to death."

In college, where education occurs both inside and outside the classroom, legend quests offer a significant kind of experiential learning. Since many freshmen have gone on such journeys as high school students, they know how to organize new ones. The complexity of the college campus and its folklore encourages exploration, as does the transitional life stage of freshman year. As Simon J. Bronner observes, "The college campus resounds with talk of the strange and wondrous" (1995: 143). Sometimes students discover supernatural dimensions of familiar campus buildings or landscape features. Often they go off campus in cars to investigate sites associated with local legends. Simultaneously offering safety and danger, the car becomes a crucial part of the discovery process.

In this digital age, college students can easily preview locations they want to visit by surfing the Internet. For example, New Jersey students who have heard about the Sunken House of Ramapo College in Mahwah can find eight photos of the house on the *Abandoned New Jersey* website, which offers directions to the site (2003). Once they have seen the photos, prospective visitors can decide whether or not they want to take the risk of climbing down into the house's flooded interior. One student told me that he had gone down under the water, taking pictures of the house to bring back for his friends. His pride in undertaking this rather risky quest shone through his matter-of-fact description of underwater photography.

Many students have gone on legend quests in the southern United States, where local landmarks remind students of tragedies related to slavery and the Civil War. In their book *Whispers on the Color Line* (2001), Gary Alan Fine and Patricia A. Turner comment on the subtleties of rumors and legends about racial issues. Intriguingly, some southern legend quests emphasize race-related tension without clearly identifying the tension's source. Such is the case in the story of "Maxwell's Crossing," narrated by the folklorist Joseph P. Goodwin in December 1974. Goodwin graduated from the University of Alabama at Tuscaloosa in the spring of 1974; the legend quest that he describes here took place while he was a student at the University of Alabama.

Maxwell's Crossing

The Maxwell's Crossing story is actually a ghost story which I found out about while working on a place-name study of Tuscaloosa County, Alabama.

I found out more about it late one night when several of us went out
there. There were six or seven other guys my age, and one girl, same age,
in a pick-up truck.

Legend has it that the family had a black man (perhaps a slave) working for them. He was seven feet tall. When young people would come
out to the Maxwell's Crossing area, he would chase them away. The family finally moved from the plantation, but the black man stayed there. He
continued to chase the people off when they would come out there. Then
he began killing them and driving their cars into the river. He was finally
arrested and hung in the silo on the plantation (the silo is still standing).
He supposedly still roams the area.

The road (a dirt road) that goes there is thirteen miles long, and has
thirteen wooden bridges on it. The trees overhang the road so that it looks
like a tunnel, and it is always foggy. When anyone goes out there, they are
supposed to tell someone where they are going, so that if they aren't back
in a reasonable length of time, someone can come looking for them.

You aren't supposed to stop while you're there, because the black man
will be able to get in the car or slit the tires or somesuch. At the crossing
itself, one can see a light, either red or green. (It's actually a signal light
on the railroad track, and can only be seen from one spot, since the track
curves). If the light is green, all is well; however, if it is red, the persons
seeing it are never supposed to come away from Maxwell's Crossing alive.
Fortunately, it was green the night we went.

This story asks unanswerable questions. Who is the black man, and why
does he pursue young visitors so ruthlessly? Goodwin says that the man
worked for a family on their plantation, where he was "perhaps a slave." We
can assume that the family members were white and that the black man relied
on them for financial support, so whether or not he was a slave, his relationship to the family made him their dependent. When the family moved away,
he stayed on the plantation, chasing away young (and presumably white) visitors who wanted to find him. His determination to get rid of the visitors and
their insistence upon finding him suggest that the crux of this legend quest is
young people's need to confront racial tensions head-on. Locating the black
man is not easy, and a successful search may have horrifying consequences—
but the search itself is exciting and suspenseful.

All we know about the black man's appearance is his height. Unusually tall
and extremely hostile, he resembles Candyman, the murderous, hook-handed

killer in the movie by that same name (1992). In *Candyman*, based on a story by Clive Barker (1985), a legend explains why the vengeful spirit wants to kill people: when a young black artist fell in love with a white woman, her family punished him by cutting off his hand and dooming him to a slow, painful death. No such backstory explains the killer's anger in "Maxwell's Crossing," but the extremity of his reaction to visitors—killing them, then driving their cars into the river—makes it clear that he angrily seeks revenge. In the absence of more specific information, we can connect his vengefulness with slavery. After white law enforcement officials hang him from the silo on his home plantation, he has another reason for revenge. Without a trial and without due process of law, he has been lynched, not justly punished.

Students who want to find this vengeful ghost must look for a series of signs steeped in folk tradition. Supposedly, the dirt road to Maxwell's Crossing is exactly thirteen miles long, with thirteen wooden bridges. Highlighting the unlucky number thirteen heightens suspense, as does description of the trees over the road; the road "looks like a tunnel, and it is always foggy." Shady lanes shrouded in fog are notorious for inexplicable disappearances; some folk legends speak of horses, buggies, and cars being swallowed up on such pathways. However, the most important sign of danger is the signal light at the crossing itself. If the light is green, the questers will get away safely; if it is red, they may die a terrible death. Both red and green have symbolic and otherworldly meaning.[1] Visitors to Maxwell's Crossing who see a green light can breathe a sigh of relief after their visit to this dangerous location, which lets them take—and then quickly reject—the role of an intruder who deserves punishment for racial injustice.

Another story from Joseph P. Goodwin, also told in December 1974, presents a different kind of quest: a search for a scene from the past with little fear of dangerous consequences. Its setting, the University of Alabama's Smith Hall, seems calm and safe compared to the fog-shrouded forest surrounding Maxwell's Crossing.

Dr. Smith's Ghost

Smith Hall, which is the Alabama Museum of Natural History, is located on the University campus. Several people have told me about this, including Debbie H., whose father is chairman of the geology department, and who has his office in Smith Hall. I have been there two or three times about two o'clock in the morning, but I never met the ghost.

The only experience we had there (two other guys and two girls, all about my age) was when we gave up and had just gotten outside. Three other guys who came while we were there (we didn't know them) came running out, claiming they had heard him. We all went back in, got very quiet, and suddenly there was a noise, sort of like a piece of plaster falling from the ceiling (which was two floors above us, the next floor being a balcony).

Needless to say, we ran out as quickly as we could, and if there was anyone else in the building, they were probably really frightened when they heard us running down those wooden stairs. The next time we went, it was an entirely uneventful visit.

As the story goes, Dr. Smith still visits the building where he taught classes in the 1920s. You can hear him walking down the aisles and through the halls, tapping his yardstick or pointer as he walks. You can hear the students rustling through their notebooks, and you can hear them talking as they change classes. You can also hear what sounds like a group of elementary school students touring the museum. Although you can tell that these are people talking, you can't make out the words.

This story vividly describes college students' repeated efforts to come face-to-face with ghosts from a previous era. At the story's beginning, it is not clear that a legend quest is taking place. Goodwin mentions that he was in Smith Hall early in the morning several times, but he does not say why. Later, when he says that he and his friends "gave up" and went back outside, we realize that their objective was to find Dr. Smith's ghost.

This ghost's name reminds students that the halls where they attend classes have intriguing histories. Walking the corridors of the hall whose name matches his own, Dr. Smith represents past faculty members who contributed to the university's development. He serves as a foundational ghost who fosters pride in the university's past.

Both Dr. Smith and the other ghosts that accompany him make their presence known through startling sounds. When Goodwin and his friends search for the ghost, they hear "a noise, sort of like a piece of plaster falling from the ceiling." Sudden noises of this kind serve as omens of death in folklore of the southern United States. The *Frank C. Brown Collection of North Carolina Folklore* indicates that plaster falling in a room is "a sure sign of death to some member of the family"; more specifically, "If the plastering in a college building falls, someone intimately connected with the college will die"

(Hand 1964: 26). These University of Alabama students look for a ghost, not evidence of deaths to come, but their interpretation of the sound of falling plaster neatly fits existing folk belief. It also fits the pattern of risk-taking that characterizes legend quests. If you come too close to a ghost, you may risk becoming a ghost yourself.

Goodwin explains that the sound of Dr. Smith walking, "tapping his yard-stick or pointer as he walks," is just one of several spectral phenomena that happen during nocturnal visits to Smith Hall. Other sounds include students "rustling through their notebooks" and children touring the museum, speaking in low, unintelligible voices. Dr. Smith's noisy presence seems to make it possible for other sounds of the 1920s to break into the present. Child ghosts, often mentioned by college students, play an important role here. Subdued and innocent, barely audible, the children add an eerie sense of liveliness to the scene. College students who have heard any of these sounds can take pride in completing a successful legend quest—but they will probably not want to stay in the building very long afterward.

Legend Cycles

The first few days of freshman year offer entering students one of their best chances to learn about campus ghost stories. When they listen to upperclass-men and faculty members speak at orientation, freshmen become familiar with legend cycles that form part of their institution's identity. Two examples of institutionally supported legend cycles are the stories of the Black Lady at Henderson State University and Sara at Mansfield University, discussed in chapter 5. At both of those universities, many students have visited the sites associated with the ghost: the Black Lady's cliff and Sara's stairwell. Accounts of such exciting experiences enrich old legend cycles, refreshing their value for new students.

Students are not the only members of a campus community who visit haunted sites on campus; sometimes faculty and staff members do too. Their participation in the development of campus traditions makes a strong impression on students. A few folklorists have taken an interest in faculty and staff members' nurturance of legend cycles. One especially interesting article is Helen Gilbert's study of the legend of the drowned monk at Saint John's University and Abbey in Collegeville, Minnesota (1975). As Gilbert explains, the death of a young workman engaged in construction of the Abbey's church in the late 1800s—on record as a historical fact—drew the interest of a professor, Father Hilary, who first told his version of the workman's story in 1966. Father Hilary told students that a monk working on a building project drowned after his abbot told him to take a leaky boat to Chapel Island. The monk's mother demanded compensation for the loss of her son, but the abbot refused. When the church's dedication took place, the mother flung herself down on the floor, vowing that she would return. Later that same day, she perished in a horse-and-buggy accident. One year later, when the monks were celebrating the anniversary of the church's dedication, wet tracks moved up the center aisle to the abbot's throne.

Father Hilary's legend of the dead construction worker creates a dramatic scenario of injustice and retribution, with the shocking appearance of a ghost at the end. To some extent, this narrative reminds the listener of the Old English epic *Beowulf*. To avenge the death of her son Grendel, Grendel's mother rises from the depths of her lake to kill everyone who was responsible for his death. Helen Gilbert explains that the threatened return of the monk and his mother forms the stable core of the Saint John's legend cycle (1975: 75). Often told at freshman orientation, this set of stories has given new students an initiation into the "community of believers" (76).

Father Stephen Hess, a Saint John's University alumnus who joined the faculty and the brotherhood at his home institution, knew the stories of the drowned monk and his mother very well.[2] In December 1974, shortly before the publication of Helen Gilbert's study, he explained that he and other faculty members at Saint John's had repeatedly warned students not to go out to Chapel Island, where students enjoyed drinking and smoking marijuana. Sometimes he put his warning in the form of a story, as follows.

The Ghost of the Brother

Two students were out canoeing on Lake Sagatagan late one night. It was a dark night and the air was very still. As they were canoeing near Chapel Island, they suddenly encountered the sound of large splashes of water close to the canoe. They heard no one, just the splashes, which simply terrified them. They knew that the objects thrown in were very large and that the person throwing them was a very strong and powerful individual, for the distance from nearest land was considerable. Strangely (and luckily), however, they were never hit. They paddled from the area and returned safely to tell their story. They and others immediately recognized it must have been the ghost of the brother out on Chapel Island.

Father Stephen's story describes a frightening trip to Chapel Island that would, presumably, keep students from making such expeditions themselves. Who would want to encounter a "very strong and powerful" ghost that paddles quietly across the lake, throwing large objects (possibly students' bodies) into the water? As described in this story, the dead monk seems dangerous, almost demonic. It is not difficult to understand why students might want to test their courage by crossing the lake, listening closely for sounds of spectral splashing.

Father Stephen himself could not resist the temptation to look for the dead brother's ghost. One night, in the company of a friend, he undertook his own legend quest, as a curious student would do. His description follows.

Charged with Possibility

I can only remember once going out of my way for a scary experience. A friend and I decided one nice spring evening to go on his motorcycle to Chapel Island. We specifically chose to go around midnight so that we might run into the ghost of the old brother. This happened about four years ago and though it was kind of a joke to us, I remember being somewhat excited and scared that we would actually see or experience something. We arrived at just about midnight. The air was charged with possibility. The situation was so scary that we decided not to stick around but leave before anything could happen. We saw nothing and later attributed the failure to the presence and noisiness of the motorcycle.

In this intriguing story, Father Stephen eloquently expresses what many legend questers have felt: "The air was charged with possibility." Frightened and expectant, he and his friend decide to clear out before anything happens. Note that he has done just what he warned students not to do: take a trip to the island to find the ghost. As both a faculty member and an alumnus of the university, he slips into the role of questing student quite easily. His eagerness to investigate the haunted site shows that he takes the possibility very seriously. As a member of what Helen Gilbert calls the "community of believers," he needs to enter the legend cycle's web of enchantment. He does not, however, want to go in too far. Feeling a sense of uncanny possibilities has confirmed his belief in the ghost and strengthened his role as a protector of students.

Haunted Houses

As legend scholars have shown, one of the most frequent inspirers of a "good scare" is a house associated with death. Sylvia Grider's essay "The Haunted House in Literature, Popular Culture, and Tradition" (1999) persuasively demonstrates how consistently the Gothic novel, the oral ghost story, and various forms of American popular culture have portrayed a certain kind of house as a source of supernatural danger. The haunted house, "the ugly stepsister of the enchanted castle" (193), usually includes such features as a "gambrel roof, turrets or towers, and broken or boarded-up windows with 'spooky' inhabitants peeking out" (181). Traditionally, it stands on a hilltop or in another isolated location.

One notorious haunted house is the Massapequa House on Long Island. Variously known as the Massapequa Hell House and the Massapequa Satan House, this building draws carloads of college and high school students, especially around Halloween. Alison, a senior at the University of Buffalo, told this story in March 2004.

Massapequa House

If you live in Long Island, you've definitely heard of the Massapequa House . . . it's right off the Southern State Parkway. The best part is that this eerie home stands right in the middle of a residential neighborhood. Supposedly the place is haunted, and it definitely looks that way. The house is extremely old, and appears like a cemetery due to the towering metal fence that surrounds the entire house. There are drapes the color of blood in every window, and a hearse in the driveway.

I don't know the story of what went on inside the house; but I do know that when you park your car outside, candles are placed in the windows. AND . . . the number of candles lit in the windows corresponds to the *number of people in your car.*

A few summers ago, my friends and I took a ride out to the house one night. When we got out of the car to take a closer look, we saw a small flickering light appear in one of the windows. At this point, we all jumped back in the car as fast as we could, and got the hell out of there!!!!!!!!!!!!!!!!!!!

What happens in Alison's story might be described as a drive-by legend quest. Leaving the comfort and safety of their car for only a moment, these

A candle in a window suggests danger or death.
Photograph by Geoffrey Gould.

college students wait to see how many candles will appear in a certain window. They are prepared to drive away quickly, since they know they may be in danger if they see a number of candles that matches the number of people in their car. A glimpse of one flickering light is enough to make them get "the hell out" of the Massapequa Hell House's vicinity. Because danger seems imminent but avoidable, the quest succeeds.

Sometimes, however, proximity to the house is enough to scare young questers away. Alison's story shows how strongly the Massapequa House evokes images of death: with drapes "the color of blood" and "a hearse in the driveway," the place "appears like a cemetery." Clearly, confrontation with death motivates this visit, which lets students take the role of potential victims or corpses. In contemporary American culture, we tend to separate death from everyday life. Jessica Mitford's *The American Way of Death Revisited* notes that ever since the late nineteenth century, families have tended to let specialists care for their deceased loved ones (1998: 148–49). Young people who have not learned much about death may need to seek it out within the framework of a haunted house. The Massapequa House, like the spooky edifice on a hilltop in the movie *Edward Scissorhands* (1990), is an architectural monstrosity that represents death in the midst of everyday life.

Why do candles in a window work so well as symbols of death and danger? At funerals, candles often illuminate the rooms where solemn burial services take place. Folk tradition tells us that a burning candle shows whether we are safe or in danger (Motifs E765.1.1, "Life bound up with candle" and D2061.2.2.6, "Candle burned causes victim to waste away"). The *Frank C. Brown Collection of North Carolina Folklore* also connects candles with mortality: "To see a coffin in the candle betokens death" (Hand 1964: 44). Matching the number of candles to the number of people in a car brings a dead metaphor to life: seeing such a sight, students know that their number is up. If they don't drive away quickly, their own deaths may follow.

Unlike the Massapequa House, which is located in the middle of a city, another haunted house fourteen miles southeast of Rexburg, Idaho, once stood alone at the edge of a canyon. In 1982 its owner burned it down, fearing that young people sneaking in to experience supernatural events might get hurt. Before that happened, Ricks College student Todd Wightman drove to the house with his friend Doug. He told this long, suspenseful story in the winter of 1984.[3]

Huge Yellow Eyes

On a July evening of 1981, my friend Doug and I were fishing below the broken Teton Dam. We decided on the spur of the moment to go find out about the Haunted House that many people had talked about. So, after taking our fish home, we set out in my dad's pick-up truck to see what this place was all about. Neither one of us had been there before, so my sister Jodi gave us directions to get there. It was after midnight when we arrived at the farmer's field that we needed to cross to get to the canyon where the house was located.

There were two dirt roads that crossed the potato (spud) field that supposedly led to the house. We weren't sure which one to take, but the funny thing was we both knew by a very evil feeling that we had chosen the right one. I had feelings of turning back, but we went on in, winding down the bumpy road until we reached the bottom of the small canyon or gully where the house is located. We parked the truck and then started toward the trees where the house was hidden. The ridiculous thing about this night was the full moon. We just laughed it off and continued down a small grassy road that a vehicle would barely pass.

As we were walking past the thick trees (where we later found the house to be), I heard something move in the trees. I didn't say anything to Doug because I didn't want him to think I was hearing things. Finally Doug stopped and said, "Did you hear that?" I told him I had. But we continued on, not wanting to be pansies. I became very nervous because the same sound kept occurring as if something was stalking us in the trees. Each time we would stop, it would stop.

We only had one flashlight, and Doug had it. He shined it into the trees but they were just too thick to see anything. We passed the trees and came upon a large clearing or meadow and the moving sound stopped. Whatever it was planned to stay in the trees and not come out. Doug began to shine the light about the area and suddenly the light hit on what I assumed to be trailer reflectors because they were spread so far apart. Instantaneously I discovered my perception to be incorrect because the reflectors started moving in unison. It was obvious to me that it was a large head with an eye span [of a size] that I had never seen [before].

In the few seconds we were watching we tried to see more of what it was. I figured later that it was about 30 yards away. All that I could see was a large black outlined figure with huge yellow eyes. Suddenly it started moving with large sounding thuds and Doug exclaimed, "What the heck!" and we started running for the truck. I was in the lead until I stepped into a hole and fell down right in front of the thick trees. Doug ran past me and got into the truck and locked the doors. Thank goodness I had forgotten about the stalking thing in the trees or else I would have really freaked out. I got up and ran for the truck, Doug unlocked the door (like a good friend would), and I climbed in.

The first thing Doug said to me was, "Did you see the eye span on that thing?" I said, "What could it be? The eyes had to be at least two or three feet apart!" Doug agreed. We then decided to drive down the small grassy road past the trees and into the meadow. Upon reaching the meadow I put my lights on high beam and the thing was gone. So I turned the truck around and as we passed the trees the truck lights and the lights on the dashboard controls began to fade off and on. Then the blue light indicating high beam on the dashboard went out. After this the needle to the gas gauge spun around two or three times and broke.

By this time we were on our way out of the gully. When we reached the main road everything was back to normal except the gas gauge. It ended up being replaced because it was completely busted. After such an experience one would wonder why Doug and I went back several times. I guess we were curious to really find out [more about] what we had seen and experienced.

Believe me, we tried every logical approach to what had happened. I have checked about every sporting good store to compare the eye span between mounted moose heads and the head we saw that night. But nothing is as large or has the eye span that would be common to that area (such as an elephant). Whether or not the place is haunted is still a question in my mind. All I know is that there is a very strong evil feeling that I have never experienced anywhere [else] before. Maybe it is the imagination or just natural things occurring in an eerie setting, but there are just too many things that have happened to pass off as incidental.

This chilling story is one of ten narratives about the haunted house near Rexburg that Todd Wightman collected. All ten of the young narrators belong to the Church of Latter-day Saints. Because they share a strong faith, the narrators—all of whom are in their early twenties—connect their quest to religious issues. Their stories reflect a common interest in investigating an "evil feeling" that emanates from the house. Is the house truly haunted by an evil spirit? Each narrator answers that question in his or her own way.

Todd's story offers so many details that we feel pulled along on a frightening journey. The closer we get to the house, the more we feel an intense sense of trepidation—but we never actually get to the house. Like the cottage of the witch in the folktale "Hansel and Gretel" (AT 327A), this house stands in a wild, dangerous area where supernatural events can happen. The first sign of an evil presence is the sound of something moving in the trees: a stalker of some sort. Soon perception shifts from sound to sight. Todd and Doug think they see two trailer reflectors, spread far apart, but soon realize that these are eyes on a gargantuan head. Both young men see "a large black outlined figure with huge yellow eyes." Is this figure a wild animal or a demon? Its colors suggest demonic associations. In the popular film *Rosemary's Baby* (1968), the baby's yellow eyes prove that he is Satan's son, and all the witches wear black clothes. Color symbolism shows that whatever lurks near the haunted house's woods is both evil and dangerous.

When Todd and Doug jump back into their truck, its lights go out and its gas gauge breaks. The yellow eyes glow as the truck's lights fade, showing dominance of evil over mechanical contraptions. With desperate urgency, Todd and Doug race away. Once they get home, the last stage of their legend quest begins. No longer under an immediate threat, both young men want to learn what was pursuing them. Although they try "every logical approach to what had happened," no rational explanation makes sense. No mounted moose heads in sporting goods stores come close to the size of the eyes that they saw in the woods. Like the car's lights and gas gauge, reason has broken down, but sensory evidence has proven the presence of evil.

Graveyards

While haunted houses give students the chance to confront images of evil and death, graveyards let them stand among the remains of those who have died. Quite a few college campuses have their own graveyards; other campuses stand near municipal or church cemeteries. College students have paid many visits to these realms of the dead, hoping to find evidence of ghostly presences.

This story about an on-campus graveyard came from Brandon, a nineteen-year-old freshman at Rowan University in Glassboro, New Jersey, in April 2005.[4]

Glowing Tombstones

It was the spring of 2003 at Rowan and after going to the football game, two of my friends and I met up with some girls and decided to go to the cemetery which was on campus and said to have glowing tombstones. My friends and I had already seen the glowing tombstones. This was caused by a red neon light that reflected off of the headstones. Since I had already seen the tombstones a bunch of times before, I thought it would be fun to take the girls there.

We parked at the usual spot, because it was the only angle from which the stones glowed, and we got out. I dared my friend Don to hop the fence, knowing he had never been frightened of anything in his life. He didn't say one word in reply. I look over at him only to find him staring into the cemetery, looking as pale as ever.

I turned to see what was drawing his attention and then I saw it: around the tombstone that glowed red stood at least four or five figures in white. Each was so bright that we could almost see features from at least a hundred yards away. The figures stood motionless, showing no movement. Don and I freak out and start sprinting for the truck. The others followed even though they hadn't seen what we had. They said they didn't believe us.

Sometimes I drive by the cemetery, but the tombstones don't glow anymore because they removed the neon light, but I still get nervous driving by it.

The above story shows how campus graveyards serve as settings for social interaction and self-testing. Having seen the tombstones "a bunch of times before," Brandon decides that it would be fun to go there with his friends after a football game. This is a classic dating scenario, in which male students try to scare their female companions by showing them something spooky. Unexpectedly, "four or five figures in white" offer visual evidence that the graveyard actually is haunted. Brandon and his friends rush back to their truck, scared out of their wits.

While this legend has high entertainment value, it also warns students to show respect for the dead. Casually using their campus's graveyard for late-night trysts with young women, Brandon and his friend discover that the dead may retaliate. Alan Dundes, in his analysis of the medical school legend "The Cadaver Arm," makes the point that legends make students think about the ethics of their playful behavior: "The fact that future doctors use a cadaver arm to pay the toll suggests that they are using the limbs of others, perhaps of victims, to help pay their way in life" (1971: 32). Similarly, "Glowing Tombstones" suggests that students should not choose a graveyard as a location for dates and dares.

The story's focus on red and white reinforces its moral message. In folktales, red signals danger; red may also indicate a supernatural presence (Motifs Z141, "Red as symbolic color," and F178.1, "Red as otherworld color"). White has even stronger connotations of otherworldliness, since it has a connection to ghosts, fairies, mermaids, and other supernatural beings (Motifs D1293.3, "White as magic color"; E422.4.3, "Ghost in white"). In *Lucifer Ascending*, Bill Ellis notes that adolescents' legends of Slaybrook Corner in England in the 1960s emphasized the color red: both "a red light" and "a red ball of fire" (2004: 117). Sue Samuelson's study of adolescents' "White Witch" legends (1979) offers a similar concentration on the color white.

Brandon's story ends with a comment on the tombstones' loss of color and light: "the tombstones don't glow anymore because they removed the neon light." Without this indication of supernatural danger, the graveyard loses some of its allure. However, he says that he still "[gets] nervous driving by it." Since his legend quest demonstrated that ghosts exist, he cannot quickly discard the role of believer.

On- and off-campus graveyards offer opportunities for storytelling about the deaths of people who have died tragically. Some legend quests involve visits to the graves of children that legends identify as murder victims. One case in point is the Beaver family's cemetery, located half a mile south of the town of Esopus, New York. Gravestones from the mid- to late 1800s indicate that some of the children buried there died young. Willie Beaver, for example, died in 1883 at the age of eleven months. Other children who died young have no personal names on their headstones, just the phrase "Child of" followed by the names of their parents. Although such indefinite grave markers were not unusual in the nineteenth century, when child mortality was high, their vagueness makes them ideal for students' legend quests.

Gina, a twenty-one-year-old student at Binghamton University, told the following story in September 1994.

The Beaver Family

Oh, I saw a ghost. I've seen a lot of them, because I'm in touch with the supernatural. This guy I was going out with, we went to this place, Esopus-E-S-O-P-U-S. We went to this place, Esopus, and it's a retreat house for the brothers. You know, the Franciscan Order brothers, like priests, but they're not priests. And we were up there and Dan says, "Oh, I'm gonna show you something really cool." The whole time I'm there I felt really weird. Cause it's this really religious place.

And we go across from where the retreat place is, and there's this little cemetery, and it sounds really stupid—this already sounds too much like a vampire movie or something. The whole cemetery is this family, it's the Beaver family. The parents had like nine kids, and every child they had they killed, they killed all their kids. All their kids are buried there, and they're buried with their kids.

And we were in the cemetery and we walked up the cemetery steps; we counted thirteen steps. It was like a hundred degrees out that day—it was freezing in the cemetery, but the hair on my arms was really clammy and wet. I was so scared. I felt like someone was following me around.

We were standing by one of the graves, and Dan says, "See, between that tree and that grave is one of the youngest Beaver kids. The mother's supposed to pace." And I'm like, "Where?" and I walked through where she paces, and I got all cold, because she must—her spirit must have passed through me.

And when I turned around, all of a sudden, Dan, who had been on the other side of the cemetery, was standing right next to me. And it was so weird—we saw a ghost. We saw her pass by right in front of us. And I was so scared, and then we go to the other end, but I thought Dan was following me, and I turned around. I said, "What?"

And something touched my shoulder; somebody put their hand on my shoulder, I swear to God, and I thought it was him, the person I was with, but he was over there (gestures with arm). He was at the opposite end of the cemetery where I left him, like he'd never walked with me, and the whole time I heard footsteps right next to me and I thought that it was him, but it wasn't him, it was something else, and then we walked down the cemetery stairs and there were only nine steps. Like four steps just disappeared.

From the beginning of Gina's story, we can see that she has an affinity for the supernatural. Having grown up in an Italian American Catholic family, she knows how important it is to believe in saints and angels. She feels the sanctity of a "really religious place" like the Esopus retreat center, where visitors usually show respect for both the living and the dead. However, going on a legend quest puts adventure above respect. Once Gina and her boyfriend Dan enter the Beaver family's graveyard, they eagerly search for the graves of the nine children who were murdered by their parents. Dan's discovery of the youngest child's grave proves that the legend has substance.

When Dan tells Gina that the "mother's supposed to pace," Gina immediately walks through the area where she envisions the mother pacing. Feeling cold, Gina senses that the mother's spirit has passed through her. It is important to recognize that Gina takes the role of the mother/murderer here, walking where the mother's ghost walks and feeling the presence of her spirit. As in many other college ghost stories, a dead metaphor comes to life when Gina goes "through the paces" of the mother's ghost. Why does Gina feel such a need to do this? Because the crime of infanticide seems so shocking and unnatural, she may want to understand the mother better by taking her role. Alternatively, she may just want to find out what will happen next. Other legends, such as the story of Stepp Cemetery in southern Indiana, indicate that it is dangerous to approach the ghost of a mother mourning her baby's death (Clements and Lightfoot 1976). In a quest to investigate unnatural death, participants feel unsafe, far from their usual comfort zone.

In the last part of Gina's story, sensory disorientation suddenly occurs. Dan appears and disappears; the number of steps in the graveyard diminishes from thirteen to nine. This last part of the action resembles what happens in the popular movie *The Blair Witch Project* (1999), in which college students lose track of where they are going and wander around in a circle. Gina's final sentence has such a fluid rhythm that it sounds like stream-of-consciousness writing, with little attention to conventional syntax, and the story ends abruptly: "Like four steps just disappeared." We get the impression that Gina still feels shocked by what happened to her in the cemetery and does not want to keep talking about it any longer.

While legends like "The Beaver Family" tell of women who kill their own children, other legends describe women who die after suffering terrible abuse and injustice, then become horror figures that haunt the living. Many of these women are named Mary. Since Christianity emphasizes the suffering of both Mary, the mother of Christ, and Mary Magdalene, the choice of this name has strong religious connotations. As discussed in chapter 4, preadolescents have summoned horrifying women named Mary in mirrors (see Dundes 2002; Langlois 1978; and Tucker 2005b). "Mary's Grave" sites exist in various parts of the United States; legends about these sites have identified Mary as both a victim of rape and murder and a protector of young women. Linda McCoy Ray's essay "The Legend of Bloody Mary's Grave" (1976) presents a collection of such legends in one part of Indiana; "Long Island Folklore: Mary's Grave" (2005) and other websites have documented Mary's grave locations in New York State, offering good leads to folklorists with an interest in legend research.

The following legend came from Steve, a Binghamton University student, in March 2004.[5]

Mary's Grave

This girl Mary back when Long Island was all farmland, it was very rurally developed and a lot of it was just land. This girl Mary was born into this family; she was born into a farming family in Nessaquogue. When she was born, there were complications with her birth that caused her mother to pass away within a day or two. She was an only child and her father raised her on the farm.

Mary didn't exactly have a good childhood, because her father always blamed her for the death of his wife. So growing up, her father basically used to rape and beat Mary on a daily basis, and puberty rolled around and Mary eventually got pregnant from the raping. But her father, being a devout Christian and believing abortion is murder, her father forced her to have the child.

A couple months later, through the fact that she now had the child to raise and her father still constantly beat her, one night Mary snapped. In the middle of the night around one to two in the morning, she took her baby to the barn-house and in a satanic ritual, she slaughtered all the animals in the barn-house. She then proceeded to take her baby and herself, she climbed up to the storage area on top of the barn, hung her baby from the rafters and then hung herself.

Eventually her father, not knowing where she was, went out to the barnyard and found the gruesome scene, and to save his family and his family's name the embarrassment of what happened, he buried Mary and her baby in an area that is now basically eroding. The area that he buried her in is now Long Beach, Long Island. There, if you go down to a certain area and you start calling Mary's name, you're supposed to start hearing a girl crying and hear a baby crying, and people have actually claimed to see Mary walking along the road carrying her child.

Personally the most fucked up thing that ever happened to me—there is this pond, that is right near this general area where she was supposed to live called Rhododendron Drive, and this area is Creepy as HELL, I went down there one day, with a couple of friends and just to test it we started calling to Mary, and literally before our eyes, this trail of fog around this foggy figure started walking across the lake, and just stopped in the middle of the lake, then came up off the lake about 4–5 feet and just stopped there in mid-air. My friend said he heard someone crying. I was like WHOA we're leavin'.

And this story is true too . . . if you don't believe me you can go to one of the web sites and check it out for yourself.

Steve, this story's narrator, expresses shock about what happened to Mary. The story of her life and death is painful and difficult to tell. Showing how much Mary's story has upset him, Steve says that seeing her ghost is "the most fucked up thing that ever happened" to him. Mary's ghost not only proves the existence of supernatural forces but also drives home the point that such suffering has really happened. Her story may seem fictional, because she belongs to the tradition of *la llorona*, the weeping woman who kills her child;

her misty form after death resembles ghosts of the Victorian era. In legend quests, however, what has seemed fictional can suddenly become real.

Mary, a domestic violence victim who kills herself and her child, inspires both pity and horror. A doomed sufferer, Mary represents millions of women who have undergone similar torment. As Elaine J. Lawless explains in her book *Women Escaping Violence* (2001), evidence of domestic violence suggests that "the figures are probably not reflective of even *one-tenth* of the number of women who are actually beaten, abused, and violated, but who never report it" (42). Because women hesitate to speak about such devastating, life-threatening situations, narrative can serve as an important "herstory" (13). Lawless includes the life stories of four women—Sherry, Margaret, Teresa, and Cathy—in her book. Legends about "Mary's Grave" express the horror felt by all women who have been trapped by domestic violence and sexual abuse. Less personal than the stories in Lawless's book, yet eerily reflective of them all, Mary's story demands attention.

Because the legend of Mary's grave is so disturbing, it interrupts and redefines people's concentration on their everyday life. As Jeffrey Andrew Weinstock suggests, a ghost "interrupts the presentness of the present" with stories that insist upon reassessment of the past (2004: 5). While young visitors to Mary's grave seek excitement and danger, they also discover that there is more to women's history than official records reveal.

Another legend complex about a suffering woman focuses on the sadness of losing a husband and children. Students at Utah State University have narrated various versions of the legend of the "Weeping Widow," whose statue stands in Logan Cemetery next to their campus. This text came from Jalyn Rinderknecht, a Utah State University freshman, in January 1987.[6]

"Cry, Lady, Cry"

It's been said for years that if you go up to see the Weeping Widow, this is what you're supposed to do to get her to cry. Shine your car lights on her and then run around her chanting cry, lady, cry.

Well, one night we did that exact process and tears began to run down her face. It really looked as though she were crying.

Many Utah State University freshmen have visited the locally famous "Weeping Widow" statue. Jalyn's story shows us how students approached the statue in the late 1980s. Following older students' advice, they shone their car's headlights at the statue, then ran around the statue in a circle, chanting, "Cry, lady, cry." If she looked like she was crying, the legend quest succeeded. A story like this one would, of course, encourage further visits to the cemetery.

Weeping statues are well known in Europe, especially in Germany and Switzerland (Motif D1625). Paintings of the Virgin Mary have also been seen weeping (Motif K1972.2). Many such weeping works of art have a connection to legends about heart-breaking situations. Although the legend of the Weeping Widow of Logan Cemetery has varied according to its teller, usually the reason for the statue's tears is the tragic loss of her children.

College students visiting the Logan Cemetery late at night have one major goal: to make the legend of the Weeping Widow come true. If they make the statue weep by chanting "Cry, lady, cry," they prove that they have the power to bring an inanimate object to life. Like the young witches and wizards at Harry Potter's Hogwarts Academy (Rowling 1997), they take important roles in an exciting scenario. Through legend quests like this one, students transform a quiet cemetery into a place of power and enchantment.

Films and Video Cameras

By watching horror movies and by making movies of their own, students enrich their perceptions of legend quests. Some horror movies, such as Shirley Jackson's *The Haunting* (1999) and Stephen King's *Rose Red* (2002), involve exploration of a spooky place. *The Blair Witch Project* (1999) not only shows college students venturing into a haunted domain in Burkittsville, Maryland, but also suggests that their adventure really happened. Such filmed enactments of legend quests increase students' expectations. In his essay "Folklore and Film: Some Thoughts on Baughman Z500–599" (1996), Larry Danielson notes that horror movies intensify traditional plots and motifs. Besides giving new shock value to old concepts, horror films suggest patterns for investigations of places that have become famous locally through legend-telling. The increasing availability of video and digital technology has made it easy for students to make their own recordings, which help to provide visual evidence of whether or not something astonishing has actually taken place.

Certain horror films have exerted an especially powerful influence. In *Legend and Belief*, Linda Dégh makes the point that *The Exorcist* (1974), along with several other films, "opened a new chapter in perennial theological and scientific debates concerning the devil and exorcism" (2001: 249). On college campuses, this debate was reflected in students' stories. Shortly after *The Exorcist* opened, college students told terrifying legends about successful and unsuccessful exorcisms on their own campuses. At Mount Saint Mary's College in Emmitsburg, Maryland, for example, the folklorist Marie Campbell collected legends about black masses, shredded seminarians, and dramatic exorcisms.[7]

The Internet Movie Database (http://imdb.com) offers a long list of facts and anecdotes about *The Exorcist*, including some that help to explain college students' fascination with the movie. Filmed on the campuses of both Georgetown University and Fordham University, *The Exorcist* attracted the attention of students living nearby. During the filming of the scene where a stuntman fell down seventy-five steps at the end of M Street, students at Georgetown University in Washington, D.C., charged people five dollars each to watch the action from their rooftops. Several scenes were filmed at Fordham University's freshman residence hall, Hughes Hall. Father William O'Malley, a priest and a member of Fordham's faculty, played the role of Father Dyer in the film. For many years, Father O'Malley has told students about his experiences as an actor in *The Exorcist* while showing the students the movie on the same floor of the building where it was filmed.

Besides its connections to student life on two campuses, *The Exorcist* has had a certain mystique because of legends about deaths of its cast and crew. Supposedly nine people died while the film was in production, and a mysterious fire ruined the set during a weekend. Two actors, Jack MacGowran and Vasiliki Maliaros, died before the film came out. Since Jack MacGowran played the role of Burke Dennings, who fell down the steps on M Street "with his head turned completely around, facing backwards," both the film and this tragic death gave people the impression that the steps were dangerous. It is not surprising that these steps have become a legend quest destination for Georgetown University students.

George, a freshman at Georgetown University, told the following story in April 2005.

The Exorcist Stairs

OK, well when I first came to Gtown, everyone kept telling me about "the exorcist stairs" and how unbelievable they were and that I should check them out. So one day I ventured out with some of my friends to see what all the hype was about. So we walked along M Street, right before it meets Key Bridge until we reached the infamous gas station. At the far end of the gas station was a HUGE stone black wall that went as high as we could see and all the way in the right corner was a dark and mysterious alleyway.

We walked up to it and all we saw were stairs, really scary, all black cement, and it was nighttime, so it was especially dark. I've never seen the movie *The Exorcist* before, but all my friends who had seen it said those were the stairs from one of the scenes. They all seemed scared when they saw them because they were exactly from the movie, and when I said we should climb them they got really scared.

I kept asking about them and I found out that most of the movie was filmed on campus at Georgetown. At the top of the stairs there's a house that was also used for the movie, and an empty abandoned lot that everyone thinks is haunted. I also found out that the priest who the movie was based on, the real guy who actually performed the exorcist, was a priest and professor at Georgetown.

People must really believe that house is haunted, because it's right off campus and is a lucrative spot to build new dorms. There's always construction or some kind of activity going on there, but nothing seems to ever get accomplished. It's an abandoned lot on an otherwise overcrowded and really busy campus. It's strange. I don't think the stairs themselves are haunted, but they are probably the creepiest things on this campus.

Lots of people I know use those stairs when they go jogging, because they get a good workout . . . but I try to avoid those stairs, they're just plain old creepy. I get this weird feeling every time I walk up or down them.

George's story shows that the "Exorcist Stairs" function as a landmark for initiation of new students at Georgetown. Older students urge freshmen to visit the steps, saying that the steps are "unbelievable": marvelous, worth investigating. Although the steps are in the middle of a fast-moving city, not isolated or hard to find, they serve as the object of a legend quest closely related to shocking events on film and in reality.

George describes his journey with his friends along M Street, up to one end of "the infamous gas station." Georgetown students know that this is the Exxon station at the bottom of the "Exorcist Stairs," where crimes have taken place: for example, two men were shot there in February 1999. To the side of the gas station, "a HUGE stone black wall" and "a dark and mysterious alley-way" create a sense of menace. Darkness, a high black wall, and memories of past crimes keep students on edge, reminding them that danger may strike unexpectedly.

It is interesting to note that George, who has *not* watched *The Exorcist*, is the one who urges the group of friends to climb the stairs. While his friends feel frightened about the stairs being "exactly from the movie," George can take the role of leader without troubling memories. To him, the stairs seem exciting because of their connection to both a well known horror movie and his university's campus. George enjoys learning that "a priest and professor at Georgetown" played the part of Father Merrin, the exorcist in the movie. This is, however, untrue; Max von Sydow, the son of folklorist Carl Wilhelm von Sydow, plays the part of Father Merrin. The fact that a Fordham profes-sor acted in the movie makes it seem plausible that a Georgetown professor participated too—and few students will check the movie's cast, more than thirty years after its production.

Although we might expect George to go into detail about his friends' climb up the stairs, he says nothing about that, so we can assume that the climb was uneventful. He seems more interested in the futility of construc-tion on an abandoned lot, which creates a sense of supernatural blight. As in many other campus ghost stories, the metaphor of construction fits the initia-tory situation in which new students live and work. As they build new lives for themselves away from home, they may find meaning in legends about the construction of their campus or its environs. But on this construction site, "nothing seems to ever get accomplished." Perhaps stories about the filming of *The Exorcist* have made the construction workers too nervous to work.

Ultimately, however, this story is not so much about construction as it is about getting a "weird feeling" on each visit to a landmark that brings a movie to life. Students who have already been scared and shocked by *The Exorcist* cannot forget its vivid visual imagery; even those who have never seen the movie find its presence to be unforgettable. On a staircase where a movie character died, close to a gas station where people suffered assault and injury, painful incidents from real life merge with frightening suggestions of supernatural invasion. Through the intensity of film, a run-down staircase near a vacant lot becomes an exciting destination for a legend quest that tests students' ability to handle fear.

While students enjoy visiting sites immortalized by horror movies, they like to make movies of their own even more. Local landmarks offer good potential for movie-making, especially if they are in secluded locations. One such place that has fascinated both high school and college students is Briarcliff Lodge in the Hudson Valley. Built in 1902, Briarcliff was known as King's College from 1955 to 1994. John, a Binghamton University freshman, told this story in October 2004, just before Halloween.

Briarcliff

Years and years ago a lodge was built in Briarcliff. The lodge did great business when it first opened. Many people stayed there, as its location was in the middle of a high traffic area. However, after a couple years strange occurrences started to happen there. It became a very popular place for suicides, murders and vanishings. Death loomed over the lodge and it was soon closed and abandoned for having this bad reputation.

Some years later Kings College was built over the old foundation of this lodge. Just like the lodge the college was successful in its early years. Many students attended the school and enjoyed their experiences there. Yet, after some time, strange occurrences started to happen at the school as well. Numerous amounts of students began to commit suicide. People actually traveled there specifically to commit suicide from other colleges. Murders became more frequent, as did kidnappings and vanishings. Soon, due to this reputation, the college was forced to close. This happened many years ago, and the college is now a ghost town.

My friends and I decided it would be a fun time to go to the abandoned college and make a video of the trip. Three friends and I drove to the college at night and entered the old, crumpled main building. The building was in fact decaying, as it consisted of rubble, rocks, and debris.

Upon entering the building we heard strange noises that faded, grew louder, and then faded again. As the four of us walked into the main building we heard the footsteps of about twenty people walking. Things were clattering down the halls and strange noises were heard from the high windows of the buildings. We took the time to zoom up to each window to look inside with our flashlights.

We didn't realize this at the time, but by inspecting the video we realized that in one of the windows where noises were coming from you can distinctly see a face lean into the window and then lean out again. It is a clear image of a human face. However, we didn't see this image at the time, so we continued to explore the building.

Upon entering the stairwell to go up, the footsteps came back, as well as faint sounds of people whispering and murmurs. The video camera had full battery and was in perfectly good condition, yet it mysteriously turned off during this time. The camera gave no indication that it stopped recording, and my friends and I thought that it was in fact still recording. Only when reviewing the tape did we realize that it had shut off by itself for no reason. We wandered the house for 15 more minutes that the camera did not record. Everything on the camera said it was still recording, yet the film was blank. The noises kept coming closer and then going far away again, but we were never able to discover what was making the noise. We left the college confused and scared.

One interesting feature of this story is its generalization of the events that made Briarcliff a spooky place. Although John mentions a number of deaths, including suicides, murders, and disappearances, none of these seem vivid or clear. "Death loomed over the lodge" sounds like a vague threat from a piece of pulp fiction. There are, however, two good reasons why John gives no specific details. Like the Massapequa House, Briarcliff is a haunted mansion, so deaths must have occurred there. And this is a story about an elaborate legend quest, so what happened in the past seems less meaningful than what will happen to the intrepid visitors.

Why do John and his three friends want to enter the "old, crumpled main building" of Briarcliff? Their main goal is to make a video that they can share with others. TV shows like *Fear Factor* have encouraged young people to videotape their own exploits, proving their courage in tough situations. As John and his friends enter the main building, they watch their camera carefully to make sure that it will produce a good record of their adventure.

The videocamera, however, has a mind of its own. Although it is in perfectly good condition, it mysteriously turns itself off, giving "no indication that it stopped recording." John says there is "no reason" why the videocamera would do such a thing; the solution to this conundrum must be supernatural, not rational. After the legend quest has ended, the students see that their videocamera has recorded a face leaning in and out of the window through which they heard noises. Although they thought they were aware of what was happening, their recording machine saw more than they did. This contrast between human perception and mechanical capabilities unnerves the students. Nonetheless, their quest has succeeded. They have escaped from Briarcliff unharmed, carrying a video that offers proof of their bravery in confronting supernatural activity.

Whether or not they use advanced technology, college students learn important lessons from legend quests. They learn about supernatural presences that seem real and past injustices that seem almost unbearably painful, as well as deaths that impinge on everyday life. As they talk about what happened, they remember the intensity of their emotions during confrontations with the supernatural. Like the hero of "The Youth Who Wanted to Learn What Fear Is," they come to terms with their fears and move on.

While learning valuable lessons, students enjoy spending time in the enchanted realm of their college campus and its environs; they also enjoy telling stories about their discoveries. Cryptic, mysterious, and compelling, these stories have high entertainment value. Last year my student Naomi, a sophomore, wrote, "I enjoy hearing ghost stories because they are thrilling and usually keep me on the edge of my seat. Certainty is not *always* satisfying."[8] Naomi speaks for many of us who have studied supernatural experiences. We search for answers, but the search itself is what matters most.

NOTES

Chapter One. Campus Ghostlore

1. This request appeared on a national housing listserv on November 13, 2000.

2. My article "Ghosts in Mirrors: Reflections of the Self," published in the *Journal of American Folklore* in 2005, includes some of the legends that I collected from students in Sullivan Hall (pseudonym). Several of these legends appear in chapter 4.

3. In addition to the work of Alan Dundes, an essay by Michael P. Carroll (1992) offers a thought-provoking psychoanalytic approach to college legends.

4. I have not identified the ethnicity of all of the legend-tellers in this book, as most of the texts that I obtained from archives did not include ethnic data. When available information about a teller's ethnicity has a bearing on the story's traditionality, I have identified the teller's ethnic group.

5. Two excellent sources of Asian ghostlore are *Ghosts and the Japanese* (1994), by Michiko Iwasaka and Barre Toelken, and *The Woman Warrior*, by Maxine Hong Kingston (1976).

6. Authors of early collections and analyses of adolescent folklore include Joanne Parochetti (1965), Daniel Barnes (1966), Linda Dégh (1968a, 1968b, 1969a, 1969b), and others.

7. Paul Lee, a student at Binghamton University, collected this story in November 2004.

8. Berkeley students have told legends about Pedro since the 1940s. For analysis of Pedro stories, see Rosalie Hankey (1944) and Alan Dundes (1968).

9. Emory University's "Traditions and Rituals" website explains that Dooley was first mentioned in an article titled "Reflections of the Skeleton" in Emory's literary journal, *The Phoenix*, in October 1899. He made his first appearance at "Dooley's Frolics" in 1941 (Hauck 2005). Although the author of this website expresses concern about Dooley's vitality and involvement in campus life, there seems to be no problem now. In the early summer of 2006, Lord James W. Dooley had 1,937 friends listed on Facebook. I am proud to be one of those friends myself. In the spring of 2006, one of the students in my introductory folklore class followed Dooley's example by dressing up in a skeleton costume and running into our classroom with a large squirt gun, spraying the front of the room. The other students and I were delighted by this display of campus spirit.

10. Sweet Briar's website, "Ghosts of Sweet Briar College" (2005), includes stories of encounters with Daisy and her mother told by students, alumnae, and members of the college's faculty and staff.

11. The University of Northern Iowa's website "Halloween Traditions and Ghosts at UNI," compiled by Gail Briddle (2001), provides many details about the development of campus ghostlore from the late nineteenth century to the present.

12. A particularly interesting segment of Bed, Bath & Beyond's "Survival 101" website is its set of "College Memoirs" (2005), which trace one student's difficulties in leaving home and adjusting to college life.

13. One detailed hazing website is Hank Nuwer's "Unofficial Clearinghouse to Track Hazing Deaths and Incidents" (2005).

14. For example, in the fall of 1966, David Truman, president of Mount Holyoke College, told the other entering freshmen and me that although we had all worked hard to get good grades in high school, 50 percent of us would be in the lower half of our class in college.

15. For analysis of children's ghost stories that sound scary at first but culminate in a funny punchline, see Elizabeth Tucker's "Tradition and Creativity in the Storytelling of Pre-adolescent Girls" (1977) and John Vlach's "'One Black Eye and Other Horrors'" (1971).

16. Joanna Pelizzoni, a student at Binghamton University, collected this information from a twenty-year-old female student at Randolph-Macon in November 2004.

17. At Rush Rhees library at the University of Rochester, librarians have offered an annual Halloween event called the Rush Rhees Scare Fair. This event "gets students into the library, gives them a gentle introduction to the stacks—which many find scary, not to mention confusing—and helps them know that librarians are fun, approachable people" (Bultrago 2005). Of course, the ghost of Pete Nicosia has been an important part of this Halloween celebration. Students at the University of Rochester are fortunate to have such a pleasant, yet spine-chilling initiation into the horrors of library research.

18. This legend about Logan's Lyric Theatre is included in Tucker, *Campus Legends* (2005a: 73).

19. Barbara Popadak's story, narrated in August 1972, comes from the Utah State University collection of the Fife Folklore Archive, L2.1.8.5.1.

20. June Baskett's story, collected in January 1965, is part of her term paper, "Folklore Collection: Scare Stories Found in Women's Dormitories," which is part of the Folklife Archive of Western Kentucky University in Bowling Green, Kentucky.

21. Although the dogs in this story bark, not howl, their awareness of death conforms to Motif B733.2, "Dogs howling indicates death."

Chapter Two. Sensory Evidence

1. This information was collected by Binghamton University student Zachary Betters in April 2005. A similar focus on visual images of a ghost can be found in Michael L. Crawford's study of the "Faceless Nun" legend cycle, "Legends from St. Mary-of-the-Woods College" (1974). For a thorough study of the meaning of images on glass, see Barbara Allen, "The 'Image on Glass': Technology, Tradition, and the Emergence of Folklore" (1982).

2. Kristin Lau, a student at Binghamton University, collected this legend about Fordham University's "ghost exorcist" in November 2004. For more information about Fordham's connection to the filming of *The Exorcist* (1973), see chapter 8.

3. This quotation comes from act 1, scene 5 of Shakespeare's *Hamlet* (lines 166–67). Gillian Bennett discusses the ghost of Hamlet's father in *Alas, Poor Ghost!* (1999: 139–45).

4. Sigmund Freud and D. E. Oppenheim scrutinize encounters with ghosts during dreams in their small but significant book *Dreams in Folklore*. Analyzing two narratives about men's dreams of female ghosts, they find that such dreams have symbolic value. In one narrative, a beautiful young female spirit leads a man toward treasure; in another, a female spirit of unspecified age asks a man to accompany her to her grave in a churchyard. After the ghosts lead them forward, the two male dreamers defecate in their beds. Both ghosts, according to Freud and Oppenheim, reflect "an anxiety which could perhaps be traced back to an effort to suppress the achievement of satisfaction in bed" (1958: 42).

5. The popular television show *The Twilight Zone* used elevators as vehicles of transition from reality to fantasy; in the 1985 movie titled *The Twilight Zone*, one episode was called "The Elevator."

6. MTV's *Fear* and NBC's *Fear Factor* have been popular with college students.

7. Marble ghost stories are well known on college campuses in other parts of the world. College students have told marble ghost legends in mainland China and Singapore during the past several years. For example, students at Temasek Junior College in eastern Singapore have exchanged stories about construction workers placing marbles between floors of student apartment buildings, so that ghosts can use the marbles as playthings. See "Temasek Junior College Online Forums" (2004).

8. In the popular movie *The Exorcism of Emily Rose* (2005), the haunting of Emily's residence hall room begins after a container of pencils falls over. This movie was based on Felicitas Goodman's anthropological study *The Exorcism of Anneliese Michel* (1981).

9. A selection of legends about outrageous pranks can be found in Tucker, *Campus Legends* (41–42, 93–96).

10. BarBara Lee's work as an exorcist is described by Linda Dégh in *Legend and Belief* (2001: 274–90).

11. Recent figures on marijuana usage can be found on the website *Info-Facts-Marijuana* (2006).

Chapter Three. Ghostly Warnings

1. In the late-fifteenth-century play *Mankind*, for example, actors playing the parts of vices encouraged audience members to laugh at Mankind when he tried to behave virtuously. For information on a 1998 performance of *Mankind*, see "Duquesne University Medieval and Renaissance Players Present Mankind" (1999). A good source of morality and miracle play texts is E. Martin Browne's *Religious Drama 2: Mystery and Morality Plays* (1977).

2. "Footsteps in the Attic" was collected by Binghamton University student Jacqueline Minichiello in April 2005.

3. The sense of moving away from conventional time while taking drugs is comparable to what happens to characters in British folktales and ballads who unexpectedly enter Fairyland, where time passes differently from time in the primary world.

4. Although some scholars question the reliability of Wikipedia, the online encyclopedia that allows visitors to add and edit entries, I have found it to be a helpful source of information on campus druglore, especially in relation to folk names. The version of Wikipedia's "Adderall" article that I read in June 2006 had been updated two months before; it will continue to be updated as new information becomes available.

5. "Sleeping at the Same Table" was collected by Jacqueline Minichiello in April 2005.

6. "!! EM PLEH" was collected by Binghamton University student Samantha Shulman in November 2004.Other college ghost stories feature ghosts that write backward. In the Gettysburg College ghost story "Blue Boy," for example, a female student sees a boy with a blue face at her third-floor window, then finds the words "EM PLEH" written in the frost on the window's outside surface (Nesbitt 1991: 78–79).

Chapter Four. Troubling Encounters

1. According to Dan Norder, "some people say that if you walk by a mirror in total darkness, regardless of whether you are trying to summon her or not, Bloody Mary will get you" (1999). For college students and others well versed in folklore of the supernatural, knowing can function as passive summoning.

2. Studies of the "Bloody Mary"/"Mary Worth" phenomenon include Langlois (1978), Bronner (1988: 168), and Dundes (2002). Dundes's Freudian analysis, based upon many texts collected from preadolescent girls, finds that anxiety about the onset of menstruation underlies "Bloody Mary" rituals. A significant shift to study of the mirror rituals of older adolescents occurs in Bill Ellis's "Table-Setting and Mirror Gazing," a chapter of *Lucifer Ascending* (2003: 142–73). Also noteworthy are psychologists' studies of images seen in mirrors as "illusions" (e.g., Schwartz and Fjeld 1968).

3. In *The Great Mother: An Analysis of the Archetype* (1963), Erich Neumann analyzes female deities who both protect and hurt: Kali, Hecate, and others. Some initiation ceremonies for girls feature a representation of the Great Mother; my article about the Guéré panther woman, who menaces initiates with a sharp knife, is one case in point (1987).

4. The name "Sullivan Hall" is a pseudonym.

5. As Faculty Master of the residential area, I worked closely with resident assistants and resident directors, planned academic and social programs, offered informal counseling to students, and attended area events. Because I was often in the halls late at night, I knew more about students' activities and stories than I would have known as a regular faculty member.

6. Mirror magic is a well-known form of divination practiced by young women who want to learn about their future husbands. Emelyn Gardner's *Folklore of the Schoharie Hills* describes a number of rituals which, with their focus on inversion, bear some resemblance to witchcraft rituals (1937: 277). An Irish legend tells of a girl practicing love magic who dies after seeing a terrifying figure in the mirror (Wilde 1890: 118–19). Irish witches scratch their victims horribly (Gregory 1920: 202). The *Handwörterbuch des deutschen Aberglaubens* tells of young women who repeated the name of their beloved three times and then saw the devil's face in the mirror, since the young men of their choice were not

right for them (Hoffmann-Krayer 1938: 558). It is possible that some legends of ghosts in mirrors are descendants of this sequence of early European love magic and punishment. The appearance of another face next to one's own may be seen as a death omen (559). Relevant motifs include D1163, "Magic mirror"; G303.6.1.4, "Devil appears when woman looks at herself in mirror after sunset"; and T11.7, "Love through sight in magic mirror."

7. In "Pain, Pleasure and the Spectral: The Barfing Ghost of Burford Hall," Jeannie B. Thomas explains that the supernatural lore of a college residence hall "picks up and carries concerns about political issues of the era in which the legends are circulated, and this political focus changes with the times" (1991: 28). Many college ghost stories are situated in the politically turbulent era of the 1960s and 1970s.

8. The terms "ostension" and "ostensive," referring to the enactment of legend events, were introduced by Linda Dégh in 1983.

9. Good sources on the "Satanic panic" phenomenon are Jeffrey Victor's *Satanic Panic* (1993) and Bill Ellis's *Raising the Devil* (2000).

10. This legend was collected by Hal, a Binghamton University student, in April 2003.

11. Jessica Montera, a student at Binghamton University, collected this narrative in November 2004.

12. For a thorough description of the RA's job, see Gregory Blimling, *The Resident Assistant* (1995). Blimling identifies the RA as a role model, a counselor, a teacher, and a student.

Chapter Five. Desperate Lovers

1. For example, see "Sigma Kappa Sorority: Beta Sigma Chapter at Purdue University" (2004).

2. One good example of a thwarted lover in nineteenth-century literature is Bertha, Mr. Rochester's hidden wife in Charlotte Brontë's *Jane Eyre* (first published in 1847). Like a ghost, Bertha makes her presence known through maniacal laughter, mystifying and frightening young Jane. After Jane becomes engaged to Mr. Rochester, Bertha goes on a wild rampage through the house and sets fire to Jane's bed, burning the house down. Her intense rage and despair mirror the feelings of female characters in ghost stories who have suffered a similar fate. Sandra M. Gilbert and Susan Gubar analyze parallels between Jane and Bertha in *The Madwoman in the Attic* (1979: 360–62).

3. Alicia Maston, a student at Binghamton University, collected this narrative in March 2005.

4. For more details on the subject of fraternity/sorority pressures, see Alexandra Robbins, *Pledged: The Secret Life of Sororities* (2005).

5. This discussion with a member of Mansfield's library faculty took place in late February 2005.

6. As Max Lüthi explains in his essay "Aspects of the Märchen and the Legend" (1976), glass adds radiance and beauty to the folktale. In legends, as well, it can seem beautiful and mysterious. Sara's imprisonment within a glass stairwell seems comparable to the

entombment of Snow White in a glass coffin in the Grimms' folktale # 53 (Aarne-Thompson tale type 709).

7. In children's ghost stories such as "Bloody Fingers," a ghost stands at the bottom of the staircase, waiting to be vanquished by a brave child (see Tucker 1977 for versions of this story). For older adolescents, stairways represent challenges appropriate to their age group.

8. See, for example, the story of "The Pregnant Nun" in Tucker, *Campus Legends* (2005a: 80).

9. The earliest and most detailed account of the trees' history is George O. Johnson's "Weena and Connestoga: A Legend which Centers around Two Trees in the Heart of Athens" (1924).

10. In the Greek myth of Baucis and Philemon, Philemon turns into an oak tree and Baucis turns into a linden tree. It is noteworthy that oaks have been perceived over a long period of time as "manly" trees. For interesting details regarding Ovid's choice of the oak and linden trees, see Patrick Hunt, "Arborisms in Ovid's Baucis and Philemon from *Metamorphoses* 8.620–720" (2005).

11. Another ghost that fits this pattern is Lucy, who haunts Sessions House at Smith College in Northampton, Massachusetts. Smith students say that Lucy had trysts with her British lover, Gentleman Johnny Burgoyne, on Sessions House's secret staircase. Later, the staircase became a hiding place for slaves following the Underground Railroad. See "Living at Smith" (2005).

Chapter Six. Wailing Women

1. One good study of *"La Llorona"* stories is Judith S. Beatty's and Edward Garcia Kraul's *La Llorona: Encounters with the Weeping Woman* (2004).

2. For more details about this distinction between folktale and legend features, see Max Lüthi's "Aspects of the Märchen and the Legend" (1976).

3. Wolfgang Mieder offers a feminist analysis of this proverb in his "A Proverb a Day Keeps No Chauvinism Away" (1985).

4. Grace Housholder's essay "A Man Works from Sun to Sun, but a Woman's Work Is Never Done" (1999) applies this well-known proverb to American women's work patterns.

5. For details about the actual disappearance of a student at Miami University of Ohio who left all his things behind, as if he had just gone to the bathroom, see Walter Havighurst's "The Miami Years, 1809–1984" (1996).

6. The concept of the "Final Girl" was introduced by Carol Clover in *Men, Women and Chain Saws: Gender in the Modern Horror Film* (1992).

7. Interview with Professor Nancy C. McEntire at the annual meeting of the International Society for Contemporary Legend Research in Copenhagen, Denmark, May 30, 2006. Further details concerning Barb's recent exploits can be found on the popular website "Haunted Places in Indiana," http://theshadowlands.net/places/indiana.htm. This website notes that students can detect Barb's presence by hearing her vomit and cry.

8. Another example of a women's residence hall that contains a significant portrait is Agnes Howard Hall at West Virginia Wesleyan University. Agnes Howard, one of the first students who attended West Virginia Wesleyan in its early days as a Normal School, died young. Students say that her ghost resides in an old apartment in the building's tower. Each year, students make a door tag to identify Agnes's room.

9. Interview with a female Colvin Hall staff member in December 2005.

10. Interview with Sarah Gingrich, resident director of Cheney Hall at the State University of New York at Cortland, on November 29, 2005.

11. I was touched by Christina Hope's determination to help Shelley's spirit leave the campus where she died and go to heaven. Christina's effort reminded me of the work of BarBara Lee, the exorcist with whom I did some fieldwork under Linda Dégh's direction as a graduate student at Indiana University. Described in Dégh's *Legend and Belief*, BarBara Lee had a spiritual vocation to send troubled souls to heaven (2001: 274–84).

12. E-mail communication from Christina Hope, June 5, 2006.

13. Two previous assaults on the Stony Brook campus are described in some detail in Scott Higham's "Firearms on Campus Debated" (1983).

14. Other outcomes of good fantasy, according to Tolkien's essay "On Fairy Stories," include escape from the tedium of daily life and recovery of a clear viewpoint (1965: 55–70).

Chapter Seven. Spectral Indians

1. An article by Rick DelVecchio in the *San Francisco Chronicle* (2005) describes what happened when developers and archeologists excavated a large shell mound in Emeryville, California, between 1997 and 2002, so that they could clear the site for a new shopping mall. Archeologists discovered hundreds of human remains from the Ohlone mound-building culture, which had come to an end before Spanish explorers arrived in the area. Bodies that had been ceremoniously interred in pairs and in groups were removed and reburied in an unmarked grave on the site. Many workers, including descendants of the Ohlone, felt deeply troubled by the disturbance of the graves. Filmmaker Andrés Cediel, who made the documentary "Shellmound," tactfully commented, "There are unresolved issues here."

2. The story of the use of Delaware John's skeleton bears a haunting resemblance to Wendy Rose's poem "Truganinny," which describes the public display of an Aboriginal woman's body for more than eighty years (2000: 1158).

3. For Dartmouth students' discussion of the Indian mascot in relation to their college's charter, see John McWilliams and Cortney Scott, "The Indian's Long History" (1996).

4. Dartmouth student Benjamin Wallace-Wells interprets Dartmouth's mascot as a reference to early education of Indians in his *Dartmouth Review* article "The Indian and the Rock" (1998).

5. Scholars have disagreed about the number of children who died while residing at Indian boarding schools. Ward Churchill, author of *Kill the Indian, Save the Man* (2004), has suggested that half of the children at Indian boarding schools died, while Brenda J. Child, author of *Boarding School Seasons* (1998), has said that fewer children died

and that the exact number of deaths cannot be known. For information on that debate, see Morson 2006.

6. "John Sithins" is a pseudonym.

7. Another important study on this subject is Rayna Green's "The Only Good Indian" (1973), which examines the meaning of dead Indians in American vernacular culture.

8. Among the American graves that visitors have covered with coins are the resting places of Dred Scott, Patsy Cline, Frank Sinatra, Benjamin Franklin, Nathaniel Hawthorne, James Dean, Paul Revere, Samuel Adams, and Baby Jerry Ogata, who died at the Manzanar War Relocation Center for Asian Americans in Owens Valley, California. Placing a coin on a grave reflects the ancient Greek custom of offering money to Charon, the ferryman on the River Styx, for safe passage to the realm of the dead. Nineteenth-century Mohawks in western Canada, Sa Sa Na's homeland, would have preferred tobacco as a grave offering.

9. Among these films, some of the most popular have been *Child's Play* (1988) and its sequels, especially *Bride of Chucky* (1998).

10. Early films in which whites struggle with bloodthirsty, destructive Indians include *A Frontier Soldier of Fortune* (1912), *The Indian Massacre* (1912), and *Iola's Promise* (1912). Later films such as *Geronimo* (1962) offer less extreme characterizations; *Dances with Wolves* (1990) made a serious effort to portray Indians in a realistic way, but the older stereotypes are still well known.

11. Joanna Pelizzoni collected this story in November 2004.

Chapter Eight. Legend Quests

1. Applicable motifs include D1293.1, "Red as magic color"; 1293.2, "Green as magic color"; F178.1, "Red as otherworld color"; F178.2, "Green as otherworld color"; Z141, "Symbolic color: red"; and Z145.1, "Green as symbolic of martyrdom."

2. Father Stephen Hess's name is a pseudonym. The two stories of his that I include here come from Linda Dégh's legend archive. For historical information on the drowning of Brother Anselm Bartholmy at St. John's in 1890, see David Klingeman, "Monk Drowns in Lake Sagatagan" (2004).

3. Todd Wightman told his own story as part of his paper "The Haunted House" (1984), written at Utah State University. This paper belongs to the Fife Folklore Archive (84–061).

4. This narrative was collected by Binghamton University student Ken Shiraiwa in April 2005.

5. Dianne Harris, a student at Binghamton University, collected this legend in March 2004.

6. Jalyn Rinderknecht's story, told in January 1987, comes from the Fife Folklore Archive (FA L2.2.2.1.1.2.2).

7. While visiting Mount Saint Mary's archive in the summer of 2002, I found a number of exorcism legends that Marie Campbell's students had collected shortly after *The Exorcist* was released. I also saw several legends about exorcisms on the Mount Saint Mary's campus that Campbell had sent to Linda Dégh in the mid-1970s.

8. Naomi, a Binghamton University student, made this comment in April 2005.

REFERENCES CITED

Abandoned New Jersey. 2003. http://www.abandonednj.com, accessed May 20, 2006.

Adams, David Wallace. 1997. *Education for Extinction: American Indians and the Boarding School Experience, 1875–1928*. Lawrence: University Press of Kansas.

Allen, Barbara. 1982. The "Image on Glass": Technology, Tradition, and the Emergence of Folklore. *Western Folklore* 41: 85–103.

Alvord, Lori Arviso, and Elizabeth Cohen van Pelt. 2000. *The Scalpel and the Silver Bear: The First Navajo Woman Surgeon Combines Western Medicine and Traditional Healing*. New York: Bantam.

Amato, Jennifer. 2005. R.U. Scared? Duo Chronicles Campus Lore. *Sentinel*. North Brunswick Township, New Jersey. October 27. http://nbs.gmnews.com/news/2005/1027/Front_Page/005.html, accessed November 4, 2006.

Anderson, Joan Wester. 2004. *In the Arms of Angels: True Stories of Heavenly Guardians*. Chicago: Loyola Press.

Andriano, Joseph. 1993. *Our Ladies of Darkness: Feminine Daemonology in Male Gothic Fiction*. University Park: Pennsylvania State University Press.

Babula, Justin. 1992. Ghost Stories of Mt. Mary's College. Unpublished student paper, Mount Saint Mary's College. May 1.

Baker, Ronald L. 1982. *Hoosier Folk Legends*. Bloomington: Indiana University Press.

Barefoot, Daniel W. 2004. *Haunted Halls of Ivy: Ghosts of Southern Colleges and Universities*. Winston-Salem, NC: John F. Blair.

Barker, Clive. 1985. The Forbidden. In *Clive Barker's Books of Blood 5*. Aylesbury, England: Sphere Books, pp. 1–54.

Barnes, Daniel R. 1966. Some Functional Horror Stories on the Kansas University Campus. *Southern Folklore Quarterly* 30(3): 312–31.

Baskett, June. 1965. Folklore Collection: Scare Stories Found in Girls' Dormitories. Unpublished student paper, Western Kentucky University. Folklife Archives, Department of Library Special Collections. January 24.

Beatty, Judith S., and Edward Garcia Kraul, eds. 2004. *La Llorona: Encounters with the Weeping Woman*. Santa Fe: Sunstone Press.

Bennett, Gillian. 1999. *Alas, Poor Ghost! Traditions of Belief in Story and Discourse*. Logan: Utah State University Press.

Bergland, Renée L. 2000. *The National Uncanny: Indian Ghosts and American Subjects*. Hanover: University Press of New England.

Birkrem, Nancy. 2001. The Ghosts of the Mandelles. http://cob.mtholyoke.edu/offices/library/arch/ref/ghost/mandelle.htm, accessed July 22, 2004.

Blimling, Gregory. 1995. *The Resident Assistant*. Dubuque, IA: Kendall/Hunt Publishing Company.

Bordelon, Brian. 1991. Believe It or Not. *Gumbo* 4(3): 8–12.

Boyer, Ernest L. 1987. *College: The Undergraduate Experience in America.* New York: Harper and Row.

Bradley, Marian Zimmer. 1984. *The Mists of Avalon.* New York: Random House.

Briddle, Gail. 2001. Halloween Traditions and Ghosts at UNI. http://www.library.uni.edu/speccoll/halloween.html, accessed June 5, 2005.

Britt, Robert Roy. 2006. Higher Education Fuels Stronger Belief in Ghosts. *Yahoo! News.* January 20, 2006. http://news.yahoo.com/s/space/Highereducationfuelsstrongerbelief inghosts, accessed January 21.

Brogan, Kathleen. 1998. *Cultural Haunting: Ghosts and Ethnicity in Recent American Literature.* Charlottesville: University of Virginia Press.

Bronner, Simon J. 1986. *Grasping Things.* Lexington: University Press of Kentucky.

———. 1995. *Piled Higher and Deeper: The Folklore of Student Life.* Little Rock, AR: August House.

Brontë, Charlotte. 1954. *Jane Eyre.* New York: John C. Winston Company.

Brown, Alan. 2000. *Shadows and Cypress: Southern Ghost Stories.* Jackson: University Press of Mississippi.

———. 2004. *Stories from the Haunted South.* Jackson: University Press of Mississippi.

Brown, Dorothy Moulding. 1938. Legends of Wisconsin Springs. *Wisconsin Archeologist* 18(3): 79–86.

Brown, John Norris. 2005a. The Lovers' Trees of Tennessee Wesleyan. *Ghosts and Spirits of Tennessee.* http://johnnorrisbrown.com/paranormal-tn/wesleyan, accessed June 8, 2005.

———. 2005b. University of Tennessee. *Ghosts and Spirits of Tennessee.* http://johnnorris brown.com/paranormal-tn/utk/index.htm, accessed June 11, 2005.

———. 2006. Forgotten Ohio: Ohio University. http://www.forgottenoh.com/ou.html, accessed January 2, 2006.

Brown, Roger. 1987. Colvin Hall Haunted by Good-Natured Ghost. *The Maine Campus,* p. 1. October 30.

Browne, E. Martin. 1977. *Religious Drama 2: Mystery and Morality Plays.* Gloucester, MA: Peter Smith.

Browne, Ray. 1976. *"A Night with the Hants" and Other Alabama Folk Experiences.* Bowling Green, OH: Popular Press.

Bruchac, Joseph. 1993. Bone Girl. In *Earth Song, Sky Spirit,* ed. Clifford E. Trafzer, pp. 235–44. New York: Anchor Books.

Brudvig, Jon L. 1996. The College of William and Mary. In *Encyclopedia of North American Indians,* ed. Frederick E. Hoxie, p. 71. Boston: Houghton Mifflin.

Brunvand, Jan Harold. 1981. *The Vanishing Hitchhiker.* New York: Norton.

———. 1984. *The Choking Doberman.* New York: Norton.

———. 1989. *Curses! Broiled Again!* New York: Norton.

———. 2004. The Vanishing "Urban Legend." *Midwest Folklore* 30(2): 5–20.

Bultrago, Jason. 2005. Haunting Rush Rhees. University of Rochester *Campus Times.* October 27. http://www.campustimes.org/media/storage/paper371/news/2005/10/27/Features/Haunting.Rush.Rhees-1035375.shtml, accessed June 25, 2006.

Burke, Carol. 2005. Personal interview. May 25.

Burr, George Lincoln. 1914. *Narratives of the Witchcraft Cases, 1648–1706*. New York: Charles Scribner's Sons.

Butler, Judith. 1999. *Gender Trouble: Feminism and the Subversion of Identity*. New York: Routledge.

Campbell, Joseph. 1968 [1949]. *The Hero with a Thousand Faces*. Princeton: Princeton University Press.

Carroll, Lewis. 1946. *Through the Looking-Glass and What Alice Found There*. New York: Random House.

Carroll, Michael P. 1992. Allomotifs and the Psychoanalytic Study of Folk Narratives: Another Look at "The Roommate's Death." *Folklore* 103: 225–34.

Child, Brenda J. 1998. *Boarding School Seasons: American Indian Families*, Lincoln: University of Nebraska Press.

Christie, Agatha. 2000. *By the Pricking of My Thumbs: Tommy and Tuppence Series*. New York: Signet.

Churchill, Ward. 2006. *Kill the Indian, Save the Man: The Genocidal Impact of American Indian Residential Schools*. San Francisco: City Lights Books.

Clements, William M., and William E. Lightfoot. 1972. The Legend of Stepp Cemetery. *Indiana Folklore* 5(1): 92–135.

Clover, Carol. 1992. *Men, Women, and Chain Saws: Gender in the Modern Horror Film*. Princeton: Princeton University Press.

College Town Ghost Stories. 2001. *Everything 2*. December 14. http://www.everything2.com/index.pl?node_id=1217455, accessed October 6, 2005.

Colmant, Stephen A. 2006. Haskell Cemetery: A Symbol for Healing and Growth. http://www.dincoalition.org/related_issues/haskellcemetery.pdf, accessed April 15, 2006.

Condie Cunningham's Door. 2004. *The Award-Winning Rick & Bubba Web Site*. http://www.rickandbubba.com/index.asp?pg=13DaysofHorror-CondieCunninghamsDoor.asp, accessed May 5, 2005.

Conway, Jill Ker. 2001. *A Woman's Education*. New York: Alfred A. Knopf.

Corsbie-Massay, Charisse. 2005. Personal interview. May 26.

Crawford, Michael L. 1974. Legends from St. Mary-of-the-Woods College. *Indiana Folklore* 7(1–2): 53–75.

Curti, Merle, and Vernon Carstensen. 1949. *The University of Wisconsin: A History, 1848–1925*, vol. 2. Madison: University of Wisconsin Press.

Dalby, Richard, ed. 2002. *Victorian and Edwardian Ghost Stories*. New York: Metro Books.

Danielson, Larry. 1996. Folklore and Film: Some Thoughts on Baughman Z500–599. In *Contemporary Legend: A Reader*, ed. Gillian Bennett and Paul Smith, pp. 55–68. New York: Garland.

DeCaro, Frank. 2003. E-mail communication. June 3.

De Voragine, Jacobus. 1993. *The Golden Legend*. Trans. William Granger Ryan. Princeton: Princeton University Press.

Dégh, Linda. 1968a. The Boy Friend's Death. *Indiana Folklore* 1(1): 101–6.

———. 1968b. The Hook. *Indiana Folklore* 1(1): 92–100.

———. 1969a. The Haunted Bridges near Avon and Danville and Their Role in Legend Formation. *Indiana Folklore* 2: 54–89.

————. 1969b. The Roommate's Death and Other Related Dormitory Stories in Formation. *Indiana Folklore* 2(2): 55–74.

————. 1971. The "Belief Legend" in Modern Society. In *American Folk Legend: A Symposium*, ed. Wayland D. Hand, pp. 55–68. Berkeley: University of California Press.

————. 2001. *Legend and Belief*. Bloomington: Indiana University Press.

Dégh, Linda, and Andrew Vázsonyi. 1983. Does the Word "Dog" Bite? Ostensive Action: A Means of Legend Telling. *Journal of Folklore Research* 20: 5–34.

Deloria, Philip J. 1998. *Playing Indian*. New Haven: Yale University Press.

DelVecchio, Rick. 2005. Emeryville: Filmmaker tells story of forgotten Indian burial ground disrupted by quest for retail. *San Francisco Chronicle*. March 25. http://www.sfgate.com/cgi-bin/article.cgifile=/chronicle/archive/2005/03/25/EBGQGBQQG21.DTL, accessed July 4, 2005.

Dickens, Charles. 1937. *Great Expectations*. Edinburgh: R and R Clark Ltd.

Dorson, Richard M. 1959. *American Folklore*. Chicago: University of Chicago Press.

————. 1973. *America in Legend*. New York: Pantheon Books.

Douglas, Mary. 1966. *Purity and Danger*. New York: Praeger.

Douglas, Todd. 2001. Dual Personality. *Timber Processing*. November/ December. http://www.panelworldmag.com/.../display.cfm?Magazine Key=5&IssueKey=430&SectionKey=614&ArticleKey=1911, accessed July 9, 2006.

Dundes, Alan. 1968. One Hundred Years of California Traditions. *California Monthly* 78 (5): 19–32.

————. 1971. On the Psychology of Legend. In *American Folk Legend: A Symposium*, ed. Wayland D. Hand, pp. 21–36. Berkeley: University of California Press.

————. 1972. Seeing Is Believing. *Natural History* 81(5): 8, 10–12, 86–87.

————. 1996. The Ballad of "The Walled-Up Wife." In *The Walled-Up Wife: A Casebook*, ed. Alan Dundes, pp. 185–204. Madison: University of Wisconsin Press.

————. 2002. Bloody Mary in the Mirror. In *Bloody Mary in the Mirror: Essays in Psychoanalytic Folkloristics*. Jackson: University Press of Mississippi.

————. 2004. As the Crow Flies: A Straightforward Study of Lineal Worldview in American Folk Speech. In *What Goes Around Comes Around: The Circulation of Proverbs in Contemporary Life*, ed. Kimberly J. Lau, Peter Tokofsky, and Stephen D. Winick, pp. 171–87. Logan: Utah State University Press.

Duquesne University Medieval and Renaissance Players Present Mankind. 1999. http://www.engl.duq.edu/servus/M_R_Players/mankind2.html, accessed June 3, 2006.

Eakins, Paul. 2001. The Ghosts of Haskell. *Topeka Capital-Journal*. November 4. http://www.cjonline.com/cgi-bin, accessed July 14, 2005.

Eliade, Mircea. 1958. *Rites and Symbols of Initiation: The Mysteries of Birth and Rebirth*. New York: Harper and Row.

Ellis, Bill. 1982. "Ralph and Rudy": The Audience's Role in Recreating a Camp Legend. *Western Folklore* 41: 169–91.

————. 1982–83. Legend-Tripping in Ohio: A Behavioral Study. In *Papers in Comparative Studies*, vol. 2, ed. Daniel Barnes, Rosemary O. Joyce, and Steven Swann Jones, pp. 61–73. Columbus, OH: Center for Comparative Studies in the Humanities.

————. 1994. Speak to the Devil: Ouija Board Rituals among American Adolescents. *Contemporary Legend* 4: 61–90.

————. 2003. *Aliens, Ghosts, and Cults: Legends We Live*. Jackson: University Press of Mississippi.

————. 2004. *Lucifer Ascending: The Occult in Folklore and Popular Culture*. Lexington: University Press of Kentucky.

Erdoes, Richard, and Alfonso Ortiz, eds. 1984. *American Indian Myths and Legends*. New York: Pantheon Books.

Erikson, Erik H. 1965. *Childhood and Society*. London: Penguin Books. "The Excite Chat Ghost." 2005. http://www.geocities.com/Hollywood/Camera/9599/mandy.htm, accessed August 1, 2005.

Fine, Gary Alan, and Patricia A. Turner. 2001. *Whispers on the Color Line*. Berkeley: University of California Press.

Finucane, R. C. 1996. *Ghosts: Appearances of the Dead and Cultural Transformation*. Buffalo, NY: Prometheus Books.

Fish, Lydia M. 1976. Jesus on the Thruway: The Vanishing Hitchhiker Strikes Again. *Indiana Folklore* 9: 5–13.

Fox, William S. 1990. The Roommate's Suicide and the 4.0. In *A Nest of Vipers: Perspectives on Contemporary Legend V*, ed. Gillian Bennett and Paul Smith, pp. 69–76. Sheffield, England: Sheffield Academic Press.

Fraiberg, Selma. 1959. *The Magic Years: Understanding and Handling the Problems of Early Childhood*. New York: Scribner.

Frankel, Richard. 1998. *The Adolescent Psyche: Jungian and Winncottian Perspectives*. New York: Routledge.

Frazier, Charles. 2003. *Cold Mountain*. New York: Random House.

Freud, Sigmund, and D. E. Oppenheim. 1958. *Dreams in Folklore*. New York: International Universities Press.

Gardner, Emelyn. 1977 [1937]. *Folklore from the Schoharie Hills*. Chicago: Lakeside Press.

Gardner, John N. 1989. *Freshman Year Experience: Options toward Success*. New York: John Wiley and Sons.

Ghost Hunt. 2003. *The Maine Campus Online*. http://www.mainecampus.com. November 3. Accessed November 17, 2005.

Ghost: Residence Hall's Spirit Another Dying Tradition. 1986. *Ball State Daily News*, pp. 4–5. October 31.

Ghost Stories Told by Students. 1998. *Wells College Library*. http://aurora.wells.edu/~library/ghosts.htm, accessed November 1, 2004.

Ghosts of Sweet Briar College. 2005. http://ghosts.sbc.edu, accessed March 19, 2005.

Gilbert, Helen. 1975. The Crack in the Abbey Floor: A Laboratory Analysis of a Legend. *Indiana Folklore* 8(1–2): 61–78.

Gilbert, Sandra M., and Susan Gubar. 1979. *The Madwoman in the Attic: The Woman Writer and the Nineteenth-Century Literary Imagination*. New Haven: Yale University Press.

Glassie, Henry H. 2006. Personal interview. October 21.

Glimm, James York. 1983. *Flat-Landers and Ridge-Runners*. Pittsburgh: University of Pittsburgh Press.

Goldenberg, Naomi. 1976. A Feminist Critique of Jung. *Signs: A Journal of Women in Culture and Society* 2(2): 443–49.

Goldstein, Diane. 2004. *Once Upon a Virus: AIDS Legends and Vernacular Risk Perception.* Logan: Utah State University Press.

Goodman, Felicitas. 1981. *The Exorcism of Anneliese Michel.* New York: Doubleday.

Gordon, Avery F. 1997. *Ghostly Matters: Haunting and the Sociological Imagination.* Minneapolis: University of Minnesota Press.

Grant, Glenn. 1996. *Obake Files: Ghostly Encounters in Supernatural Hawai'i.* Honolulu: Mutual Publishing.

Green, Rayna. 1973. The Only Good Indian: The Image of the Indian in Vernacular Culture. Ph.D. diss., Indiana University.

Greenberg, Andrea. 1973. Drugged and Seduced: A Contemporary Legend. *New York Folklore Quarterly* 29(2): 131–58.

Gregory, Isabella A. 1920. *Visions and Beliefs in the West of Ireland.* Vol. 1. New York: G. P. Putnam's Sons.

Grider, Sylvia. 1973. Dormitory Legend-Telling in Progress: Fall, 1971–Winter, 1973. *Indiana Folklore* 6(1): 1–32.

———. 1999. The Haunted House in Literature, Popular Culture, and Tradition: A Consistent Image. *Contemporary Legend,* new series 2: 174–204.

The Grimms' German Folktales. 1960. Trans. Francis P. Magoun Jr. and Alexander H. Krappe. Carbondale: Southern Illinois University Press.

Hall, Gary. 1973. The Big Tunnel: Legends and Legend-Telling. *Indiana Folklore* 6: 139–73.

Hall, Robert. 1993. Red Banks, Oneota, and the Winnebago: Views from a Distant Rock. *Wisconsin Archeologist* 74(1–4): 10–79.

Halloween Traditions and Ghosts at UNI. 2001. http://www.library.uni.edu/speccoll/halloween.html, accessed July 29, 2003.

Hand, Wayland D. et al., eds. 1964. *The Frank C. Brown Collection of North Carolina Folklore,* vol. 7. Durham: Duke University Press.

Hankey, Rosalie. 1944. Campus Folklore and California's "Pedro." *California Folklore Quarterly* 3: 29–35.

Haring, Lee, and Mark Breslerman. 1977. The Cropsey Maniac. *New York Folklore* 3: 15–27.

Hauck, Dennis William. 1996. *Haunted Places: The National Directory.* New York: Penguin Books.

Hauk, Gary S. 1999. *A Legacy of Heart and Mind: Emory since 1836.* Atlanta: Emory University.

———. 2005. ". . . but Dooley goes on forever." *Traditions and Rituals of Emory University.* http://emoryhistory.emory.edu/traditions/Dooleystory.html, accessed June 24, 2006.

Haunted Denver, Colorado. 2005. http://www.legendsofamerica.com/CO-Denver-Ghosts2.html, accessed December 11, 2005.

Haunted Places in Indiana. 2006. http://theshadowlands.net/places/indiana.htm, accessed June 4, 2006.

Haunted Places in New York. 2005. Juicee News Daily. http://www.juiceenewsdaily.com/1004/news/haunted_new_york, accessed December 3, 2005.

Havighurst, Walter. 1996. The Miami Years, 1809–1984. http://www.lib.muohio.edu/myindex.html., accessed May 18, 2005.

Hawthorne, Nathaniel. 1978. *The Scarlet Letter*, ed. Sculley Bradley. New York: Norton.

Hesse, Hermann. 1961. *Steppenwolf*, trans. Basil Creighton. New York: Holt, Rinehart and Winston.

Higham, Scott. 1983. Firearms on Campuses Debated. *New York Times*. Sec. 11, p. 5. May 15.

Hillman, James. 1964. *Suicide and the Soul*. Dallas: Spring Publications.

Hingson, Ralph W., et al. 2002. Magnitude of Alcohol-Related Mortality and Morbidity among U.S. College Students Ages 18–24. *Journal of Studies on Alcohol* 63(2): 136–44.

Hoffmann-Krayer, Edouard, and Hanns Bachtold-Staubli, eds. 1938. *Handwörterbuch des deutschen Aberglaubens*, vol. 9. Berlin: Walter de Gruyter.

Hope, Christina. 2004. The Hauntings of Sheahan Hall. http://www.christinahope.com/shelley_project/what/what.htm, accessed June 4, 2006.

Horn, Miriam. 1999. *Rebels in White Gloves*. New York: Times Books.

Housholder, Grace. 1999. A Man Works from Sun to Sun, but a Woman's Work is Never Done. *The News-Sun*. November 4. http://www.kpcnews.net/special-sections/reflections2/index.html, accessed June 8, 2006.

Hufford, David. 1982. *The Terror That Comes in the Night*. Philadelphia: University of Pennsylvania Press.

———. 1995. Beings without Bodies: An Experience-Centered Theory of the Belief in Spirits. In *Out of the Ordinary: Folklore and the Supernatural*, ed. Barbara Walker, pp. 11–45. Logan: Utah State University Press.

Humphrey, Hubert H. 1976. *The Education of a Public Man: My Life and Politics*. Garden City, NY: Doubleday.

Hunt, Patrick. 2005. Arborisms in Ovid's Baucis and Philemon from *Metamorphoses* 8. 620–720. *Philolog*. http://traumwerk.stanford.edu/Philology/2005/12, accessed July 2, 2006.

Hyatt, Harry M. 1965. *Folk-Lore from Adams County, Illinois*. New York: Memoirs of the Alma Egan Hyatt Foundation. InfoFacts-Marijuana. 2006. National Institute on Drug Abuse. http://www.nida.nih.gov/InfoFacts/marijuana.html, accessed June 6, 2006.

Irving, Washington. 1980. *The Legend of Sleepy Hollow*. New York: Sleepy Hollow Press.

Iwasaka, Michiko, and Barre Toelken. 1994. *Ghosts and the Japanese: Cultural Experience in Japanese Death Legends*. Logan: Utah State University Press.

Jacobi, Jolande. 1959. *Complex, Archetype, Symbol in the Psychology of C. G. Jung*, trans. Ralph Manheim. Princeton: Princeton University Press.

James, Henry. 1999. *The Turn of the Screw*. Norton Critical Edition. New York: Norton.

Johnson, George O. 1924. Weena and Connestoga: A Legend Which Centers around Two Trees in the Heart of Athens. *Tennessee Historical Magazine* 8: 153–66.

Johnson, Nola. 1966. Folklore Collection. Unpublished student paper, University of Maine. Northeast Folklore Archive, # 217 (CP133). Fall.

Jones, Louis C. 1944. The Ghosts of New York: An Analytical Study. *Journal of American Folklore* 57:226 (October–December): 237–54.

Jung, C. G. 1961. *Memories, Dreams, Reflections.* New York: Random House.

———. 1968. *Man and His Symbols.* New York: Dell.

———. 1970. *Four Archetypes,* trans. R. F. C. Hull. Princeton: Princeton University Press.

Jung, Emma. 1981. *Animus and Anima.* New York: Spring Publications.

Karo, Aaron. 2002. *Ruminations on College Life.* New York: Simon and Schuster.

Kelley, Charles Greg. 1992. Joseph E. Brown Hall: A Case Study of One University Legend. *Contemporary Legend* 2: 137–53.

Kelly, Courtney E., and Lauren Moscowitch. 2005. Case File: Cleveland Hall. Unpublished student paper, Binghamton University. May 5.

Kibbey, Ann. 1982. Mutations of the Supernatural: Witchcraft, Remarkable Providences, and the Power of Puritan Men. *American Quarterly* 34: 125–48.

Kiepenheuer, Kaspar. 1990. *Crossing the Bridge: A Jungian Approach to Adolescence,* trans. Karen R. Schneider. La Salle, IL: Open Court.

Kilby, Clyde S. 1969. Meaning in *The Lord of the Rings.* In *Shadows of Imagination: The Fantasies of C. S. Lewis, J. R. R. Tolkien, and Charles Williams,* ed. Mark R. Hillegas, pp. 70–80. Carbondale: Southern Illinois University Press.

King, Stephen. 1980. *The Dead Zone.* New York: Mass Market.

———. 1981. *Fire-Starter.* New York: Signet.

Kingston, Maxine Hong. 1976. *The Woman Warrior: Memoirs of a Girlhood among Ghosts.* New York: Vintage International.

Klingeman, David. 2004. Monk Drowns in Lake Sagatagan. http://www.csbsju.edu/sjuarchives/info/ask/drowning.html, accessed June 9, 2005.

Kolek, Ethan A. 2006. Recreational Prescription Drug Use among College Students. *NASPA Journal* 43(1): 19–39.

Krouth, Kim. 1997. Wisconsin Indians' Legendary Landscape: A Critical Review of Dorothy Moulding Brown's Folklore Articles in the *Wisconsin Archeologist.* Unpublished student paper, University of Wisconsin. October 14.

Langlois, Janet. 1978. "Mary Whales, I Believe in You": Myth and Ritual Subdued. *Indiana Folklore* 11(1): 5–33.

Largey, Gale. 1984. *Life at Mansfield: A Visual Reminiscence.* Mansfield, PA: Mansfield University.

Lau, Kimberly J. 1998. On the Rhetorical Use of Legend: U.C. Berkeley Campus Lore as a Strategy for Coded Protest. *Contemporary Legend,* new series 1: 1–20.

Lauter, Estella, and Carol Schreier Rupprecht, eds. 1985. *Feminist Archetypal Theory.* Knoxville: University of Tennessee Press.

Lawless, Elaine J. 2001. *Women Escaping Violence: Empowerment through Narrative.* Columbia: University of Missouri Press.

———. 2002. The Monster in the House: Legend Characteristics of the "Cycles of Violence" Narrative Prototype. *Contemporary Legend* n.s. 5: 24–49.

Leary, James P. 1973. The Boondocks Monster of Camp Wapehani. *Indiana Folklore* 6 (2): 174–90.

Lewis, C. S. 1950. *The Lion, the Witch and the Wardrobe.* New York: HarperCollins.

Lewis, Matthew. 1998. *The Monk.* New York: Oxford University Press.

Living at Smith. 2005. http://www.smith.edu/sao.reslife/houses/sessions.php, accessed November 8, 2005.

Long Island Folklore: Mary's Grave. 2005. http://lioddities.com/Folklore/mg.html, accessed December 15, 2005.

Longfellow, Henry Wadsworth. 1992. *The Song of Hiawatha.* London: J. M. Dent.

Lüthi, Max. 1976. Aspects of the Märchen and the Legend. In *Folklore Genres,* ed. Dan Ben-Amos, pp. 17–34. Austin: University of Texas Press.

Magliocco, Sabina. 2004. *Witching Culture: Folklore and Neo-Paganism in America.* Philadelphia: University of Pennsylvania Press.

Marcia, James E. 1966. Development and Validation of Ego Identity Status. *Journal of Personality and Social Psychology* 3: 551–58.

Marr, Carolyn. 2006. Assimilation through Education: Indian Boarding Schools in the Pacific Northwest. http://www.english.uiuc.edu/maps/poets/a-f/erdrich/boarding/marr.htm, accessed March 11, 2006.

Marx, Leo. 1964. *The Machine in the Garden: Technology and the Pastoral Ideal in America.* New York: Oxford University Press.

McNeil, W. K. 1985. *Ghost Stories from the American South.* New York: Dell.

McWilliams, John, and Cortney Scott. 1996. The Indian's Long History. *Dartmouth Review.* October 23. http://www.dartreview.com/archives/1996/10/23/the_indians_long_history.php, accessed December 11, 2005.

Mead, Margaret. 1972. *Blackberry Winter: My Earlier Years.* New York: Morrow.

Mechling, Jay. 1980. The Magic of the Boy Scout Campfire. *Journal of American Folklore* 93 (367): 35–56.

Meiklejohn, Benjamin. 1992. The Ghost of Colvin Hall. Northeast Folklore Archive, Maine Folklife Center. Fall.

Mieder, Wolfgang. 1985. A Proverb a Day Keeps No Chauvinism Away. *Proverbium* 2: 273–77.

Mitford, Jessica. 1998. *The American Way of Death Revisited.* New York: Knopf.

Montagu, Ashley. 1978. *Touching: The Human Significance of the Skin,* 2nd ed. New York: Harper and Row.

Montell, William Lynwood. 1975. *Ghosts along the Cumberland: Deathlore in the Kentucky Foothills.* Knoxville: University of Tennessee Press.

Montevallo Ghost Stories. 2006. http://www.montevallo.edu/library/spotlight/ghoststories.shtm, accessed March 2, 2006.

Montgomery, James Riley, Stanley J. Folmsbee, and Lee Seifert Greene. 1994. *To Foster Knowledge: A History of the University of Tennessee, 1794–1970.* Knoxville: University of Tennessee Press.

Morison, Samuel Eliot. 1935. *The Founding of Harvard College.* Cambridge: Harvard University Press.

Morrison, Toni. 1988. *Beloved.* New York: Penguin.

Morson, Berny. 2006. Photo latest fuel in Churchill flap. *Rocky Mountain News.* May 16. http://www.rockymountainnews.com/drmn/education/Article/0,1299,DRMN_957_4701982,00.html, accessed July 7, 2006.

Moyer, William. 2004. Historic Cemetery Regains Bygone Grandeur. *Press and Sun-Bulletin.* September 14. http://www.pressconnects.com, accessed March 20, 2005.

Mudge House. 2005. *Carnegie Mellon Housing Services.* http://www.housing.cmu.edu/buildings/mudge, accessed February 12, 2006.

Munn, Debra D. 1994. *Big Sky Ghosts: Eerie True Tales of Montana,* vol. 2. Boulder, CO: Pruett Publishing Company.

Murphy, Gardner, and Herbert L. Klemme. 1966. Unfinished Business. *Journal of the American Society for Psychical Research* 60(4): 306–20.

Nadolny, Marcia. 1966. Dorm Stories. Unpublished student paper, University of Maine. Northeast Folklore Archive # 308 (CP 180). Fall.

Nathan, Rebekah. 2005. *My Freshman Year: What a Professor Learned by Becoming a Student.* Ithaca, NY: Cornell University Press.

Nellsch, Katy, and Heather Tinnin. 1999. "Aren't you glad you didn't turn on the light?" College Ghost Stories and the Reasons for Their Telling. Unpublished student paper, University of Northern Colorado. Fall.

Nesbitt, Mark V. 1991. *Ghosts of Gettysburg.* Gettysburg: Thomas Publications.

Neumann, Erich. 1972. *The Great Mother: An Analysis of the Archetype.* Princeton: Princeton University Press.

Newbrough, John. 1998 [1882]. *A New Bible in the Words of Jehovih and His Angel Embassadors,* vol. 2. Whitefish, MT: Kessinger Publishing Company.

Newland, Donna. 1965. College-lore. Unpublished student paper, Wayne State University. Folklore Collection, Labor History Archive, Reuther Library.

Norder, Dan. 1999. Bloody Mary, Mary Worth, and Other Variants of a Modern Legend. *Mythology Web.* January. http://www.mythology.com/bloodymary.html, accessed July 9, 2002.

Norkunas, Martha. 2002. *Monuments and Memory: History and Representation in Lowell, Massachusetts.* Washington and London: Smithsonian Institution Press.

Notestein, Lucy Lilian. 1971. *Wooster of the Middle West,* vol. 1. Kent, OH: Kent State University Press.

Nuwer, Hank. 2005. "Unofficial Clearinghouse to Track Hazing Deaths and Incidents." http://hazing.hanknuwer.com, accessed August 1, 2005.

Ong, Walter J. 1982. *Orality and Literacy: The Technologizing of the World.* New York: Methuen.

Ovid. 1955. *Metamorphoses,* trans. Rolfe Humphries. Bloomington: Indiana University Press.

OxyContin. 2005. Drug Facts: Office of National Drug Control Policy. http://www.whitehousedrugpolicy.gov/drugfact/oxycontin/index.html, accessed June 4, 2006.

Pappas, Thomas. 1978. Ghostlore of Michigan. Unpublished student paper, Wayne State University. Folklore Collection, Labor History Archive, Reuther Library.

Parochetti, JoAnn Stephens. 1965. Scary Stories from Purdue. *Keystone Folklore* 10: 49–57.

Peacock, Molly. 1998. *Paradise, Piece by Piece.* New York: Riverhead Books.

Pierpoint, Mary. 2001. Ghosts of the Past Called on to Help Haskell Wetlands. *Indian Country Today.* November 2. http://www.indiancountry.com/content.cfm?id=2779, accessed June 6, 2005.

Porter, Matthew. 2000. Ghosts in Pres Park. Unpublished student e-mail communication, George Mason University. Northern Virginia Folklore Archive #2000–067.

Preston, Cathy Lynn. 2005. "The Macky Murder": Historical Moment, Campus Legend, and a Sense of Place. Paper presented at the twenty-third annual meeting of the International Society for Contemporary Legend Research, Athens, Georgia. May 26.

Propp, Vladimir. 1968. *Morphology of the Folktale*. Austin: University of Texas Press.

Puckett, Newbell Niles. 1981. *Popular Beliefs and Superstitions: A Compendium of American Folklore from the Ohio Collection of Newbell Niles Puckett*, ed. Wayland D. Hand et al. Boston: G. K. Hall.

Raftery, Kathleen. 1989. Vomit is a Five-Letter Word. Unpublished student paper, Binghamton University.

Random House College Dictionary. 1980. Revised ed. New York: Random House.

Rawlings, Kerri. 2000. "Daisy Drove My Car." Ghosts of Sweet Briar College. http://ghosts.sbc.edu/students1/html, accessed July 9, 2004.

Richardson, Anne. 2003. *Possessions*. Cambridge: Harvard University Press.

Ritchie, William A. 1980. *The Archaeology of New York State*. Revised ed. New York: Harbor Hill.

Robbins, Alexandra. 2005. *Pledged: The Secret Life of Sororities*. New York: Hyperion.

Rose, Wendy. 2000. Truganniny. In *Anthology of Modern American Poetry*, ed. Cary Nelson et al., p. 1158. London: Oxford University Press.

Rowling, J. K. 1997. *Harry Potter and the Sorcerer's Stone*. New York: Scholastic.

———. 1999. *Harry Potter and the Chamber of Secrets*. New York: Scholastic.

Ryden, Kent C. 1993. *Mapping the Invisible Landscape: Folklore, Writing, and the Sense of Place*. Iowa City: University of Iowa Press.

Samuelson, Sue. 1979. The White Witch: An Analysis of an Adolescent Legend. *Indiana Folklore* 12(1): 18–38.

Santino, Jack. 1994. *Halloween and Other Festivals of Death and Life*. Knoxville: University of Tennessee Press.

Scary Urban Legends: Ghosts, Amityville, Strange & Weird Folklore. 2006. http://www.geocities.com/sayswamp/folklore.htm, accessed November 4, 2006.

Sceurman, Mark, and Mark Moran. 2005. Weird New Jersey. http://www.weirdnj.com, accessed October 10, 2005.

Schonhardt, Sara. 2001. Wilson Hall Boasts History of Haunting. *The Post Online*. Ohio University. http://www.thepost.ohiou.edu/archives3/nov01/110101/t2.html, accessed March 10, 2004.

Schwartz, Luis H., and Stanton P. Fjeld. 1968. Illusions Induced by the Self-Reflected Image. *Journal of Nervous and Mental Disease* 146: 277–84.

Seaman, Barrett. 2005. *Binge: What Your College Student Won't Tell You. Campus Life in an Age of Disconnection and Excess*. New York: John Wiley and Sons, 2005.

Shoback, Doug. 1999. Oh, the Stories They Tell: Legends about the University of Northern Colorado as Told by Students. Unpublished student paper, University of Northern Colorado. Spring.

Sigma Kappa Sorority: Beta Sigma Chapter at Purdue University. 2004. http://web.ics.purdue.edu/~sigmakap/betasig.html, accessed March 10, 2006.

Smelcer, John E. 2006. *Stealing Indians*. New York: Henry Holt.

Sollors, Werner. 1986. *Beyond Ethnicity: Consent and Descent in American Culture*. New York: Oxford University Press.

Steppenwolf Theatre Company. 2004–2005. Theatre Superstitions. *Backstage Archive*, vol. 1. http://www.steppenwolf.org/backstage/article.aspx?id=23, accessed November 4, 2006.

Stohlman, Martha Lou Lemmon. 1956. *The Story of Sweet Briar College*. Sweet Briar, VA: Alumnae Association of Sweet Briar College.

Stoller, Paul. 1989. *The Taste of Ethnographic Things: The Senses in Anthropology*. Philadelphia: University of Pennsylvania Press.

Sunken House of Ramapo College. *Abandoned New Jersey*. http://www.abandonednj.com/exp/sunkenhouse/sunkenhouse.htm, accessed June 7, 2006.

Survival 101: College Memoirs. 2005. *Bed, Bath & Beyond*. http://www.bedbathandbeyond.com/Bts01_SurvMemoirsHome.asp?order_num=-1, accessed June 2, 2005.

Taylor, L. B., Jr. 1999. *The Ghosts of Williamsburg*, vol. 2. Lynchburg: Progress Printing Company.

Temasek Junior College Online Forums: Do you believe in ghosts? 2004. http://forum.tjc.edu.sg/topic.asp?ARCHIVE=true&TOPIC_ID=3142&whichpage+3, accessed April 10, 2005.

Thigpen, Kenneth A., Jr. 1971. Adolescent Legends in Brown County: A Survey. *Indiana Folklore* 4(2): 141–215.

Thomas, Jeannie B. 1991. Pain, Pleasure, and the Spectral: The Barfing Ghost of Burford Hall. *Folklore Forum* 24(2): 27–38.

Thompson, Stith. 1966. *Motif-Index of Folk-Literature*. Rev. ed., 6 vols. Bloomington: Indiana University Press.

———. 1968. *One Hundred Favorite Folktales*. Bloomington: Indiana University Press.

Tipton, Mary Frances. 1996. *Years Rich and Fruitful: University of Montevallo*. Montevallo, AL: University of Montevallo Press.

Toelken, Barre. 1968. The Folklore of Academe. In *The Study of American Folklore*, ed. Jan Harold Brunvand, pp. 317–37. New York: Norton.

———. 2003. *The Anguish of Snails: Native American Folklore in the West*. Logan: Utah State University Press.

Tolkien, J. R. R. 1965. "On Fairy Stories." In *Tree and Leaf*. Boston: Houghton Mifflin.

———. 1977. *The Silmarillion*. New York: Ballantine Books.

Tracy, Alison. 2004. Uncanny Afflictions: Spectral Evidence and the Puritan Crisis of Subjectivity. In *Spectral America: Phantoms and the National Imagination*, ed. Jeffrey Andrew Weinstock, pp. 18–39. Madison: University of Wisconsin Press.

Tucker, Elizabeth. 1977. Tradition and Creativity in the Storytelling of Pre-Adolescent Girls. Ph.D. diss., Indiana University.

———. 1980. Concepts of Space in Children's Narratives. In *Folklore on Two Continents: Essays in Honor of Linda Dégh*. Bloomington, IN: Trickster Press, 19–25.

———. 1987. The Guéré Excision Festival. In *Time Out of Time: Essays on the Festival*, ed. Alessandro Falassi, pp. 276–85. Albuquerque: University of New Mexico Press.

———. 2005a. *Campus Legends*. Westport, CT: Greenwood Press.

————. 2005b. Ghosts in Mirrors: Reflections of the Self. *Journal of American Folklore* 118 (468): 186–203.

————. 2005c. Spectral Indians, Desecrated Burial Grounds. *Voices: The Journal of New York Folklore* 31(1–2): 10–13.

Turkle, Sherry. 1995. *Life on the Screen: Identity in the Age of the Internet.* New York: Simon and Schuster.

Turner, Victor W. 1967. *The Forest of Symbols: Aspects of Ndembu Ritual.* Ithaca, NY: Cornell University Press.

Twain, Mark. 1899. *The Adventures of Tom Sawyer.* Hartford: American Publishing Company.

————. 1900. *How to Tell a Story and Other Essays.* Hartford: American Publishing Company.

Van Gennep, Arnold. 1960. *The Rites of Passage.* Chicago: University of Chicago Press.

Versaggi, Nina. 2004. E-mail communication. October 22.

Victor, Jeffrey. 1993. *Satanic Panic.* Chicago: Open Court.

Villard, Lisa. 1976. The Legends of the Mount. Unpublished student paper, Mount Saint Mary's University. December.

Vlach, John. 1971. One Black Eye and Other Horrors: A Case for the Humorous Anti-Legend. *Indiana Folklore* 4: 95–140.

Walker, Barbara, ed. 1995. *Out of the Ordinary: Folklore and the Supernatural.* Logan: Utah State University Press.

Walker, Steven F. 1995. *Jung and the Jungians on Myth.* New York: Garland.

Wallace-Wells, Benjamin. 1998. The Indian and the Rock. *Dartmouth Review.* November 17. http://69.57.157.207/issues/11.17.98/editrock.html, accessed February 3, 2006.

Warshaw, Robin. 1988. *I Never Called It Rape: The Ms. Report on Recognizing, Fighting, and Surviving Date and Acquaintance Rape.* New York: Harper and Row.

Waterman, A. S. 1985. Identity in the Context of Adolescent Psychology. In *Identity in Adolescence: Processes and Contents,* ed. A. S. Waterman, pp. 5–24. San Francisco: Jossey-Bass.

————. 1993. Developmental Perspectives on Identity Formation: From Adolescence to Adulthood. In *Ego Identity: A Handbook for Psychosocial Research,* ed. J. E. Marcia, A. S. Waterman, D. R. Matteson, S. L. Archer, and J. L. Orlofsky, pp. 42–68. New York: Springer-Verlag.

Waterman, A. S., and S. L. Archer. 1979. Ego Identity Status and Expressive Writing among High School and College Students. *Journal of Youth and Adolescence* 8: 327–41.

Waterman, A. S., E. Kohutis, and J. Pulone. 1977. The Role of Expressive Writing in Identity Formation. *Developmental Psychology* 13: 286–87.

Waterman, A. S., and C. K. Waterman. 1971. A Longitudinal Study of Changes in Ego Identity Status during the Freshman Year at College. *Developmental Psychology* 5: 167–73.

Weinstein, Sheri. 2004. Technologies of Vision: Spiritualism and Science in Nineteenth-Century America. In *Spectral America: Phantoms and the National Imagination,* ed. Jeffrey Andrew Weinstock, pp. 124–40. Madison: University of Wisconsin Press.

Weinstock, Jeffrey Andrew, ed. 2004. *Spectral America: Phantoms and the National Imagination.* Madison: University of Wisconsin Press.

Widdowson, John D. A. 1977. *If You Don't Be Good: Verbal Social Control in Newfoundland.* St. John's, Newfoundland: Memorial University.

Wightman, Todd. 1984. The Haunted House. Unpublished student paper, Utah State University. Fife Folklore Archive 84–061. Winter.

Wilde, Jane-Francesca. 1890. *Ancient Cures, Charms, and Usages of Ireland.* London: Ward and Downey.

Wilson, Richard. 1984. *Syracuse University: The Critical Years.* Syracuse: Syracuse University.

Windham, Kathryn Tucker, and Margaret Gillis Figh. 1983. *13 Alabama Ghosts and Jeffrey.* Huntsville: Strode Publishers.

Wolfreys, Julian. 2002. *Victorian Hauntings: Spectrality, Gothic, the Uncanny and Literature.* London: Palgrave Macmillan.

Yeates, Geoff. 1994. *Cambridge College Ghosts.* Norwich: Jarrold Publishing.

INDEX OF TALE TYPES AND MOTIFS

GENERAL INDEX

11–12, 153–81; library, 34–35; lovelorn, 115–33; marble, 53–62; mirror, 94–107; orientation, 23–25; professor, 10, 187–89; slave, 4, 11, 16; theater, 35–36
Gilbert, Helen, 22, 189–90
Gilbert, Sandra M., 215
Glassie, Henry, 53
Glimm, James York, 127
"Golden Arm, The," 63
Goldenberg, Naomi, 98
Goodwin, Joseph P., 185–89
Gordon, Avery F., 8–9, 59, 153
Gothic novel, 6, 8
Gould, Geoffrey, 168
Gould, Peter, vii
Grant, Glen, 64
Green, Rayna, 218
Greenberg, Andrea, 40, 71
Grider, Sylvia Ann, 22, 192
Grimm brothers, 5
Gubar, Susan, 215
Gus, ghost of Binghamton University, 105–6

Halloween, 18–19, 47, 192
hants. *See* ghosts
Harris, Mackenzie, 12
Harvard University, 159
Haskell babies, 163
Haskell Indian Nations University, 162–65
haunted houses, 192–97
Haunting, The (movie), 63, 204
Havighurst, Walter, 216
Hawthorne, Nathaniel, 102
Henderson State University, 128–29
Henken, Elissa R., 118–19
Hesse, Hermann, 96
Hiawatha, 167
Hillman, James, 106–7, 123
Hingson, Ralph W., 74, 135
Hofstra University, 105
Hollcroft, Temple R., 157

Hope, Christina, 150–51
Housholder, Grace, 216
Howard, Agnes, ghost of West Virginia Wesleyan, 217
Hufford, David J., 65
Humphrey, Hubert, 45
Huntingdon College, 93, 129
Hyatt, Harry M., 59

Indiana State University, 105
Indiana University, 27, 51–53, 67
initiation, 21–22, 30–31, 50–51, 62, 71, 95–96, 106, 108, 112, 181, 190, 206, 212
Instant Messaging, 12–13, 43, 46, 73, 75, 87–90
International Society for Contemporary Legend Research, 51
Iroquois Confederacy, 172
Isabella, ghost of Northwestern State University, 131–33

Jacobi, Jolande, 104
James, Henry, 8
Johns Hopkins University, 30–31
Johnson, George O., 216
Jones, Louis C., 9
Jung, C. G., 97, 101, 121
Jung, Emma, 99–100, 102
Jungian analysis, 94–115, 128–29

Karo, Aaron, 20, 74
Kelley, Charles Greg, 68–69
Kelly, Courtney, 60–62
Kemeny, John, 159
Kenyon College, 26
Kibbey, Ann, 7
Kilby, Clyde S., 26
King, Stephen, 84, 169, 204
King's College, 208
Kingston, Maxine Hong, 65
Klemme, Herbert L., 49
Klepenheuer, Kaspar, 106
Kolek, Ethan A., 84

Oppenheim, D. E., 47
Ortiz, Alfonso, 156
ostensive play, 100–1, 107
Ouija board, 102, 105
Oxford University, 147–48

Pappas, Thomas, 167
Parochetti, Joanne, 211
Peacock, Molly, 44
Pedro, ghost of the University of California
   at Berkeley, 12
Pelizzoni, Joanna, 212, 218
Pennsylvania State University at Schuylkill
   Haven, 65–67
Pennsylvania State University at University
   Park, 12
Phillips, Justin, 57–58
Poltergeist (movie), 90, 112
Preston, Cathy Lynn, 135
Propp, Vladimir, 76
Puritans, 7–8, 59

Raftery, Kathleen, 75
Ramapo College, 185
Randolph-Macon College, 27
rape, 40–41, 74, 134–35
Red Lady of Huntingdon College, 93,
   129
Reed, Mary, 34
revenants. *See* ghosts
Revolutionary War, 30, 130
Rhode Island School of Design, 55
Ricks College, 194
Rinderknecht, Jalyn, 203
Ring, The (movie), 80, 90
Ritchie, William A., 172
Robbins, Alexandra, 215
"Roommate's Death, The," 93
Rose Red (movie), 204
Rosemary's Baby (movie), 196
Rowan University, 197
Rowling, J. K., 96, 179
Rutgers University, 29, 35, 111
Ryden, Kent C., 25–26

Saint Alexis, 71–72
Saint Anthony, 11
Saint Catherine of Alexandria, 11, 147–48
Saint Christopher, 11
Saint Frideswida, 148
Saint John's University, 22, 189–91
Saint Jude, 11
Saint Thomas Aquinas, 11
Saint-Mary-of-the-Woods College, 212
Salem witch trials, 62–63
Samuelson, Sue, 198
Sara, ghost of Mansfield University,
   123–27, 147, 189
Scary Movie, 81
Scary Movie 2, 81
Schamberg, William, ghost of Ball State
   University, 32
Schreier Rupprecht, Carol, 97–98
Schulman, Samantha, 214
Seaman, Barrett, 73–74, 117
séance, 132
Seton, Ernest Thompson, 154
Shakespeare, William, 35, 43, 47
Shiraiwa, Ken, 218
Shoback, Doug, 70
Sixth Sense (movie), 63
Skull and Bones, secret society at Yale,
   106
Smelcer, John E., 162
Smith College, 68, 116, 216
Sollors, Werner, 166
sororities, 10, 117–20
Southern Methodist University, 12
Speck, Richard, 136
spectral evidence, 7, 62
Sperling, Shelley, 149–51
spirits. *See* ghosts
spiritualism, 8
State University of New York at Buffalo,
   192
State University of New York at Cortland,
   145–49
State University of New York at
   Morrisville, 171

Printed in the USA
CPSIA information can be obtained
at www.ICGtesting.com
JSHW020056290723
45459JS00001B/76